The Live-Streaming Handbook will teach you how to present live-video shows from your phone and stream them straight to Facebook and Twitter. With this book and your favourite social media apps, you will be able to run your own TV station for your home or work.

Peter Stewart, an experienced TV and radio presenter, producer and author, now shares the training he's given to professional broadcasters, with you! From structuring and developing a show to establishing an effective online persona and getting more people to watch you. The book includes dozens of tried-and-tested formats for your live-video show, alongside case studies highlighting how businesses and professionals are using live-streaming in their brand and marketing strategies.

Also included are:

▶ With a Foreword by Al Roker (NBC's *The Today Show*)

▶ practical steps for using popular live-streaming apps, such as Facebook Live and Twitter;

▶ nearly 80 colour images of live-streaming events, screenshots and gadgets;

▶ a detailed walk-through of how to successfully present and produce your live-streaming show;

▶ advice on analysing and exploiting viewer metrics to increase followers;

▶ more than 130 quotes of real-world advice from expert producers of online media content;

▶ over 700 links to online case studies, articles, research and background reading.

With this extensive manual you will gain a competitive edge in the world of online live-streaming. This book is invaluable to entrepreneurs, professionals and students working in journalism, public relations, marketing and digital media, as well as general readers interested in live-streaming at home.

Peter Stewart is a journalist, presenter and author with 30 years' experience in BBC and commercial TV and radio. He's produced hundreds of live-streams of his own and for clients, has trained BBC reporters and Oxfam field staff, and was a panellist at the inaugural 'Periscope Summit' in New York City, USA.

'Peter's abilities as a practitioner and strategist in live video have always impressed me. He represents a special ability to connect voice and community to brand. This book shares that know-how in a witty and concise way. Love it.'

Ryan Bell, *Director of Digital Strategy Hydro Studios, USA*

'In *The Live-Streaming Handbook* Peter Stewart has created a bite sized bible for anyone wanting to do and teach mobile streaming. From developing streams, choosing apps, platforms, strategies, presenting styles, real-time interactions and analytics, this book unleashes the power of the mobile TV station we carry in our pockets.'

Ivo Brumm, *Coordinator and Lecturer in Media Industries,*
Department of Communications and Media,
La Trobe University, Australia

'If you are considering using live streaming, this is an indispensable handbook for media professionals and students. It offers ideas for content themes, practical advice for using popular live stream apps and guidance on how to promote your live events to attract more viewers to your live and replay streams.'

Krishna De, *Digital Communications and Social Business Strategist*

'The concisely informative *Live-Streaming Handbook* challenges readers to cast aside long-held tenets about television production practices. Live streaming is visual communication in its newest and leanest form, and the language of minimalist video production is changing. Stewart's spirited, easily digestible chapters guide readers through the maze of decisions about platform choices, equipment and techniques.'

Bruce Mimms, *Professor of Mass Media,*
Southeast Missouri State University, USA

'Peter's detailed guide is an incredible resource for businesses and individuals alike, providing all the necessary tools for those wanting to grow their brand or connect with a community via live-stream broadcasting.'

Aaron Roth, *VP, Sales & Marketing, Arkon Resources, USA*

'Welcome to the future – a comprehensive guide to live-streaming, from the tools and platforms available to do it, to the essential ethical and practical considerations you'll need to take into account. Whether you are just starting out, or already riding the wave of this exciting phenomenon, Stewart's book will inspire journalists to safely make the most of this opportunity and develop a live-streaming strategy that will boost your news organisation on social.'

Caroline Scott, *video journalist and Senior Reporter at Journalism.co.uk*

'Do you want more customers? Do you want people to be more likely to buy from you rather than your competitor? Then you need to embrace video. Video and, in particular, LIVE video is a game-changer for marketers. *The Live-Streaming Handbook* written by Peter Stewart is an absolute MUST read for anyone who wants to get into the live-streaming game and the earlier you do, the faster your business will grow. Peter masterfully lays out everything you need from a game plan, equipment, promotional strategies and more. I highly recommend this book to anyone looking to grow their business with video.'

Andrea Vahl, *social media consultant and speaker, co-author of* Facebook Marketing All-in-One for Dummies *and co-founder of Social Media Manager School*

The Live-Streaming Handbook

How to Create Live-Video for Social Media on Your Phone and Desktop

Peter Stewart

Routledge
Taylor & Francis Group

LONDON AND NEW YORK

First published 2018
by Routledge
2 Park Square, Milton Park, Abingdon, Oxon OX14 4RN

and by Routledge
711 Third Avenue, New York, NY 10017

Routledge is an imprint of the Taylor & Francis Group, an informa business

British Library Cataloguing-in-Publication Data
A catalogue record for this book is available from the British Library

Library of Congress Cataloging-in-Publication Data
Names: Stewart, Peter, 1967– author.
Title: The live-streaming handbook : how to create great live video on your
    phone, for Facebook and Twitter / Peter Stewart.
Description: London ; New York : Routledge, 2018.
Identifiers: LCCN 2017023113 | ISBN 9781138630048 (hardback : alk. paper)
    | ISBN 9781138630055 (pbk. : alk. paper) | ISBN 9781315209883 (ebook)
Subjects: LCSH: Streaming technology (Telecommunications)—Handbooks,
    manuals, etc. | Smartphones—Handbooks, manuals, etc.
Classification: LCC TK5105.386 .S726 2018 | DDC 006.7—dc23
LC record available at https://lccn.loc.gov/2017023113

ISBN: 978-1-138-63004-8 (hbk)
ISBN: 978-1-138-63005-5 (pbk)
ISBN: 978-1-315-20988-3 (ebk)

Typeset in Warnock Pro
by Apex CoVantage, LLC

To my parents, Margaret and John.

They were born before the start of World War Two, and the first TV programme they saw was the coronation of Queen Elizabeth II in 1952.

Now, anyone can go live to the world with a mobile phone.

Technology has changed. My love for them remains constant.

Contents

PART I So you want to go live?

1 Why love live?   3

In this introductory chapter, both sides of the live-streaming story: the facts, the stats (which suggest that we are entering a perfect time to 'go live'), and also the reputational risks of producing 'raw' video. Live-streaming is not a fad, it's the future. And it's shaking up social. I'll explain why and how you can take advantage.

2 Facebook Live   12

The facts and the features of the live-video app of this media monster. The basics of how to go live, what icons to tap and what settings to adjust, plus a look at in-show adverts to help you make money while you live-stream.

3 Twitter Go Live/Periscope   27

There's a look at the differences between going live with these two apps, the features and the formats and what settings to tap and toggle.

4 YouTube   49

The options and advantages of using YouTube to live-stream from, including what to press and select and how Super Chat can help you monetize your broadcast.

5 Other live-streaming apps and software   55

It's not just the Big Three social media platforms that offer live-streaming services. In this chapter, there's a quick view of 'the best of the rest', some of which have direct integration with Facebook. Plus the software and services you can use to add extra graphics, captions and videos to your live-stream to make your show more pro, a live-video production company that could help make you a star, and businesses that can help you analyse your analytics.

PART II Live-stream themes

6 Your live-stream strategy   67

Live-streaming is a tool, not a strategy in itself. If you want to get results, you need to consider live-video as just one part of your marketing mix: live-video doesn't replace other aspects, it should help fuel them. In this chapter, devising your live-stream brand guidelines, your production plan and what to do if it all goes wrong.

7 Content is king   73

This chapter has 17 different sections, each one crammed full of tried-and-tested user case studies of successful live-streams. From 'behind the scenes streams' to 'e-commerce', 'city tours', 'education and training' and even 'spying on the competition', it's a database of ideas to steal to make live-streaming work for you. And don't miss the section on 'extreme streams': using 360 cameras, drones and action-cams to bring unique places and perspectives to your viewers.

8 Focus on. . .   127

In this chapter, we take a closer look at how specific groups and businesses have integrated live-streaming into their marketing mix. By reading these more-detailed case studies, you should clearly see how live-video could be used in your field. The areas covered include journalism, conferences and events, non-profits, property sales, religion, museums and 'making money'.

PART III Pre-show production

9 How long and when it's on   177

With live-video, the consideration is, what's the tipping point between 'being interesting and worthwhile' and 'being live long enough to get a good audience'? We discuss the best time to 'go live', how long you should stream for and how often, for the greatest effect.

10 The recce   185

Let's be honest, being live creates many opportunities for failure. Just because it's live, it doesn't mean that it can be completely raw. You have to think ahead, plan and produce your content as much as you would any other part of your marketing mix. And that's what this chapter is all about.

11 Live-stream privacy, security and safety   190

Don't get caught by the courts! This is the chapter that could save your reputation, money and maybe your job. It's full of what you should avoid saying and showing in a live-stream and how to protect yourself from weirdos who may be watching you. We look at copyright, product placement, defamation and, in the section on abuse and harassment, how to deal with online trolls.

12 Tech tips and kit   213

Of course, it's great to point your camera phone at something and go live. But what if you want to take live-streaming a bit more seriously and avoid The Blair Witch Project look? This chapter is about 'equipment investment' to avoid reputational risk, with free tips and a variety of tech.

PART IV **On air**

13 Your vital title   229

Just before you start your show, Facebook Live says: "Describe your live video" and Periscope asks, "What are you seeing now?". A compelling description will help attract more people to watch your video when it is live and once it has ended. You need to spend some time coming up with an awesome title so people know why they should invest minutes and megs watching you. This is the chapter with all that help in one place.

14 Comments and reactions   236

One of the reasons live-streaming is so much more powerful than other social media is the real-time interaction between who is presenting and who is watching. Here we look at how to turn viewers from 'passive' to 'participants', and how doing this helps your end-of-show metrics, which will in turn give your stats the snowball effect.

15 Shares, follows and notifications   246

Live-streaming is all about engagement and interactivity, sharing and recommending (this is *social* media after all), and the more your viewers do this with your content, the more valuable your video becomes. In this chapter, how to build and boost your broadcast audience and have them coming back for more.

16 The presenter   254

Here is your personal pep talk for on-camera confidence: how to warm up mentally and physically; the language and tone of voice you use; your gestures; the best clothes and colours to wear and even how to stand and sit for best effect. The advice on how to make friends with the lens continues with 'rehearsal' advice, how to frame yourself on-screen and the question over whether horizontal or vertical views are best.

17 The producer   273

You need a plan for promotion, moderation and discussion with your viewers. And that's where a producer can help. And this is the chapter to tell you how.

18 The viewers   277

The audience that watches your shows isn't one homogenous group but made up of lots of different sub-sets of smaller audiences. We look at how to target four distinct groups of viewers and how to promote your show before and during your broadcast to attract them.

19 At the start of the show   286

Some people mumble and stumble through the first vital minutes. Not only does this give a bad business image for their brand, but it will also dissuade early joiners (and replay viewers) from staying with them. So here's what to do in the first 111 seconds, so you thrive when you go live.

Or, 'How To Make It Sticky'. It's easy to get caught up in the moment when you are presenting on a live-video. After all, there's a lot to think about. In this chapter, the considerations to have when you are in mid-flow. Simply the best advice on how to successfully engage and inspire, explain and entertain.

Before you start a show, you need to know where you are going, so you know when you have arrived. But when you get there, what then? This chapter is all about how to end on a high before you say goodbye.

PART V **Post-show production**

Of course, after you end your show, you can turn off your phone, turn off your mind and turn to other things. That's the simplest post-production. But it's probably best to finish the job you started. In this part, I'll tell you why you need to have a 'Post-Show Strategy', starting with saving and reposting your video.

Or 'Replays, Republishing, Repurposing and Resurrecting'. You've invested time and effort in getting this far, so this chapter is all about getting as much juice as possible from the fruits of your labour, so you can reach a new audience. It includes the 'Ultimate RRR Workflow' and how to strengthen your relationship with your viewers through a policy of post-promotion.

You need to analyse your viewing data so you can evaluate and optimize your live-stream show. Here, I mention 'retention', 'reach', explain what a 'viewer' actually is and discuss how to interrogate your impact stats. This data-mining will help you realise what is working and what isn't, so you can improve your videos and become a live-stream superstar.

Figures

Foreword

By NBC's Al Roker

I have always loved tech.

When I was 9 years old I discovered I could record the audio from a live TV broadcast by running a wire from the speaker to the 'line in' of a reel-to-reel tape recorder. In 1992 I started a website because I saw it as another way to use the latest technology to communicate with people.

And, as I've been live on TV for over 40 years, it makes perfect sense for me to love live-streaming too, or as I'd like to call it, 'social broadcasting'.

It's like radio was in the 1920s: nobody knows what it's going to be, but I do think we are on the cusp of something big.

Live-streaming bridges television and social media, offering huge audiences, viewer interaction and commerce opportunities. With just a few taps on the screen of your cell phone, you can broadcast on all the major social media platforms. The ultimate convergence of social media and broadcasting, live-streaming is more powerful than either of them. And going live creates real-time data and analytics way beyond anything we have seen previously.

Those of us who understand and believe in the power of live-video know that it's special because of its ability to connect all of us as human beings. There's a certain unpredictability about it. It's in the moment, it's happening in real time and most importantly it's a shared experience. Not just in your 'neck of the woods', live-video connects people around the world: it is truly unique and engaging.

Live-streaming will create new formats, programs and opportunities currently not even being considered. I'm so convinced of that, it's why my company Roker Media is now working with talent, producers and some of the world's biggest brands to create professional live-programming optimized to reach and engage select audiences.

And with time, effort and the advice in this book, you're also in a great place to take advantage of these developments and be at the forefront of this new technology.

So whether you are in marketing for a big brand, own a small mom-and-pop store or work for a non-profit, or maybe you just want to entertain or tell the world what's on your mind, do read and learn from this fantastic book. Explore everything that goes into creating a successful live broadcast from planning to promotion to production to post-mortem.

There's advice on how to identify clear live-streaming goals and objectives, the kind of gear you need to produce a live-video, presenting skills (my tip: don't tell me you're going to be the next Martha Stewart or Oprah . . . No, you're not! Be yourself!) and how to avoid rookie mistakes (at the end of one Facebook Live, I forgot to take my mic off before going to the bathroom; my viewers literally heard me 'live-streaming'!).

Finally, there's a section on how to identify your key performance indicators to capture insight on what's working and what you can improve.

With 30 years' experience in TV and radio broadcasting for the likes of the BBC, Peter's now sharing his secrets, and with this 360-view of live-video, you'll be well-equipped with a comprehensive plan of action so you can go live every day, like me!

Thanks so much for buying this book, and good luck with your live-streams.

Al Roker
New York City
April 2017

Al Roker is an established media personality, described as a 'contemporary Renaissance man' due to his early adoption of tech. Al was the first NBC *Today Show* personality to develop his own website, jump head-first into social media, and was instrumental in bringing live-streaming to a wider audience. In addition to heading up Roker Media (http://rokermedia.live/), Al is CEO of Al Roker Entertainment, Inc., a multimedia company involved in the development and production of television programs and branded entertainment.

FIGURE 0.1 Al Roker
Credit: http://rokermedia.live/

FIGURE 0.2 Behind the scenes on the production of 'pro' live-streams

Preface

That device in your pocket or bag is way more than just a phone. As well as a computer, games console and messaging device, it's now also a TV station.

Just as blogging made everyone a 'newspaper reporter', live-video streaming can make you a 'television presenter'.

I'm Peter Stewart and I've got qualifications in PR, sales and marketing and have worked in broadcast media for nearly 30 years. So I know quite a bit about video, audio, live and recorded production techniques, presentation, journalism and social media. As a trainer and consultant, through one-to-one sessions, seminars and several books, I've taught professionals 'how to do TV': developing formats, structuring programmes and building relationships with the audience.

And now it's time for me to help you, by sharing the secrets of live broadcasting that until now, only the pros knew.

You don't need a studio or editing suite. You don't need a team of technicians. And you don't need a camera costing several thousand pounds or dollars. Because with your humble cell phone you can transmit live-video pictures to anyone on Earth. You can show them where you are and tell them what you know, connect with them, build friendships and boost your business.

By investing in this Handbook, you have given yourself a great opportunity to master one of the most exciting and innovative developments in social media for years.

▶ INCLUDED IN THIS BOOK

▶ An introduction to the big main social media live-streaming apps, what they do and which one is best for you

▶ The greatest ways to plan for your 'dream stream' and how to avoid huge mistakes

▶ Why you need to plan, tease and feed

▶ How to connect and engage, to grow and keep your audience

▶ Brilliant tips on writing a show title to grab attention and turn followers into viewers

▶ Great ways to rehearse your first show and conquer the fear factor

▶ When to do a show, how to structure it and how long it should be on for, how often . . . and what time of day

▶ How to open and close a show . . . and keep it going

▶ Why you need to start when you start . . . and pause before you stop

▶ The reason you need to say 'hello' but not 'good morning'

▶ Magic ways to make your shows more creative and compelling

▶ Top tips on presenting, where to go, what to show, what to say, how to act and even what to wear

▶ The four kinds of viewers and how to keep them watching for longer

▶ What to do after the show to keep the relationship alive

▶ How to build your personal or business brand with live-streaming

▶ How to get seen, shared and generate revenue

▶ The kit you need . . . or may not need!

▶ What to look for when you review your show to make it better the next time

▶ A strategy to pre-promote and back-promote your show and reasons why you should

There are also tips and tricks, dos and don'ts and hundreds of examples of shows and formats from farmers to theme parks, churches to shops, plumbers to police . . . plus ideas for salons, chefs, teachers, charities and a whole lot more; and hundreds of links to useful websites, articles and stories with even more information and inspiration.

Who is the handbook for?

It's for you at home live-streaming your family vacation or kid's birthday, but also for:

▶ **Government PRs, communications officers and media relations staff** – so they can better communicate with the public and promote the area in which they serve.

▶ **Marketing and social media staff** – who want to contact their customers and colleagues and attract new ones.

▶ **NGOs, non-profit, church and community outreach staff** – who need to have effective connections and communications on a budget with their supporters and neighbourhoods.

▶ **Small and large business owners** – whether they're online or on the high street and want to promote their goods, skills and services.

▶ **Experts** – who want to position themselves as key figures in their niche area.

▶ **Vloggers, amateur hobbyists and local groups** – who want to connect with other enthusiasts.

▶ **Celebrities** – who want to chat one-to-one with their fans.

▶ **Aspiring celebrities** – who want to get comfortable with interaction, appearing on screen, reacting live and building a digital showcase for their personality.

▶ **Journalists and citizen reporters** – who are keen on covering breaking news and interacting with their existing audiences in a new way.

Indeed, this book is for anyone who wants to connect, befriend or sell, wants to be a social media superstar, or who wants to have greater impact when they stream from their smartphone.

Why do you need this book?

Using the apps is pretty straightforward, right? And surely anyone with a phone in their pocket can broadcast?

Well, it's like many things from baking a cake to running a business. Most people can make a pretty decent go of it, but there are many tricks and subtleties that you need to know if you are going to get the most out of your investment of time.

This is an in-depth, comprehensive training programme to give you a competitive advantage to help you succeed. I'll show you what to do to increase the number of people who see your broadcast, how they engage with it and how it performs. I will help you cut your 'trial and error time' by cutting out your own experimentation and fast-track your success by showing what I know has worked for professional broadcasters for decades.

Now, let's work together to get content from your phone to their phone, and make your 'live' thrive.

Peter Stewart
London
October 2017

A few quick points

Many other guides to social media platforms concentrate on just one app, say Facebook *or* Instagram *or* LinkedIn. This book is looking at the techniques and tech of a feature which is common to several apps: live-streaming video.

New live-streaming apps are being launched on a regular basis: at the time of writing there are probably around 20 'main' ones which have a bit of traction in their take-up. These fall into two broad categories:

▶ **Video-conferencing style platforms** – these give the opportunity to have *several* guests at a time (one at least allows up to 100 guests who can contribute, that's *guests*, not *viewers*). These are often paid-for, and used for in-house conferencing, public training, workshops, community discussion forums and talking-head discussion shows. They are characterised by being mainly laptop-based and used by people in a static indoor location, on an internal Wi-Fi system. Examples include Blab (now closed down) and BlueJeans' onSocial.

▶ **Mobile, phone app platforms** – these are often free and use Wi-Fi and cellular connections on a mobile phone. Although they can be used for an individual talking directly to the camera, and indeed may give you the facility to invite a few people to chat on-screen at one time, 'mobile' is the key. They are often better used outside to show other people something happening in the moment: a city scene, a shared experience, a unique perspective. Examples include Facebook Live and Twitter's Periscope app.

This book tends to concentrate on the second category, and I'll be referring most to the popular platforms right now: Facebook Live, Twitter Go Live/Periscope and YouTube, although most of what's here can be applied to almost any live-video app.

Another point: those apps not only have different layouts and features on Android and iOS devices, but they are also constantly evolving. What each app does and what you need to tap to make it happen, even where the buttons are, changes on an almost weekly basis. For those reasons, I have written about *production and presentation advice* for live-streaming on these apps (advice that hardly changes), rather than spending too much space giving a walk-through of how to set each one up and every single feature.

A note on the use of images and screenshots: Staff at the live-stream platforms inform me that the copyright of any video content lies with *individual broadcasters*. During the production of this book, I have gone to great lengths to find those who produced the streams from which I wanted to request images. I am immensely grateful to those who have granted me permission. Obviously, this book cannot include an image for every case study, and on occasion that may be because the request went unanswered or was declined, or I was unable to trace the copyright owner.

All links were checked at the time of writing. Ebook readers can click and be taken directly to the article. As full web addresses are very unwieldly to reproduce, other readers can use this tip: in Google put the name of the article (say, *Best Facebook Live Publishers of 2016*) followed by "site:" (without the quote marks) and then immediately after the colon, put in the short website reference given in the text (www.news whip.com/). The article should be the first result.

And a quick point about the reproduction quality of images. As you will understand, it is inevitable that taking a screenshot on a mobile phone, of a live-stream which was itself broadcast on a mobile phone (and may have been a moving 'action shot' or from a 360 camera), will not result in as pin-sharp an image as one might get in a professional photographic or TV studio. Additionally, some images here lack the comments and reactions that you might expect on (or under) a live-stream video. That may be because previous screen layouts didn't show these, or because when the photo was taken, either the comments were hidden for privacy reasons or the image was taken after the stream had been live and on a desktop rather than a mobile device.

Acknowledgements

First, my gratitude for **Al Roker** and his colleagues at http://rokermedia.live/, **Ron Pruett** and **Jon Burk**, for their generous assistance with the Foreword.

For advice and fact-checking (although any mistakes are mine), **Krishna De** (www.krishna.me), who is my co-host on the weekly *LiveStream Insiders* programme on Facebook, and who keeps me updated with technical changes to the app. Krishna also proof-read much of this book.

Marc Blank-Settle (@marcsettle) and other colleagues of ours at the BBC, such as **Nick Garnett**, who have always been quick to help with answering questions about mojo and live-streaming that have had me stumped; **Glen Mulcahy** (*https://tvvj.wordpress.com/*), whose MoJoCon ('mobile journalism conference') events in Ireland (*https://mojocon.rte.ie* and the associated Facebook group) have kept me updated with all aspects of using mobile phones for content production (seriously, the best conferences I have attended); **Alex Pettitt** (www.alexpettitt.tv), who along with **Mark Shaw** (www.markshaw.biz) provided the early-days inspiration for my interest in live-streaming. Alex has also allowed the reproduction of some images from his streams.

▶ FOR WRITTEN CONTRIBUTIONS

Mitch Jackson (www.streaming.lawyer) for his help on the legal issues specifically regarding trolls and his generosity for allowing me to reproduce some of his work. **Sam Martin**, online media consultant (www.sociallysam.com), has allowed me to use longer extracts of some of her material, as has **Caroline Avakian** (www.socialbrite.org @CarolineAvakian).

▶ SEVERAL PEOPLE AND BUSINESSES HAVE HELPED WITH IMAGES

Corinne Podger, Lecturer in Mobile, Video and Multimedia Journalism, Macleay College, Melbourne and Sydney, Australia; **Alfred Joyner** at the *International Business Times*; **Andy Dangerfield** at *BuzzFeed News*; **Aaron Roth** at www.arkon.com

kindly offered not only images of their line of stands, tripods and mounts but also a discount for readers of this book; **Enrique Frisancho** at www.shoulderpod.com provided images of their range of phone grips and mounts; **Paul Kaufman** and colleagues at IK Multimedia Production SRL (ikmultimedia.com) for images of some of their products; **Christian Payne** (@Documentally) was generous by sharing some of his images from years of live-streaming before it became commonplace; **Jessica Robinson** and **Bryan C. Keene** at The J. Paul Getty Museum in L.A.; **Claire Wilson** at www.socialbakers.com; **Rich Birch** at www.unseminary.com; **Belive.tv** and **Jeff Adams**; **Philippe Laurent** at goeasylive; https://switcherstudio.com/, https://manycam.com/ and https://stream.live/; **Carlos Phoenix** and **Anthony Lenzo** at www. livestreamingmaster.com; the team at **Greenpeace**; **Charles Hodgson** of *View News*, Australia; **Claire Waddington**; **Dan Moore**; **Mitch Oates**. A special thanks to **Paul Ronzheimer**, who I liaised with regarding image use while he was in Mosul; **David McClelland** at www.davidmcclelland.co.uk; **Angela Nicholson** at www.camerajabber.com; and **Jane Wickens**.

Also thanks to all those experts whose quotes I have used throughout and, of course, **Facebook**, **Twitter** and **Periscope**. Although they do not endorse this book per se, without them this book would not have been written.

Finally, the team at **Taylor & Francis** publishers, including **Niall Kennedy** and **Kitty Imbert**.

Thanks to everyone who has helped me with this project. Bear in mind as you read that the apps, platforms, technology and plug-ins are ever-changing; however, any actual mistakes or inaccuracies are mine alone, and I'd be grateful if you draw those to my attention so they can be corrected for future editions.

PART I
So you want to go live?

We start with an overview of what live-streaming is and why you should fire up your phone to use it. (Hint: If you jump in now and begin to create an audience for yourself, you'll be taking advantage of the hype, as well as getting ahead of your competitors.)

Then we take a look at the top apps and how they differ, so you can choose the best one for your needs.

There's also a chapter devoted to the 'best of the rest': the other apps which may not be as well-known as the 'top three' but have their own particular features and strengths.

1

Why love live?

▶ **INTRODUCTION**

As you have bought this book, you are at least a little bit interested in live-streaming! But maybe you need a bit more convincing? After all, streaming can be daunting, and as well as the rewards there are also risks.

In this chapter, both sides of the live-streaming story are presented: the facts and stats (which suggest that we are entering a perfect time to 'go live') but also the reputational risks of producing 'raw' video.

> *In order to remain competitive and relevant, innovative marketers must keep an eye out for what's new, what's hot, and what's trending on the social media platform, and should also incorporate these new ways of connecting and communication into their strategies.*
>
> Ken Bock[1]

I believe that live-streaming is not a fad; it's the future. And it's shaking up social.

▶ **WHAT IS LIVE-STREAMING?**

Although all live-streaming apps vary slightly, they all allow you to broadcast live-video content that can be viewed on a phone, tablet, computer or TV. It's a bit like Facetiming or Skyping all your followers at once.

You immediately have your own live TV station and can broadcast from wherever you are through your cell phone. You'll have your audience literally in the palm of your hand.

With most live-streaming apps, viewers send you written comments and 'reactions' (icons such as thumbs-up or hearts), which appear on the screen. The broadcasts are saved on your page, account or profile until you delete them.

▶ THE FACTS

How did we get to crave live images?[2]

As humans, we have evolved to interpret visual information faster than the written word:

- ▶ 75 million people in the US watch videos online every day.
- ▶ Embedded videos on websites can increase traffic up to 55%.
- ▶ Merely mentioning the word 'video' in the subject line of an email can increase open rates by 13%.
- ▶ Nearly 40% of all video is watched on mobile.
- ▶ 90% of the information sent to our brains is visual: we've been trained to consume visual content as quickly as we can.[3]

Those stats suggest that people watch, but what do they subsequently do?[4]

- ▶ Shoppers who view video are 1.81 times more likely to purchase than non-viewers.
- ▶ 51.9% of marketing professionals worldwide name video as the type of content with the best ROI (Return On Investment).
- ▶ Retailers cite 40% increases in purchases as a result of video.
- ▶ In an eye-mapping study of search engine results pages (SERPS), video results commanded more attention than other listings.
- ▶ Mobile shoppers are three times more likely than desktop shoppers to view a video.

And what's the take-up in 'video marketing'?

- ▶ 51% of the top publisher companies posted to Facebook Live in September 2016, up from 10% in January[5] of that year.

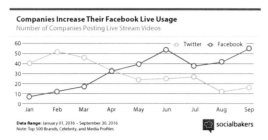

Companies Increase Their Facebook Live Usage
Number of Companies Posting Live Stream Videos

Data Range: January 01, 2016 – September 30, 2016
Note: Top 500 Brands, Celebrity, and Media Profiles

socialbakers

FIGURE 1.1 51% of media are using Facebook Live videos, but only 11% of companies do

Source: Socialbakers, Number of Companies Posting Live Stream Videos, www.socialbakers.com

▶ Almost one-fifth of US media decision-makers are planning to invest in live-stream video ads in the next six months (as of August 2016).[6]

And stats for live-video (and once-live video)?

▶ Facebook says that by 2020, 75% of all mobile data will be video.[7]

▶ Facebook Live videos are watched three times longer than regular videos[8] (on average, 20 minutes versus 2–3 minutes).[9]

▶ Native Facebook videos have a 13% organic reach and 6.3% engagement rate (much higher than the 1–3% you get on other platforms).[10]

▶ People watch 100 million hours of Facebook videos each day.[11]

Video is the current 'eye candy': it's huge and here to stay. So, adding live-streaming to your customer engagement strategy would certainly seem to be a smart thing to do.

> *Live-streaming is a new game entirely because it is dynamic, not static. Once a brand goes live, their competitors must follow. Customers will come to expect it. They won't want tired, off-the-shelf archived videos. Live broadcasting on a cell phone is the missing link between TV and social media. Period.*
>
> Ron C. Pruett[12]

▶ THE POSITIVES OF LIVE

Mark Zuckerberg, the founder of Facebook, has said he is obsessed with live-video: when he switched on live-stream capabilities on the platform in April 2016, one-quarter of the world's population suddenly had the ability to stream.

Why now?

Live-streaming has been made more accessible because of advances in technology. First, more people have more-sophisticated but easy-to-use phones (Pew Research, www.pewinternet.org, reckons 72% of Americans own a cell phone). But there's also the following available now:

▶ 3G and 4G and nearly 5G technology

▶ Cheaper data plans

▶ Cloud technology

▶ Longer-lasting batteries

▶ Bigger screens

▶ Better cameras

Plus bigger social media networks have given us immediate access to a built-in fan base of potential viewers to make it easier to create a shared and engaged experience.

> *Online video has become a key part of the strategic business model for both brands and marketers as they seek more innovative ways to capture consumer attention. [Live-streaming has] emerged as the medium of choice not only for person-to-person sharing, but also for business-to-consumer (B2C) and business-to-business (B2B) communication.*

Dylan Mortensen[13]

Live-streaming is . . .

Fast – setting up these apps is quick and easy, and shooting is simplicity itself. In just a few seconds (it takes about ten to fire up a Facebook Live), you can go live from the middle of the action to the whole of the world, with no post-show editing.

Mobile – you can film from anywhere, at any time. And as most of these apps are mobile-to-mobile, your viewers don't need any special equipment to watch you, and that helps them feel part of the action.

Accessible – streams have a friendly, accessible, behind-the-scenes feel. They feel more authentic and therefore make more of a connection with people than a glitzy production. Live-streaming is easy for people to consume and be involved in.

> *The true beauty of Periscope lies in its accessibility. Roger Federer used the app to cover his big game, so why not use it to cover your daughter's next varsity tennis*

match? Big-time politicians can use it to broadcast their speeches, and so can passionate grassroots activists and community organizers.

Mitch Carson[14]

And if you have a customer base which is largely on say, Facebook, then they may not be bothered by an 'amateur look'. In fact, it may appeal to them.

Inexpensive – there's no extra cost of video cameras, studios, sound gear or editing time. The apps are free and on your phone. Why pay for 'mass advertising' with all the inherent waste of being seen by those who have no interest in your brand, when you can reach a bigger and more dedicated audience through your live-stream? You have a free marketing platform in your pocket – your own broadcast channel in your bag.

Integrated – the main live-streaming apps are baked-in to three of the biggest and most powerful social media platforms on the planet: Facebook, Twitter and You-Tube. And that means you can reach a viewing audience without having to build one separately; the distribution is already integrated right there in the same app, allowing for a more rapid progression of connection and better analytics.

Page admins have access to more insights on live-video, we can plug into the page API, use a variety of cameras, pin comments, play with graphics and insert video clips and have the opportunity to live-stream in 360.

Mark Frankel[15]

All of this reduces the 'entry-barrier' of getting the message out.

Personal and relatable – Live-streaming is effectively face-to-face dialogue. In fact, it's *one-to-many communication* with an intimate 'personal touch' in a way that a speaker on stage in a conference centre can't hope to replicate. It's communication with emotion. At a time when customer service reps are a million miles away from people who use their product or service, you are an authentic face: the 'bloke behind the brand'.

Conversational – through the on-screen text features, viewers can interact live with each other, shaping the content with their questions and directions.

This connection becomes *communication* when the presenter answers and engages with viewers during and after the show, humanising their brand and appearing more open, honest and approachable.

And finally, the big one:

Live – these streams are unscripted and unpredictable, raw and real, fresh, exciting and in-the-moment content that lets viewers see the human side of a business. Nothing is better than a right-now, real-time experience. (Who wants to see a video of an event two days after it happened live?)

Live plays to the FOMO factor, the Fear Of Missing Out: feeding our basic human curiosity by seeing something now and not having to wait. And if the broadcaster chooses not to save and upload the video, then they've created one-time-to-watch urgent exclusivity for their content.

▶ THE NEGATIVES OF LIVE

Yep: it's a book about live-streaming that tells you why you may *not* want to do live-streaming!

> *Watching Justin Bieber prattle on for 30 minutes in a perfectly lit studio is only 5% more compelling than watching a random stranger do the same from their couch. Neither warrants the immediate attention the 'live' label suggests.*
>
> Matt Hackett[16]

Live-streaming is . . .

Fast – but don't rush in before you have thought through your goals, content and strategy.

Mobile – streaming or watching live, or seeing an archived show on auto-play, will use considerable data.

Accessible – are you streaming because it's the latest 'business bandwagon' to jump on, or do you have legitimate goals to justify the investment of staff and time? Live-streaming is rarely going to be polished and professional (although it can be, with extra software, time and expertise).

Inexpensive – there is a cost in terms of data, and also if you get added kit such as external mics and lights and so on. And things could get *very* expensive if you break copyright by streaming what you shouldn't, break someone's privacy, commit contempt or defamation.

> *If you're in business, then there needs to be an ROI to everything you do. If it isn't making you money, then it's not worth your time. Move on to something that actually*

benefits your business and not your ego. Stop just playing at being in business and do some god damn work! In business work equals money; time equals money.

Samantha Martin[17]

Integrated – It's great, isn't it? Having all of your content housed by someone else? It's like using one of those storage lock-ups for everything you created. And it's all free. But what happens if you break the rules and they lock you out? Or the rent goes sky-high? Or they start making money by selling access to your content? Or set up stalls alongside your lock-up and make more money from your popularity than you do?

You see where I'm going with this analogy? Take advantage of the literal *free*-dom of Facebook hosting your content, but get your viewers to *your website* where *you* can take advantage of them: creating a list, using their data, tracking their visits, selling to them direct, and making money for yourself via any adverts on your page. *Own your own content, and make money for you.*

Personal and relatable –

Creating relationships is all well and good and vital to growth, but creating relationships with people that are never going to buy from you is just a waste of your time and energy. Focus on creating relationships and content for the people that are your ideal customers.

Samantha Martin[18]

Conversational – but this is hard. It can mean a stuttering style as you try to talk and read the on-screen text comments to yourself at the same time. And it's not much of a conversation to say dozens of hellos, or to read out loud the messages that viewers can see perfectly well for themselves. Are *you* able to perform?

And finally, the big one:

Live – 'Going live' can be an excuse for content that is unfocused, ill-prepared, open-ended and rambling. Content that's boring or long-winded would often be better having been recorded and edited.

With 'live' there's no second take, and everyone will see what goes wrong, turning your live-stream into a *live-scream*. You have to be ready to think and react fast.

Consider:

> ▶ Is what I am about to do live, engaging, shareable and interactive?
>
> ▶ Is it a 'participatory and immersive experience'?
>
> ▶ Or would it be better recorded and edited?

HOW TO GET OVER THE FEAR OF 'RAW'

With great risk comes great reward.

And there's no doubt about it: raw = risky.

It also = open and honest.

Putting your brand on a live-stream takes courage: but that's returned as appreciation and loyalty when things go well.

You need to maximise the rewards and minimise the risks.

That's not to say you should start live-streaming just because you can. You need a purpose, a strategy and a way to manage that journey and to measure its outcome.

There may be a few fails, but you can guard against them to a large extent by a change of culture and coaching and a 'can-do' attitude.

Sitting still and watching while the world moves on is tantamount to running scared. Running over the edge of a cliff. Remember those stats at the front of the book? The ones about video consumption? Live-video streaming isn't going anywhere anytime soon, but businesses and brands that ignore it might well do.

Where we are now is just the tip of an iceberg. Start these apps now, build an audience and get ahead of the wave.

> *Doing anything "live" scares the living poo out of most brands . . . they'll wait and watch. And, while they do, the smaller, nimble companies will get creative. They'll experiment. They'll gain fans and followers . . . [and] market-share – something that will leave the big brands, wondering how it happened.*

Marcus Sheridan[19]

I believe that live-streaming will help you build a stronger and healthier relationship with current customers and potential prospects, with intimate and exclusive content, and real-time feedback.

The *New York Times* wrote: "many live videos are either plagued by technical malfunctions, feel contrived, drone on too long, ignore audience questions or are simply boring".[20]

This is where you start to remedy that.

▶ NOTES

1   Ken Bock, *The Country Caller Compares the Live Streaming Options on the Two Social Media Platforms*, www.thecountrycaller.com/ October 28th, 2016

2   Ramona Sukhraj, *Video Content Is King*, www.impactbnd.com/ September 10th, 2016

3   David Konigsberg, *The Future of Marketing*, http://blog.optimaltargeting.com/ August 28th, 2013

4   Dave Lloyd, *SEO for Success in Video Marketing*, https://blogs.adobe.com/ April 20th, 2015

5   Lucia Moses, *Publishers Adopt Facebook Live*, http://digiday.com/ November 9th, 2016

6   *Some US Marketers Are Already Eager to Invest in Live Stream Video*, www.emarketer.com/ August 11th, 2016

7   Carla Marshall, *By 2020, 75% of Mobile Traffic Will Be Video*, http://tubularinsights.com/ February 8th, 2016

8   Vibhi Kant, *News Feed FYI: Taking into Account Live Video When Ranking Feed*, http://newsroom.fb.com/ March 1st, 2016

9   Vibhi Kant, *Taking into Account Live Video When Ranking Feed*, http://newsroom.fb.com/ March 1st, 2016

10 *Brands Prefer Facebook Native Videos*, www.emarketer.com/ January 6th, 2016

11 Kurt Wagner, *Facebook Says Video Is Huge*, www.recode.net/ January 27th, 2016

12 Cathy Hackl, *Is Mobile Live Streaming the Missing Link Between TV and Social Media?*, www.huffingtonpost.com/ September 17th, 2015

13 Dylan Mortensen, *The Live Streaming Video Report*, http://uk.businessinsider.com/ September 23rd, 2016

14 Mitch Carson, *Connect Like Never Before With Periscope*, www.caribbeannewsnow.com/ August 17th, 2015

15 Mark Frankel, *Fill Your Boots*, https://medium.com/@markfrankel29/ December 20th, 2016

16 Matt Hackett, *Live Video: It's Not About the Content*, https://medium.com June 23rd, 2016

17 Samantha Martin, *Viva La Facebook Live*, http://sociallysam.com/ April 13th, 2016

18 Samantha Martin, *Viva La Facebook Live*, http://sociallysam.com/ April 13th, 2016

19 Marcus Sheridan, 7 Profound Implications of the "Live Stream Economy" for Brands and Businesses, www.thesaleslion.com/ (no publication date)

20 Liz Spayd, *Facebook Live: Too Much, Too Soon*, www.nytimes.com/ August 20th, 2016

2

Facebook Live

▶ **INTRODUCTION**

Facebook Live (born April 2016) is without a doubt the big beast of the live-streaming world. An absolute media monster. Why? It is:

- ▶ A trusted platform.

- ▶ A huge user base (as of Q3 of 2016, Facebook had 1.79 billion monthly active users to Twitter's 317 million).[1]

- ▶ An engaged *community*.

- ▶ Unparalleled distribution – other *stand-alone* apps can only reach people inside those apps, but Facebook Live integrates with Facebook.

- ▶ Great analytics, targeting and post-show boosting to reach a larger audience.

- ▶ Prioritising of live-video when it shares content with followers.

- ▶ Videos are kept on your page and are easily searched.

- ▶ People comment more than 10 times more on Facebook Live videos than on regular videos.

There will always be room for a Lyft where there is an Uber, a Pepsi where there is a Coke, and a Burger King where there is a McDonald's. What this does mean is the clear-cut market leader will be Facebook.

Dakota Shane[2]

FIGURE 2.1 The Facebook Live logo

Source: Facebook

In this chapter learn about the key features of Facebook Live and the advantages it has over other apps and whether it's right for your business or personal strategy. There won't be lots of tuition on 'what buttons to press', because the app is updated on such a regular basis and because features and layout are different on iOS, Android and desktop devices. However, there are lots of links to online resources.

▶ THE BASICS

Where you can broadcast

You can broadcast live-video through your:

- ▶ **Personal profile** – depending on the settings you have chosen (public, friends, etc.)

- ▶ **Business or Fan Pages** – via the Facebook Pages app (www.facebook.com/business/learn/facebook-page-manager-app) or the Facebook Mentions app (www.facebook.com/about/mentions/)

- ▶ **Facebook Group you belong to** – so, you can broadcast to your work colleagues, family or sports friends depending on the privacy settings of the group itself (and the group's own rules set up regarding who can post live-video)

- ▶ **Event page** – if you have been invited to the event and have responded as being interested in going (depending on whether the Event has 'public' or 'private' settings)

We hope this new ability to both broadcast and watch live video within Groups and Events enables people to connect more deeply with their closest friends, family and the communities of people who share their interests.

Facebook.com[3]

MODERATING 'GROUP' AND 'EVENT' LIVE-VIDEO

Live-video is a great way to engage with other members of the same Group or Event page.

But as every member who can post a status update could set up a live-stream on the page, monitoring the sheer number of them for possible violations of your own content guidelines could be very time-consuming. After all, it's easier to scan a written message than to listen to every word of a video. Therefore, you may decide to have a blanket 'no Facebook Live' rule.

Although there is no specific way in Settings to block live-video posts, there is a workaround by having *all* content to be moderated before being posted. (Tap the *'Post Approval'* box in the Group Moderation settings, and *'All posts must be approved by admin'* in the Event settings.)

Facebook won't let business pages post to a Group or Event, so you will need to use a personal account to do that, and tell your viewers of your company in the live-stream itself.

Your quick 'go-live guide'

There is much more on many of the features mentioned here throughout the book, but for now here's the bottom-line on what to do:

- ▶ Log into the Facebook for iOS app or the Facebook for Android app.

- ▶ Select your account.

- ▶ Complete the 'write something' description of what your presentation will be about, what you will show and say.

- ▶ Change the Public/Private setting if necessary (only on your Profile page). You can choose Public, Friends, Friends Except, Only Me and any interest lists that you have set up.

- ▶ Tap the 'Live' camera icon. (These steps may be in a different order depending on whether you are going to stream from a Profile or, say, Group page.)

- ▶ Describe your live-video (and geotag your location, tag other users, and add your 'mood' emoticon if you wish).

- ▶ Tap 'Go Live' and you will see a 3,2,1 countdown before you start broadcasting. Your followers will be notified that you are live, and if your video settings are public, you will be added to Facebook Live's map (on desktop only).

- ▶ You can tap on the camera icon at the top of the screen at any time to switch from your front-facing to the rear-facing camera to show your viewers different scenes (that is, one of you or one of what you can see). You can also show your view in landscape or portrait mode, but you need to start the broadcast in the orientation that you want. (This may not be available for older phones, and in iOS, you need to ensure that the Zoom feature is off.)

▶ On the screen, you will see the duration of your broadcast so far and the number of people who are watching right now. You will also see the names of those watching, the comments made by them and the emoji-type reactions that they are sending.

▶ At the end of your show, tap the Finish button.

▶ You are given the option to:

  ▷ Save the video to your phone.

  ▷ Upload it to your Profile/Page/Group/Event site. Before you do this, you have the opportunity to trim the start and end of the broadcast. So, if your first few seconds were unsteady as you composed yourself, or a bit rambling as you welcomed viewers, you can edit this off before the recording is saved and watched by others. Look for the 'trim' notification and scissors icon.

▶ See stats into:

  ▷ How many people watched your live-video at its peak

  ▷ How long they watched for

  ▷ And a visual representation of viewers over the duration of your show

▶ You can go back and delete your video if you wish.

FIGURE 2.2 The Facebook Live start-up screen

Source: Facebook

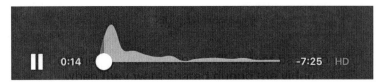

FIGURE 2.3 The 'waveform' of when you had 'peak viewership', that you see when you have completed your live-video

Source: Facebook

The map

There is no listings or comprehensive search facility for any live-stream platform, but you can see what other people across the world are broadcasting right now on Facebook at www.facebook.com/livemap/. You can only view this on your desktop.

> *A parade of strangers in their idle moments, raging and geeking out and often just staring listlessly into their cameras in real time. It is basically no one's idea of good content. I highly recommend it . . . a delightful mess.*

Claire McNear[4]

▶ FACEBOOK LIVE FEATURES

Going live from a desktop

You can also broadcast on your personal profile, business page or in Groups from a desktop PC or Mac. This will mean that the camera is steadier, thus improving quality for the broadcaster. (Indeed, you can add in peripheral cameras, not just the in-built one.)

Many people are more comfortable talking to a laptop than they are a mobile phone, and administrators of Pages can give access rights to such contributors so they can broadcast live on behalf of their company (see below).

- ▶ Use the Chrome browser and you will see the link to post live-video on your profile under the header image.
- ▶ Click the 'more' button to reveal the Facebook Live button.
- ▶ Click 'Start A Live Video' on your Facebook Page when you see the red box.
- ▶ You will need to give access to your camera and mic.
- ▶ When you are ready to start your live-stream, click the 'Go Live' button.
- ▶ A countdown timer will appear.
- ▶ You will see the duration of the live-stream at the top of the video.

- ▶ Comments from viewers will appear on the right-hand side.

- ▶ To end the live-stream, click the 'Finish' button.

- ▶ You will then get the option to delete your video or allow it to be posted to your Page or Profile.

However, part of the appeal of live-streaming is showing an event at a moment's notice when you are out and about, rather than from your home or business office.

Two-person presentations

There is the facility to add a second person to join and talk with you live on the screen. The main broadcaster invites their guest onto the show, and the two of you are shown to everyone, either as a split screen (in horizontal aspect) or picture-in-picture if in vertical mode.

You go live in the normal way, and then:

- ▶ Ask the wannabe guest to make a comment as soon as they start watching so you know that they have joined. Then, tap on their profile picture and then 'invite to broadcast'. (Alternatively, swipe the screen to see a list of all your live viewers and then invite one of them to join you on-screen.)

- ▶ The invitee will get a notification on their screen to join your live-stream. They tap 'Go Live' and they are in.

- ▶ To end the guest's broadcast, tap their live-video on the screen and then 'x'.

- ▶ They will get a message to thank them for joining the show and a prompt to share the live-stream to their followers.

Potential uses for this feature include interviews, debates, duets and collaborations. And of course by introducing an additional person, you get access to their audience as well.

Live 'contributors'

Using this feature, you can assign team members to go live without giving them full admin rights. Open your Page's settings > Page Roles > and set up a name or email as a 'live contributor'. You need to be friends with the person you add as a Contributor first, and you can remotely end their live broadcast if necessary. (See more here: www.facebook.com/facebookmedia/guides/live-contributor-role)

Pinned comments

Pages can pin particularly good comments, or ones made by the broadcaster themselves, to the bottom of a live-stream screen.

Permalinks

Pages can have all their videos at *'facebook.com/pagename/videos.'* Ongoing live-videos will be pinned to the top, making it a quick and easy way to direct users towards your page during a broadcast and to let recurring visitors know where to go.

Comments

While a show is live, or when watching a once-live show, viewers can comment with written text and send other reactions, which float across the video screen.

When watching a once-live show, any comments made are preceded by a timestamp to show at what point in the video it was sent. If you click on that stamp when watching the replay, the video will fast-forward or rewind to that point.

The emoji-type icons (Like, Love, Haha, Wow, Sad or Angry) make it easy for viewers to express an opinion in one tap, to save them from typing a sentence or phrase. Slide the comment bar across to pick which one to send. Broadcasters and viewers who want to hide all such reactions can go into 'video-only' mode to hide them. Just 'swipe right' on the screen.

Facebook allows you to use reactions for polling, with a few restrictions:

▶ You can't use a specific icon for something that doesn't match the topic (*"Choose 'heart' if you hate broccoli"*).

▶ Don't make the reactions the most prominent feature of the broadcast.

▶ Don't use reactions in a poll, where the whole live-video is a static or looping graphic.

It is quite complex to use reactions for polls, and you have to stream through another platform. There is a good 'how-to' guide here: www.interhacktives.com/2017/03/03/facebook-live-polls/

Notifications

When you are broadcasting, you can ask viewers to subscribe to your stream so they get a notification on their phone when you next go live. They do this by tapping the 'subscribe' button that appears as they watch your show.

Viewers can send an invitation to a friend to watch with them. They just tap on the 'invite' icon and select the friend they want to share the video with, and they will get a push notification.

Reminding your viewers to use these features should increase your audience.

Adjustments tray

This (tap the 'magic wand' and 'tool set') gives the presenter more control and customization over how their broadcast appears.

▶ Flip the camera horizontally or vertically.

▶ Adjust brightness settings – useful if broadcasting in a darker room.

▶ And choose whether to mirror the picture or not, so viewers see text shown on camera, the 'correct' way around.

Cross-posting live-videos

You can post your live-stream to several pages at the same time.

Filters

Use the 'magic wand' in the upper left corner of the screen to access the filters and personalise your live-video. Choose from:

▶ Normal

▶ Pop

FIGURE 2.4 A Facebook Live stream showing the invitation to follow the broadcaster, a prompt for viewers to comment and a pinned comment

Source: Facebook

FIGURE 2.5 Filter options on Facebook Live

Source: Facebook

- ▶ Classical

- ▶ Country

- ▶ Funk

- ▶ Acid designs

Masks

When you are presenting a Facebook Live, you may be able to show yourself with a Snapchat-style mask over your face. Some of these may be 'limited edition' for an event such as Hallowe'en (in 2016 they included a pumpkin and a witch).

FIGURE 2.6 Masks can be chosen by the broadcaster to 'wear' during their show

Source: Facebook

▶ Once you are live, tap the 'magic wand'.

▶ Select the mask icon in the creative tools tray at the bottom of the screen.

▶ Scroll through the options and tap on them to automatically appear on your face as you broadcast.

▶ To remove the mask, scroll left in the mask area and tap the 'no mask' sign.

Drawing on the screen

Using the 'magic wand' and then the 'pencil' icon, you can draw or doodle on your live-video as you present it, to highlight a particular part of the scene. Choose a colour and simply trace the line on your screen. Tap the 'trash can' to delete the line.

FACEBOOK AUTO-PLAYS SOUND

When followers scroll through their newsfeed, videos (live or pre-recorded) start playing with the sound on (it fades in and out as the viewer scrolls through their feed). Facebook hopes that this will keep more people engaged for longer.

▶ This may mean that noise blasts from your viewer's phone while they are in public.

▶ If they are already listening to music, that won't be interrupted. If they want to hear the *video*, they tap to make it full-screen and mute what had been playing.

What does this mean for a broadcaster?

▶ You have another opportunity (using great, compelling audio) to grab the attention of a viewer.

▶ Consider a strong 'audio opening' to your show, to entice someone to watch a 'once-live' video as they scroll past it. You will have just two or three seconds to do this.

A viewer can turn off the auto-play sound option in Facebook's settings menu: Settings > Account settings > Sounds > Videos in News Feed Start With Sound on/off.

The donate button

If you are the administrator for a non-profit organisation, you can get a 'donate' button to add to your live-videos and posts (you need to go through an official vetting process with Facebook to gain access). This will, of course, help increase donations and awareness for your charity. (Note: Facebook, like other companies, may charge a percentage fee to process credit card transactions.)

Real-time ads

These adverts make it easier to promote your broadcast and grab an audience when you are live. You can, of course, promote your show using other platforms or social media, or even run a sponsored post before the broadcast, or after it has ended. But these ads appear in newsfeeds while you are actually live.

Mid-roll ads

Some broadcasters (those with 2,000+ followers and 300+ concurrent viewers in a recent broadcast) can place adverts inside their live-streams, with a 55–45% revenue split with Facebook, in favour of the broadcaster.

- ▶ The broadcaster can choose when to take the break, and tap on the $ icon on the screen when they wish to do so.
- ▶ The live-stream must run for at least four minutes before the first advert.
- ▶ Ads, which are up to 20 seconds long, must be at least five minutes apart.
- ▶ Advertisers have limited control over which videos get their in-stream ads.
- ▶ Viewers see a countdown in the corner of the screen to indicate when you will be back.
- ▶ Viewers cannot skip through the ad.

The way live-videos are produced is likely to change to become more competitive, as broadcasters try and build suspense to keep interest through ad breaks.

Watching a live-video on your TV

You can stream videos via Apple TV, AirPlay devices, Google Chromecast and GoogleCast devices:

- ▶ Go to a video on your phone.

▶ Tap the TV button at the top right-hand corner.

▶ Select the device you want to stream via.

You can scroll through the feed and use Facebook while the video plays.

Making your show more pro

The beauty of these apps is that anyone can use them: you can go live to the world from your mobile phone. Just hold it at arm's length in front of you and show your friends what is happening in your world right now.

But it may be that you want your production to be a bit more polished. So Facebook has opened up its API (the coding), so other developers can develop programs which will enhance your live-stream. These enable you to have branding on screen (such as a logo embedded in the picture), lower-thirds (captions, such as your name and that of your company), or even to bring in other contributors or pre-recorded video. (See elsewhere for more on this topic.)

Scheduled live-streams[5]

Live-video's great, but not if your audience doesn't know when you are going to do one. You could advertise your show manually on Facebook or Twitter, but scheduling is rather more integrated and professional.

If you are using another app through which you are streaming to Facebook Live, you can make an 'announcement post' for a forthcoming show up to a week in advance. This builds a buzz around your content and such, audience anticipation will get you off to a flying start with eager viewers.

Pages can activate this through their Publishing Tools section:

▶ Select Video Library.

▶ Select Live.

▶ Copy your stream credentials (e.g. stream key or server URL).

▶ Write the description of the show.

▶ Add a custom image if you want to.

You will also be able to share a link to the broadcast or embed it in other places such as websites or blogs.

Once scheduled, an 'announcement post' will be published to your newsfeed. From that, fans can choose to get a one-time reminder just before you go live. For three minutes before the show starts, they will join a 'green room' to connect with other viewers, which adds to the community around your brand.

▶ OTHER FACEBOOK PLATFORMS

Facebook Live for Mentions

Facebook Mentions is an app that enables all kinds of public figures, including athletes, musicians, journalists and politicians, to easily connect with their audience on Facebook. There are a few features that are currently unique to this 'sub-platform'.

Before the broadcast

Team Prompts – some celebrities collaborate with their PR people on show ideas before going live, and this feature allows the staff to:

- ▶ Create drafts of Facebook Live post descriptions, so the celeb can easily review and post via Mentions when going live, and they just have to hit 'go live' and start streaming.

- ▶ Schedule reminders for them to go live.

- ▶ Publish posts from the Mentions app at a specific time, such as from an event.

Category Tags – broadcasters can add 'content tags' describing their show before they go live to increase discoverability.

Comment Moderation – those using Mentions can add words and phrases to a blacklist before they go live, which will stop comments containing those words from appearing during the broadcast. This moderation tool can help make live broadcasts friendlier and safer for viewers, reduces the amount of monitoring and blocking a broadcaster has to do while live, and so encourages them to live-stream more often.

During the broadcast

Status bar – this provides various information while the broadcaster is live:

- ▶ **Connectivity** – this indicator shows the signal strength available and whether a broadcaster is moving into a weaker area and so be more likely to be cut off.

▶ **Battery** – live-streaming takes a lot of battery power. This monitor will show the battery life so presenters can conclude before being cut off.

▶ **Audio** – this indicator shows whether you or your background location noise is too loud or soft for viewers.

After the broadcast

Trimming – this lets people using Mentions trim excess footage from the beginning and end of their live-video after the broadcast has ended. That might include any 'phone fumbling' or lengthy 'hello-to-the-show' greeting at the start or reaching for the 'stop' button at the end.

Facebook Live audio

Sometimes publishers want to tell a story with words and not video. We've even seen some Pages go live and reach audiences with audio only by adding a still image to accompany their audio broadcast. We know that people often like to listen to audio while doing other things.

Facebook.com[6]

This audio-only service from Facebook has several advantages:

▶ Maybe you are camera shy and prefer the anonymity offered by presenting a live-stream that's audio-only.

▶ It reduces the cost of streaming for the producer and the listener, making it particularly useful in a crowded area (a conference or news hot spot) or where cell coverage is weak (perhaps in a remote or developing area).

Considerations for Facebook Live Audio:

▶ It is much easier (emotionally) for a listener to turn off an audio stream than it is to turn off someone speaking to them on-camera (which is much more personal).

▶ Having said that, people usually need to *watch* video, but can consume an audio-only feed while they are doing other things.

▶ As we will see later, while shaky and grainy live-video may be 'sufferable', people turn off pretty quickly if the *sound* is bad. So this suggests that production values on Live Audio will have to be high.

Possible uses for the streams (up to four hours' duration):[7]

▶ Reports from the scene where data coverage is poor or the scene is 'too traumatic' or dangerous to show.

▶ A relay service for radio stations, particularly all-speech services.

▶ A new distribution platform for podcasts and audio blogs.

▶ A 'teaser platform' to highlight content that's on another platform and to drive people to consume it elsewhere.

Tips for using Facebook Live Audio:

▶ When you start a stream, you can use your Page's cover image as the thumbnail or you can upload a new one.

▶ Notifications are sent to a Page's Live subscribers and some of your most active followers.

▶ Android users can close Facebook and use another app and the Audio will still play. IOS users have to keep Facebook open, or the Audio will be cut.

Facebook Workplace

Facebook also runs a separate area for internal video collaboration. Workplace (https://workplace.fb.com/) is an ad-free space, separate from your personal Facebook account.

▶ NOTES

1 See: *Twitter by the Number*, https://www.omnicoreagency.com/twitter-statistics/ and *Facebook by the Numbers*, https://www.omnicoreagency.com/facebook-statistics/

2 Dakota Shane, *The Winner of the Live Streaming Battle Is Obvious . . . Here's Why*, www.socialmediaexplorer.com/ January 5th, 2017

3 Quoted at *Facebook Raises Periscope Challenge With Video Upgrades*, www.yahoo.com/ April 6th, 2016

4 Claire McNear, *The Facebook Live Map Is a Little Bit of Chaos in a Sea of Curation*, https://theringer.com/ January 10th, 2017

5 A 'How-to' Guide Is Here: https://media.fb.com/2016/10/18/scheduling-a-live-broadcast-via-the-live-api/

6 Esther Kezia Thorpe, *Why Facebook Live Audio Is Just the Beginning of Its Bid for Audio, Domination*, www.themediabriefing.com/ January 4th, 2017

7 There is a short article by Lucinda Southern on How *The Economist* Is Using Facebook Live Audio Here: https://digiday.com/media/facebook-audio-economist/

3

Twitter Go Live/ Periscope

▶ **INTRODUCTION**

You can go live within the Twitter app, or via the separate (but linked) app, Periscope[1] (born March 2015), which is owned and powered by Twitter.

The main differences are that:

- ▶ With Twitter Go Live you can easily point-and-stream with one tap, but with Periscope you have more options before you go live.

- ▶ Although live-streams via Twitter and those via Periscope can each appear in your Twitter feed, with Periscope you can limit your audience to within that app or to certain groups of people.

- ▶ Twitter Go Live live-streams are not curated, but Periscope streams are archived within your account.

- ▶ Periscope users can search via content topics and a map, so videos are more easily discovered.

- ▶ The Periscope app also has additional features such as (but not limited to): ways to easily block nuisance commenters (who may send offensive or annoying messages to the screen), a feature to hide your location, the facility to draw on the screen and metrics to more easily see who has interacted with your video.

FIGURE 3.1 The Periscope logo

Source: Periscope

So Twitter Go Live is quick and easy, but if you use Periscope you will still get the same exposure on your Twitter feed but considerably more features.

The use of the name 'Periscope' is a bit confusing. For the first 18 months, Periscope was in the main, a separate app to Twitter. Although it is owned by Twitter and the two apps 'talk to' each other, people needed Periscope to go live or to watch and comment in someone else's live-stream.

At the time of this writing, integration is still not complete. Although you can now go live directly from the Twitter app and can watch live and 'once-live' shows in your Twitter feed, you still need the separate Periscope phone app to see specific analytics and search for other broadcasts.

Twitter has shied away from simply calling its live-video service, say, 'Twitter Live' (as Facebook has done with Facebook Live), although it does now refer to a 'Go Live' brand, which is "powered by Periscope".

The Twitter/Periscope link

A huge strength of Periscope is its link with Twitter. Indeed, Twitter is really Periscope's driving force:

▶ Twitter is where people discover breaking news, and so is often used by broadcasters for this very purpose (Facebook Live is perhaps more for scheduled, longer-form content delivered to a community).

▶ It's easy for your Twitter followers to retweet your live-stream, greatly enhancing your discoverability and getting you in front of more eyeballs.

▶ Viewers can watch your video right in their Twitter feed, which 'reduces the friction' of them having to go elsewhere (e.g. following a link to a YouTube site).

▶ You can link Periscope to your Twitter profile on the web, making it easier for people to build a better relationship with you.

▶ You can turn on notifications for a specific Twitter user, including tweets that include live-video.

Periscope isn't so much channelled through Twitter but powered by it. Other live-streaming apps miss out because they don't have the promo power of the Twitter integration to help drive people to view the videos. Twitter and Periscope are a match made in heaven because they both live for 'in the moment' comment and reaction.

> *Twitter is the place where people go for real-time conversation. Facebook gives you reach, but Twitter gives you influence.*

Will Hayward[2]

Consider Twitter's Periscope as a stream of updates, whereas Facebook is a *community*, and so the two platforms may be perhaps used for different kinds of content – Twitter's Periscope to reach new viewers, Facebook to connect with the fans you already have. Twitter is considered by some to be a more obvious home for live-video than, say, Facebook:

> *Your network there is populated by people you are genuinely interested in, as opposed to people who were once seated next to you at a wedding. A live-video shared by someone you follow is more likely to interest you than one shared by a distant acquaintance.*

Casey Newton[3]

In this chapter learn about the key features of Twitter Go Live and Periscope and how they differ from other apps. That way you can work out if they are right for your business or personal strategy. There won't be lots of tuition on 'what buttons to press' in every circumstance, because the apps are updated on such a regular basis and because features, layout and terminology are different on iOS and Android devices. However, there are links to online resources which do have such information.

FACEBOOK LIVE VS. TWITTER GO LIVE/PERISCOPE

Facebook Live has perhaps:

▶ More of a community feel and

▶ There is a conversation. . .

▶ with existing followers

Twitter Go Live/Periscope:

▶ Could be considered more of a stream of updates. . .

▶ For quick snapshots of what's happening now and breaking news,

▶ And it is easier to share (re-tweet) to new followers, and more easily searched.

Periscope's 'Producer'

If you want to make your shows look more professional with a studio-quality feel, you can stream to Twitter Go Live and Periscope directly from your own camera set-up, such as:

▶ A laptop webcam

▶ A professional video camera

▶ Games such as an Xbox One

▶ Apple's ReplayKit

▶ A virtual reality headset

▶ Studio editing rigs

▶ Satellite trucks

▶ Drones

▶ Desktop streaming software like OBS

▶ Indeed, almost anything using RTMP – Real-Time Messaging Protocol – rather than your phone

This will give you the ability to manually add other elements which aren't built into the app, such as external videos, live Skype calls, sponsorship logos, custom animations and graphics and live web pages. Indeed, professional TV stations can now also distribute their traditional shows through Twitter and Periscope as well.

These additional features help strengthen your brand's polish and professionalism, although arguably get away from the raw and in-the-moment authenticity which was originally at the heart of live-streaming.

> *The easier the set-up and the bigger the audience, the more creators who'll be willing to syndicate video to Periscope or make content for it specifically.*

Josh Constine[4]

With the 'Producer', you stream your show normally, but through the app's profile settings ('additional sources') you get a stream key (a special URL) that you put into your professional equipment. This essentially makes Twitter and Periscope just the distribution method of your show. Viewers can send hearts and comments as normal. As a broadcaster, you can even make your stream or game react to viewers' feedback (the Periscope team built a game in which a bird flew faster as more viewers sent hearts).

But poor content is poor content, whatever the video quality or text overlays. So, don't consider style over substance.

Organisations and individuals can be part of the Producer programme, and there is a how-to guide here: www.periscope.tv/help/external-encoders and https://help. periscope.tv/customer/portal/articles/2600293

▶ TWITTER GO LIVE

Your quick 'go-live guide'

To start a broadcast *inside Twitter (if you don't have the Periscope app)*:

- ▶ Tap the button to compose a new tweet.
- ▶ Tap the 'live' camera icon.
- ▶ Put in a title (this is the text that makes up the tweet with your live-video playing underneath).
- ▶ Frame your shot.
- ▶ Tap 'Go LIVE'.

During the show, viewers who see your broadcast on their timelines can tap to watch. If they have Periscope, they can watch through that app and send comments and appreciative heart icons (a 'feedback mechanism' which we will look at later) by tapping the screen.

Your live (or 'once-live') video can be seen:

▶ In Twitter, attached to a tweet in:

    ▷ The Twitter feed belonging to you, the broadcaster

    ▷ The feeds of those who follow you, if Twitter has pushed that tweet to their timeline (you never get sent all the tweets of everyone you follow)

▶ PERISCOPE

You can also go live through the Periscope app. There are additional features available specifically in Periscope, which give you much more control over your broadcast. For example, you can keep the broadcast within the Periscope app itself (so it's not distributed on Twitter), and you can decide which group of people within Periscope can see it. Periscope also gives you a 'channel' for all your archive shows.

The first-time set-up

Because Periscope isn't *entirely* integrated with Twitter, it takes a bit of setting up. Not all of your personal details will migrate across, and many of the icons are not ones you see in Twitter.

When you use Periscope for the first time, your Twitter bio and picture will show up, and then you'll be offered a list of people you may want to follow, based on who you follow on Twitter.

Of course, you don't need to follow on Periscope everyone you follow on Twitter, so choose them carefully:

▶ People you follow may reciprocate by following you.

▶ The more people you follow, the more push notifications you may be sent.

You can unfollow people later if you change your mind; for example, if they do too many shows or the content is not what you had anticipated.

Your quick 'go-live guide'

There is more, much more, on each of these features throughout the book, but here's the bottom line on what to do:

▶ Open the Periscope app.

▶ Tap on the 'people' icon and then the 'person' icon to ensure that you are about to stream through the correct Periscope account that you have permissions to use (there is no on-screen logo when you go live to remind you). *Having several accounts is useful if you want to follow and respond to one set of people professionally and another on a more personal basis.*

▶ Tap the 'broadcast' button.

▶ Tap 'public' to choose who you would like to broadcast to.

▶ Write a short description of your show (where it says *"what are you seeing now?"*).

▶ Tap the 'arrow' icon to choose whether or not to have your location publicised.

▶ Tap the 'speech bubble' icon to toggle who can comment in your show.

▶ Tap the Twitter bird depending on whether you would like your live-stream also shown on your Twitter feed.

▶ Compose your shot. Make sure that you have this first shot as something creative, colourful and interesting, as it will be what the once-live show will auto-play in your followers' Twitter feed. (You can change the view you show by double-tapping the screen before you go live, or during the show.)

▶ Tap the 'Go LIVE' button.

The 'watch' page

Of the five icons across the bottom of the screen, this is the first: a picture of the 'old-fashioned TV with aerial'. Tap this to watch shows by the people you follow.

On this page, you will see among other things:

▶ Featured broadcasts chosen by the Periscope team

▶ The live shows from people you follow on Periscope

▶ Shows by the people who you follow who have presented one in the last 24 hours and which have not been deleted by them

▶ Shows from the last 24 hours recommended by the people you follow

Alongside each thumbnail of a show are the title, from what account it was broadcast, its duration and total number of viewers. If a show is live right now, it will be clearly marked in red.

Periscopes do last longer than 24 hours, but after that time they will appear in each person's personal 'broadcasts list'.

Simply tap a show title to start it playing in full screen.

FEATURED SHOWS

These will have been chosen by the Periscope team (or an algorithm) as 'worth watching' because of factors such as their content, the number of viewers, the number of hearts and the reputation of the person streaming them.

The 'global listings' page

The page denoted by the 'Globe' icon is where you can find people from around the world who are presenting live shows right now or recently. You can choose the List or the Map view on this page.

The List view

Tap the 'slider' icon on the screen to sort the list of Scopes by those suggested by the Periscope curators, or by how recent they are. There are various icons to tap on this page, through which you can choose and sort the type of content that you would like to see, under headings such as travel, sports and politics. Within these categories are filters:

▶ Broadcasts, Places and People

▶ Suggested and Recent shows

▶ Highlights, where you can see a few random seconds of each stream

Each show will play automatically: tap the speaker icon in the corner of each one to hear the audio so you can listen in before you decide to 'enter the room'. Remember this feature when you are broadcasting: just because you have not seen someone join the audience, that doesn't mean they are not listening and waiting for something to make them join.

Tap the full picture to be taken to that broadcast so you can watch in full-screen mode and (if it is live) comment and send hearts. Your profile name will appear on the screen for everyone else to see, and you may be welcomed by the host with a namecheck.

When you are watching a once-live show, you can tap and hold the screen to scroll through the video. Each thumbnail video in the list will show its duration (if it has ended) and the number of viewers (watching now if the show is live or a total number for a once-live show).

The Map view

The Map view is initially on a 'world' view with a red 'hot spot' dot showing current 'live shows', and blue ones which are less than 24 hours old (as long as the broadcaster has enabled their 'location' feature – see later).

You can zoom into the map (by outward-pinching) to see the number of streams in parts of each country and then in each city or neighbourhood. Every time you zoom to a new place on the map, Periscope will reload live and 'replay' broadcasts from this new region. Tap on a dot, and you will be taken straight to that person's show.

Using the Periscope map:

- ▶ You can easily watch streams from city to city as your whim takes you.

- ▶ You can quickly go to a specific location if you know that a news event is happening there.

- ▶ You can see people who are streaming near you (and potentially have a Periscope 'meet-up' with them).

Again, you can sort the content by (using the magnifying glass) 'broadcasts', 'places' or 'people', or (with the slider) filter the content to see 'all shows' or just those which are currently live.

The main Map view also incorporates a night-time/day-time representation, to make it easier to find endless sunsets/sunrises around the world.

CHOOSING YOUR LANGUAGE

Change the setting in your Profile to indicate the language in which you would prefer to see Scope titles. It won't *translate* any titles, but it will only show titles written in that language.

What does this mean for broadcasters?

Use the location feature strategically.

You can share your location and therefore appear on this map, by tapping the 'compass' button in the broadcast screen just before you go live. This, and having your replay Scope appear as a blue dot:

▶ **Gives authenticity to your personality and brand** – viewers will know that you are 'real' and based *somewhere*, even if it is not local to them.

▶ **May give context about what you are showing and talking about** – for example, if you are at a show or describing a view.

▶ **Makes it easier for people to find you** – if you have a business that is 'location-based' (e.g. a theatre, farmers' market or café), or are at an event or tradeshow, then turn the location feature on. Then people can easily find and visit you, perhaps by taking a screenshot of the map linked to your show.

▶ **May strengthen your relationship with viewers** – who know something about where you are, maybe having visited or lived there.

If you are on location and that location is part of the content of your broadcast, it makes sense to let your viewers see the area map.

Your broadcasting page

The next page is the main ready-to-broadcast screen. Some of these buttons are self-explanatory (such as the 'quit' and 'start broadcast' ones), but let's go through the others.

Private broadcasts

You have the option to do a private broadcast (a 'closed show') by tapping the 'Public' tag at the top of the screen (layouts differ between handsets), so only certain people will be told about your show, be able to see it and be able to comment and send you hearts. (Again, this is another feature that is not available in Twitter Go Live.)

When you tap the icon, a list of mutual followers (people you follow who also follow you back) comes up to choose from. You can select as many people as you want to join a private Scope. You can also choose to put these people in a group so you can easily select them all in the future.

Why would you want to do this?

▶ It could be a confidential show about business.

▶ You could be asking someone advice and want to show them something.

▶ You could be doing a training session for a closed group and perhaps be charging for your content.

▶ You may have one Periscope account but use it for different formats, say, for personal and business use, or one for teaching piano lessons and another for violin lessons.

Of course, most times you'll want to do a public programme (the default setting) and reach a bigger audience, but in a private Scope, you can target just those to whom the content relates. (Private broadcasts don't show up in the Watch list.)

Don't worry if you forget to turn off the Twitter auto-notification before you go private! Although people can see the link and tap on it, it will take them nowhere.

Location Sharing – the 'compass' icon

If you turn the location on:

▶ You will be discoverable on the Map view.

▶ Your location will also appear on the map (under your show title when you broadcast), on which people can zoom in.

FIGURE 3.2 The main broadcast screen for Periscope

Source: Periscope

Simply toggle the 'compass' button to turn the feature on or off. The compass turns white when it is activated.

If you do not want to be approached by a fellow Periscoper, and especially if you are broadcasting from home, you may want to turn off the 'location' sharing before you go live, but then your show won't appear on the global map (although the people who follow you will still, of course, get a notification that you are live).

Having the location feature on will also mean that your 'local time' is shown on the screen during your live broadcast.

Decide who can comment

Tap on the 'speech bubble' icon and the only people who will be able to comment will be the people who you follow. The developers have assumed that those are the people who you have taken a conscious decision to 'pre-approve', as it were, and so this reduces the likelihood of 'outsiders' or trolls from spoiling your show. **Note that the default, greyed-out position lets everybody comment, and highlighting the button permits only your followers.**

Notifications through Twitter

If you tap on the 'Twitter bird' in this screen, then your show will also be streamed through your Twitter account. Having your video publicised on your Twitter feed gives it a 'longer tail' and increases the chances of more people seeing the show. In effect, now you are on two social networks.

Your Periscope followers will (if they have opted in for this) also be sent a 'push notification' to their phone, together with a Twitter chirp.

Your broadcast title

The number-one mistake newbies make is not putting in a title at all, or putting one in that doesn't 'sell' their show.

The title is what is tweeted, and it is in the push notification, too. It's also what will describe your show in the Watch menu. So make sure that it is a real attention-grabber, to persuade people to tap and watch. It should be:

- ▶ short
- ▶ tempting

- ▶ clickable

- ▶ but true

If you do not give your show a title now, you will not be able to add it later. Neither will you be able to change a title that you have added.

The 'activity' page

Leave the broadcasting page ('x' it out) and go to the fourth tab, the 'bell' icon. This is where you can quickly see who has recently watched a show of yours or followed you. Like the 'notifications' tab in Twitter, go here to find who to thank for their support.

The 'people' page

The final main icon is of the 'group of people'. This is where you can find details of other people, and from where you can create your own profile and check some of your basic stats.

Here we have Trending Scopers: people who have been picked by an algorithm (and then hand-checked by Periscope staff, for taste and decency). Being on this list is valuable because it gives you more exposure: people who don't follow you and would not know of your existence get to see you for the first time. It's an opportunity to showcase your best work.

The list is reconfigured each 24 hours, and you are likely to appear on it if:

- ▶ You have a (reasonably) high number of viewers (500–1000).

- ▶ The time they spent watching (the 'retention rate') is high.

- ▶ The number of times that they shared the broadcast is high.

- ▶ The number of times those shares were through Twitter was high.

- ▶ The number of times those Tweets were re-tweeted was high.

The 'goalposts' for whether you are on this Trending list are likely to be ever-shifting, and only scant details are shared as to how the list is determined. You will also only see Scopers featured who have chosen the same language as you have in their Periscope Settings.

Also on this page, there is a list of accounts that you are following on Twitter but not yet on Periscope.

Your Periscope bio/profile

Tap the 'single person' icon to be taken to your Profile page. Periscope will import your profile picture and bio from the Twitter account that you connected with Periscope.

Remember this is perhaps the first thing that people will read about you, so make a great impression. Some key things to remember:

- ▶ All your Twitter bio will be imported, but not all of it will be seen on Periscope.

- ▶ Your bio is highly searchable (through the Search icon), so make sure you include key search terms in what you write and any #'s or @'s to increase your discoverability.

- ▶ Because web viewers can view your bio, put in a hyperlink that they can click through to your website, sales page or a page of resources . . . or any other site (write the full address – that is, include http://).

- ▶ Sell yourself!

You *can* change your bio (and your 'full' name) independently of Twitter, and you may want to, to reflect your different priorities when on this platform. So, your *Twitter* bio may talk about your job and what kind of RTs you do. Your *Periscope* bio will probably include the content of the shows you present and how often.

You could even change your bio on a daily basis, incorporating a trail for your upcoming shows.

Not all of the bio will be immediately visible, so you may need to scroll down. Bear this in mind when you re-write it: think what words other people may use to search for you, and put those key words at the top and make sure that the bio doesn't cut off mid-word or phrase.

Twitter 'verified' badges (the 'blue tick' for celebrities, influencers, VIPs and corporations) appear in the Users section and in Search as well. This means that it is easier to check that the person who you're following, or who is commenting in your stream, is who they claim to be.

Your Periscope picture

You can also change your profile picture directly inside the app itself. This means that there's no excuse for having a default Twitter 'egg' logo as your picture on Periscope. Unless you're an egg farmer.

You could choose to have a *different* picture on Twitter and Periscope, but if your name is the same on both platforms, this may water down your brand and lead to confusion from your customers, clients or viewers. It is usually best to have a consistency of awareness across all platforms (i.e. Twitter, Periscope, Facebook, LinkedIn) as well as, for that matter, your printed stationery and website.

Your Periscope bio on the web

If you go to www.periscope.tv/username (where 'username' is the name of the Scoper), you'll see all the recent broadcasts for that person.

Have this address in your bios on other social media platforms and in your tweets: it is, if you like, your 'holding page' for your presence on Periscope. When people land there, they will see your picture, bio and details of your recent shows.

Followers and followings

Also in your Profile page, you can see how many people *you are following* (tap to see their names and profiles) and how many people *are following you* (again, tap to see who they are). Additionally, it can show those who have been blocked and also how many broadcasts you have streamed.

The list of the people who are following you on Periscope is sorted by how recently that person followed you. It makes it more awkward to find people (but arguably, you don't need to do that very often), but makes building a relationship with people much easier as you can now spot those who have started supporting you recently: their names and profiles will be at the top of this list. So every day or so, go through this process to see who they are and perhaps follow them back, watch one of their shows and make a comment, give hearts, or reach out to them on Twitter (if they are there). This is another way to build and strengthen relationships.

Also on this screen are various other lists:

> ▶ **Who you've blocked** – again, tap the button to see who you have blocked and, if you want, tap through to unblock them. Periscope says blocking "promotes transparency and accountability".

> ▶ **Your broadcasts** – an archive of your shows

> ▶ **Recently watched** – streams that you have seen

> ▶ **Superfans** – a list of your top ten viewers

> ▶ **Groups** – you can easily broadcast to a select audience, and here is where you can create each group. This feature helps you create communities of different specific interests, such as your online fans, Superfans (give them

exclusive content) or real-life friends or colleagues. Creating groups helps you draw a line between work-related and personal broadcasts and stream directly to that niche audience. As the creator of the group, you are its administrator and can decide who can join.

Superfans

This list on your bio page is the top ten viewers who are most engaged with your shows. Alongside each name is a score, which is calculated by an algorithm based on different engagement actions. Although it's different for each broadcaster-to-viewer relationship, this is based on metrics such as:

▶ Whether they follow you

▶ How often they watch

▶ How long they watch for

▶ How often they comment

▶ How many hearts they send

When a Superfan joins or comments in your show, a 'flame' icon appears next to their name so you can easily identify, welcome and thank them.

FIGURE 3.3 A user profile on Periscope

Source: Periscope, Alex Pettitt

Your Superfans are your most loyal viewers and biggest ambassadors, so use the list to get more insight into who loves you most and why. Create more meaningful relationships with them: broadcast more of the content they like and approach them on Twitter or elsewhere to strengthen your community.

You can also see which account has you as a Superfan.

Settings

Tap through here to change all of the -tions:

- ▶ Notifications
- ▶ Synchronisations
- ▶ Stabilizations
- ▶ Auto-deletions
- ▶ High definitions
- ▶ Moderations

Notifications – these toggle-options are quite straightforward. You can decide whether to be told when:

- ▶ Someone you follow goes live
- ▶ Someone you follow on Twitter goes live
- ▶ Someone shares a broadcast with you
- ▶ To be told of suggested broadcasts
- ▶ And when a user follows you

Turn them all on to get maximum engagement with others.

Synchronisations – turning this option on will sync your contacts to find people you know who are on Periscope. If you have confidential clients in your address book, you may not want to upload them for privacy reasons.

Under the 'Your Broadcasts' tab, swipe to turn on the 'Video Stabilization' (although this can cause broadcasts to be darker in low-light conditions) and turn off 'Auto-Delete After 24 Hours' (so your past shows are still visible for days to come, thus giving you more discoverability and your content a longer life). If you turn Auto-Delete on, you can still choose to keep each broadcast after it ends.

'Camera Roll' options include 'Auto-save to Camera Roll': you will want to enable this so you have a copy of your broadcast that you can then upload to other platforms, such as YouTube or your website to use as part of a blog post. You can also choose to save in high definition, although this will result in more battery and data usage. You can also tap a button to clear the cache on the app, to make it run more smoothly.

'Comment Moderation' – you will probably want to turn both of these settings 'on' to give you maximum protection from trolls.

On this page, you can also choose to have comments shown in large font, to have Periscopes auto-play (or not, or only on Wi-Fi), and choose your language (so you only see titles that you understand). You can also deactivate your account here.

The search function

You find Search under the People tab: it's the magnifying glass. You can use the Search function to help you look for people and possible content.

You can find someone specific who you want to follow or watch by putting their name in the Search box. You can use the Search function not only to search for people's names but also:

▶ Their company

▶ Any emoticon they use

▶ Their location

▶ Their industry

▶ And an advanced search: so '*Hawaii*' and '*hairdresser*' will bring up people who are hairdressers in Hawaii.

To put it another way, you can use the Search box to look for any word that people have put in the Periscope bio.

The couch mode

Another way to find content (albeit random content, so this is not actually searching) is to use Periscope's Couch Mode (www.periscope.tv/couchmode), which lets you scroll through people's live-streams just like you would click through your TV channels. It's a bit like a one-sided Chatroulette.

You don't get to choose what you want to watch, or what videos appear, and it's only available on the desktop version (i.e. not on your phone). You can't interact by giving comments or hearts, although you can see those made by other viewers. If you find either of these a distraction, click 'h' on your keyboard to make them disappear (and vice versa).

There's an arrow in the top right corner, which you can use to randomly pick the next feed if the current one is not to your taste – or use the arrow on your keyboard. If you want to watch an endless stream, just change the URL at the end with 'd = 30' and watch it switch every 30 seconds, or d = 60 or d = 90.

Pre-roll ads

Brands can buy pre-roll advertising on select Periscope video-streams, that are no longer live but still on Twitter, through Twitter's Amplify program.[5]

The 'live on air' button

Another way to promote your Scope is by having a link to it direct from the homepage of your personal website or any other page such as Facebook. Periscope provides a button that you can embed right here: www.periscope.tv/embed.

Someone viewing your webpage will initially see your Periscope username (in the blue box) and whether you are live at that moment (the button will flash red). When they click the button, they will leave your page and go to Periscope, where they will see your full profile and (if you are live) your show will start playing.

Periscope on a laptop

People can watch, comment and send hearts to your Scope from their PC/Mac on www.periscope.tv. However, to present your show you need to use a smartphone or tablet (unless you are a Periscope Producer – see elsewhere).

iPhone 3D shortcuts

If you have an iPhone 6s or 6s+, you have some shortcuts and added features not available to any other iPhone or Android user. Use the 'force touch' on the main Periscope app icon to access them:

▶ **Broadcast** – quickly start a public broadcast. This saves you pressing the app and going to the Broadcast page.

▶ **Broadcast Mutuals** – force-touching this button starts a private broadcast that only your mutual followers see (i.e. people you follow and who also follow you back). This is a great way to quickly go live to your friends or business associates.

▶ **Teleport** – this takes you to a random Scope that's live now, somewhere (anywhere!) in the world. To that extent, it is a bit like the 'Couch' feature, (viewers on the web are shown random streams). Having this feature makes your content much more discoverable (albeit, by chance!).

▶ **Search People** – pretty self-explanatory!

The Periscope VIP program

The VIP Program is for who the developers consider to be some of the 'top Scopers': those who broadcast lots of quality output. Members have access to a number of benefits, such as a special badge on their profile and a chance to be included in a rotating list of broadcasters for people to follow.

The main criteria for membership is 10,000+ average views per video, 20,000+ followers, and there are three different tiers.

Bronze – benefits include:

▶ Bronze badge on your Periscope profile

▶ Prioritisation in the people search results so that people can find you more easily

FIGURE 3.4 An example of a show created with the Periscope Producer program

Source: Alex Pettitt, Periscope

Minimum requirements:

- ▶ Average 200+ total live viewers per broadcast
- ▶ Broadcast at least twice a week on average
- ▶ Content and behaviour meets Periscope's Terms and Community Guidelines

Silver – benefits include:

- ▶ All Bronze benefits
- ▶ Silver badge on your Periscope Profile
- ▶ Included in future discovery products
- ▶ Prioritised support – They say they strive to respond to questions within 12 hours
- ▶ Private broadcasts from the Periscope team for an inside look at what they are up to
- ▶ A Slack channel with other VIPs to collaborate and build your Periscope network

Minimum Requirements:

- ▶ Average 750+ total live viewers per broadcast
- ▶ Broadcast at least twice a week on average
- ▶ Content and behaviour meets Periscope's Terms and Community Guidelines

Gold – benefits include:

- ▶ Includes all Bronze and Silver benefits
- ▶ Gold badge on your Periscope profile
- ▶ Elevated access to collaborate with the Periscope team

Minimum Requirements:

- ▶ Average 2,000+ total live viewers per broadcast
- ▶ Broadcast at least twice a week on average
- ▶ Content and behaviour meeting the Terms and Conditions

You can apply at www.periscope.tv/vipprogram.

OTHER WAYS TO WATCH PERISCOPE

Periscope is one of the apps on Apple TV boxes. Open the app (you don't need an account), and you'll be able to:

▶ See live broadcasts from around the world.

▶ Send hearts to the broadcaster.

▶ Read comments from other people watching with you.

▶ Skip to the next broadcast.

▶ Hide or show comments and hearts.

▶ Return to the main menu for an entirely fresh collection of places to go.

If a broadcast ends, Periscope will automatically take you to the next destination.

▶ Swipe up on your iPhone and tap 'Airplay'.

▶ Then tap on 'Apple TV' and turn on 'Mirroring'.

▶ And use Periscope on your iPhone as normal.

Live (and recorded) videos (yours or someone else's) can also be included in a Twitter Moment, alongside still images and text-tweets.

▶ NOTES

1 Read more about the backstory of Periscope here: Harry McCracken, *Inside Periscope*, www.fastcompany.com/

2 Will Hayward, *Joe Media Is Making TV-Like Programming for Facebook Live*, http://digiday.com/ October 10th, 2016

3 Casey Newton, *You Can Now Broadcast Live Video From the Twitter App*, www.theverge.com/ December 14th, 2016

4 Josh Constine, *Periscope Producer Lets You Stream to Twitter From Pro Cameras, Apps, VR*, techcrunch.com October 13th, 2016

5 *The Amplify Program* by @regandc: https://blog.twitter.com/2015/twitter-amplify-now-offering-video-monetization-at-scale

4

YouTube

▶ **INTRODUCTION[1]**

Live mobile streaming has been a bit of a slow development for the Google-owned site, even though it was the first major 'video site'. Your channel has to have had no live-stream restrictions in the previous 90 days and have over 1,000 subscribers.

▶ **THE MAIN ADVANTAGES**

- ▶ Your content is easily found; you have a channel page which acts as a library of all your content (essentially giving it a longer 'shelf life').

- ▶ You can easily distribute links direct to each video.

- ▶ Comments and reactions are neatly positioned under the video rather than on top of it (unlike Facebook Live and Periscope).

- ▶ To find content, the search engine is the second most-used in the world after Google.

Metrics are available such as:

- ▶ **Watching now** – for the current total of live viewers

- ▶ **Messages per minute** – to track text engagement

However, as it has no other text-based distribution platform, broadcasters are pretty much dependent on people sharing links to your YouTube content on other services such as Facebook and Twitter.

YouTube's options

When you want to create a live-stream on YouTube, you can choose to:

▶ **Stream Now** – which lets you create a live-stream in a few easy steps

▶ **Events** – which lets you choose between Quick and Custom

▷ **Quick** will create a Hangout On Air with all the standard Hangout On Air features, including quick-start streaming right from your laptop.

▷ **Custom** will create a YouTube Live Event where you control your event production and manage your own encoding settings using your preferred platform.

Your quick 'go live guide'

▶ Download the latest version of the YouTube app.

▶ Select the camera button.

▶ Grant permissions for the YouTube app to access the camera, mic and storage.

▶ If prompted, verify your channel.

▶ Select 'Go Live'.

Note: If you do not have a channel, you will be prompted to create one after selecting Go Live.

Create a mobile live-stream

▶ Select the capture button.

▶ Select 'go live' and then select a privacy setting.

▶ Optional – Select settings.

▷ Add a description.

▷ Enable or disable live chat.

▷ Enable or disable age restriction for your stream.

▷ Indicate whether your stream contains paid promotion and add a paid promotion disclosure.

▶ Select the back arrow.

▶ Select Next to take a picture for your thumbnail. You can upload a custom thumbnail (iOS only).

▶ Optional: Stream in landscape mode.

  ▷ Hold your device in landscape mode.

  ▷ Make sure that your screen rotation lock is off.

▶ Optional: To share your stream, tap 'share'.

▶ Select 'go live'.

▶ To end a stream, select 'finish', then 'OK'. An archive of the live-stream is created on your channel after the stream ends.

▶ You can edit the privacy setting (including setting it to private) or delete the archive on the 'my videos' page.

After a mobile live-stream

When your broadcast is over, an archive of the stream is created on your channel, and you have the option to edit the privacy setting (including setting it to private) or delete the archive.

Creating highlight clips

You may get more post-live viewers if you share a shorter, edited version of the live-stream after it's over. How this is done depends on whether you went live using the Stream Now or Events route.

▶ **Stream Now**

  ▷ Click Create Highlight below the player.

  ▷ Use the player timeline to set the clip start and end time with Get player time.

  ▷ Click Upload to process a highlight clip.

▶ **Events**

  ▷ Start streaming with the sync to preview feature enabled.

  ▷ Use the Preview Player timeline to mark the in and out points with Create Highlight, Set Start and Set End.

Whichever method you chose, you can repeat the process several times and can also add metadata and custom thumbnails at any time.

Comments

Chat messages can be moderated in the same way as regular chat messages. You can assign moderators, manage spam messages, block words proactively and block users from chat or remove chat messages.

Live chat is on by default and appears to the right of the screen when you are live. Icons identify different viewers: a crown for the streamer and a spanner for the moderator.

Viewers are limited to 200 characters and a maximum of three comments every 30 seconds and can't post special characters, URLs or HTML tags. Event owners are not subject to the frequency threshold.

As with other similar apps, moderators can interact with the audience and remove comments when appropriate. They can also flag, block or put users in time out.

Selecting the tick box for 'automatically block spam messages' will block simple spam such as long messages in all caps or repeated identical messages by the same user.

Moderators can also block words proactively after compiling a list of terms in the 'community settings' section. Live chats matching these words will be blocked.

Slow mode allows you to limit how frequently each user can comment by setting a time limit between comments. This is set up through the live dashboard, where you enter how many seconds each user must wait between posts. The minimum is 1 second and the maximum is 300 seconds.

Super Chat

This is a way for you as a broadcaster to monetise your streams, by allowing fans to pay to have their messages highlighted in a bright colour and pinned to the chat of a live-stream for up to five hours.

How much fans pay depends on how long the message is and how long they want it to be pinned, and depending on the currency. But at the time of writing, this is a sample of the eleven levels:

▶ £2 – 4.99 – 50 characters – no time on the ticker

▶ £10 – 19.99 – 200 characters – 5 minutes

▶ £50 – 99.99 – 250 characters – 30 minutes

▶ £200 – 299.99 – 290 characters – 2 hours

▶ £500 – 350 characters – 5 hours

Eligibility

To be eligible for Super Chat, you have to meet these requirements:

▶ Your channel is enabled for live-streaming.

▶ Your channel is monetised.

▶ Your channel has over 1,000 subscribers.

▶ You are over the age of 18.

▶ You are located in one of the available locations.

Making a purchase

Purchases on iOS are not currently supported.

▶ Select the dollar sign within a live chat. The live chat must be visible, and mobile devices must be in portrait mode.

▶ Select 'send a Super Chat'.

▶ To select an amount, either drag the slider or type your desired value.

▶ Optionally, enter your message.

▶ Select 'buy and send'.

When the transaction is complete, your public Super Chat will be sent to all viewers in the live chat. A receipt will be emailed to you as a record of the purchase.

Notes for viewers

▶ Once a Super Chat is purchased, a countdown ticker displays the remaining time for which your Super Chat will be pinned in the ticker.

▶ The creator may end the live-stream before your time in the ticker has completed. Super Chats do not transfer between streams.

▶ Your Super Chat message, channel icon and purchase amount are visible to the public.

▶ There is a site-wide daily limit of £500.

▶ You may remove your own Super Chat messages by selecting 'remove' from the menu. Removing your own message does not cause a refund.

▶ Viewers watching in landscape mode on mobile will not see the ticker. Rotate out of landscape mode to see the ticker.

Chat moderation

All chat messages, including Super Chats, are subject to moderation. Moderated Super Chats will have their username and avatar removed, as well as the message itself, obviously.

▶ **NOTE**

1   Unfortunately, YouTube would not let us use their logo in this book. They said: "We do not actively grant permission for the use of our YouTube logos on the covers or chapter headings in any publications that are not written by Google".

5

Other live-streaming apps and software

▶ INTRODUCTION

There's more to live-streaming than Facebook Live, Twitter Go Live, Periscope and YouTube. Indeed, it's becoming quite a crowded space. Open up your cell phone's app store and search for 'live video', and you'll be swamped by the number.

Now, in alphabetical order is a list of *some* of the others with a brief description of what they are able to do. Some of them:

- ▶ Stream within the individual app only.

- ▶ Can stream to Facebook but don't actually capture or archive your video themselves.

- ▶ Don't have an app, and only allow you to stream via a desktop.

But remember, even though some of them may have unique features, you need to 'fish where the fish are' and broadcast on the platform where your followers and potential viewers already live: the platform that most closely aligns with your brand. And that's likely to be on Facebook and Twitter.

> *The goal for marketers with live-streams should be to produce a single great live broadcast and attain as wide an audience as possible while also encouraging engagement.*

David Kirkpatrick[1]

FIGURE 5.1 A small sample of some of the other live-stream apps available

Sources: clockwise from top left: www.BeLive.tv, www.goeasylive.com, https://switcherstudio.com/, https://manycam.com/. Centre: https://stream.live/

So, do not waste time building up another platform and trying to get your fans to follow you over if they're already happy where they are. *Note: apps are notorious for changing or closing down often without notice (live-streamers of 2016 will remember the sudden disappearance of once-big players Meerkat, Katch and Blab). So, by the time you read this, the landscape may well have changed.*

Also consider that the more your show 'looks like TV', the further away you may be moving from the features that make live-streaming *different* from TV! That is, the accessibility, the authenticity and the interactivity. The purpose of live-streaming is so people can get programmes whose content, presentation and production are different from what they get on the networks.

Prioritise value over venue.

Now let's compare and contrast 'the best of the rest'.[2]

Live-streaming apps

Airtime – www.airtime.com

Using live-video of you and up to five friends or colleagues, you can pull in YouTube videos, Spotify music streams and gifs to share with the crowd.

Alively – https://alive.ly/

"A mobile platform for privately broadcasting, recording and sharing everyday moments while in the moment. Real moments that go beyond the highlight reel."

Appear.in – https://appear.in/

"appear.in lets you video chat with your friends. Nothing to download and no plugins to install! Create your own room and send the link on chat, Facebook Messenger, SMS, or email to invite people. Have up to 8 friends in a room."

appear.in works on the Chrome, Firefox, and Opera browsers or use the native apps on Android and iPhone.

Bambuser – http://bambuser.com/

"Stream live video from your iPhone over 3G or Wi-Fi to friends, family and followers all over the world! View incoming chat messages, broadcast in public or in private and geotag your broadcasts using GPS. Bambuser also integrates to a wide range of global platforms and social networks, such as Facebook, Twitter and Myspace and you can also embed a Bambuser channel or a specific video onto your own blog or website."

BeLive – www.BeLive.tv

Stream to Facebook Live with this app: BeLive.tv does not have a recording anywhere else; it simply provides other features:

▶ You can broadcast from your desktop, while a guest can join from either their computer or iOS app.

▶ Connect multiple cameras, choose between a split screen, picture-in-picture or give your guest the main focus. You can also add graphics and captions.

Great how-to guide: www.krishna.me/2016/belivetv-for-facebook-live/

Busker – https://busker.co/ Update: the Busker app closed down in September 2017.

This app is a bit like Periscope-meets-QVC, as it lets you sell merchandise directly to the viewer without them leaving the stream. A strong connection is built as you interact with your customer: showing the product, answering questions and building a relationship. If you are not selling anything, viewers can donate money to your cause or non-profit venture. Payment information is handled by Stripe (used by Kickstarter, Adidas, Saks Fifth Avenue and more). Once Busker approves your store and products, you can start selling, with a percentage of the sales value going to the developer.

Carrot.fm – http://carrot.fm/

"Live video chat with any expert in any field instantly, including celebrities. Or leverage your own expertise to receive calls and earn money in paid categories. Pay only for the exact minutes you talk. Connect via social media to message or video chat anyone in 10 seconds."

Chew – www.Chew.tv

This app connects a community of over 350,000 amateur and pro DJs, producers and personalities who stream live music and mix-sets. The platform is "rights compliant and licenced to the fullest extent possible". You can stream from any desktop device (through software such as OBS, Flash Media Live Encoder, Wirecast etc.) and watch on either desktop or mobile. There is no limit on the number of viewers.

Dusk – https://duskapp.tv/

This app lets you live-stream anonymously to its online community, by protecting your identity through pixelated video and voice-changed audio. It's like an anonymous version of Periscope. You could use it to discuss a topic that could provoke cyber-bullying, such as a health, political or moral issue.

Firetalk – https://firetalk.com/

With the Firetalk live-streaming app you can schedule a broadcast and also have your channel play video content, such as an archive show, while you are off-air. You can also earn money through Pay-Per-View events and Members-Only channels. There are various subscription levels.

Glide – www.glide.me/

> "Glide is the fastest live video messenger app on the planet. It combines the convenience of texting with the expressiveness of video chat. Now you and your friends/family can share real moments as they happen, and enjoy quality facetime."

Houseparty – https://joinhouse.party/

> "Splits the screen up to 8 times so everyone can talk and laugh together. Chats are organised by room, and anyone you are friends with on the app can come and join in. You can move between rooms to join with different groups of friends."

Hype – www.hy.pe/

This live-video app lets users add music and animation to their video, plus bring in photos, videos, animated GIFs, music, text and emojis. Anything can be moved around the screen and added or deleted during the live broadcast. When a viewer makes a comment, the broadcaster can pull it into the video and have it float about as a 'chat bubble'.

Instagram Live – http://blog.instagram.com/

You can broadcast a short-life live-video on Instagram Stories to your followers. Swipe right from your feed to open the camera, tap the 'Start Live Video' button and broadcast for up to an hour. Your followers will receive a notification that you've started, and your live-video will appear at the top of their newsfeeds.

You can pin a comment for everyone to see or you can turn comments off altogether; hide certain users from viewing your stream and report abusive comments; pinch to zoom in or out, but you can't add drawings as you can in Stories.

When you end, the video is completely hidden from view: it's not saved *on the platform* and can't be watched retrospectively. So you can use this to your advantage:

▶ The increased FOMO effect (Fear Of Missing Out) could encourage people to watch with more urgency and so give you more attention.

▶ As you can't use Instagram to give out information that people may need to refer back to, use the urgency of the platform to make your content more exciting, engaging and exclusive. Perhaps have one-off sales codes or clues to a competition.

So the video is not saved on Instagram, but as a broadcaster you can save your video to your phone:

▶ The video can't be saved by a viewer.

▶ The video is saved, but not the comments, like and views.

▶ You can only save a video immediately after it's finished.

▶ You could then post it right back to Instagram as a 'once-live' video.

Use this platform to share content to younger people in an environment where they are already active, and that won't need much production effort.

Kanvas – www.getkanvas.com/

Described as the app that would be created "if Snapchat and Periscope had a baby", Kanvas allows more creativity for a broadcaster with the ability to add effects, filters, GIFs, time-lapse and slow-motion videos, animations, drawings and photo slideshows. Chat live with broadcasters and react with hearts, emojis and stickers. All Kanvases are easily shared to Instagram, Tumblr, Twitter, Facebook, YouTube, Messenger, SMS and email.

Kickstarter Live – https://live.kickstarter.com/

The crowdfunding site bought the live-stream app Huzza and integrated it into their platform to "help creators generate greater support for their ideas at the earliest stages of development".[3] They say: "Every creator can now use live video to connect with backers. Stream from your studio, rehearsal space, or wherever you work. Streams integrate seamlessly into your project page. Viewers can ask questions, chat with the host, or pledge to the project right from the live broadcast."

Line – https://live.line.me/

This Japanese mobile messaging service has group video calls which can include up to 200 participants. Only four will be on-screen at any one time. By broadcasting, you can get gift items, comments and hearts from the audience.

Live4 – http://live4.io/support

"Live broadcast action-sports video with a phone or GoPro. Calling all extreme sports dare-devils. If you can do it, prove it. Do it LIVE! LIVE4 makes sharing with your phone or GoPro instantaneous. No cell coverage? No worries. LIVE4 automatically uploads video when cell coverage is back. Streaming from iPhone or GoPro camera; full remote control of starting and stopping GoPro camera; on-screen information to control free space, data uploaded, iPhone and GoPro battery level while streaming live; integration with your Facebook or Twitter account."

Manycam – https://manycam.com/

ManyCam is a free webcam software and a video switcher that allows you to use your webcam on most applications simultaneously while you live-stream or video chat. Use it on applications such as Skype, YouTube or Livestream. Record your screen, add effects, change your background and much more.

Meemee.tv – http://meemee.tv/

"Exciting new video and live broadcast portal. Empowering social media entrepreneurs with rich features including monetization, customization & Live interactive video broadcasting. Meemee.tv online channels have fantastic, unique viewing content."

Musical.ly – www.musical.ly **and live.ly**

Non-stop, 24-hour live-streaming set up for amateur music-video creators. There is a category that includes anyone capable of miming along to their favourite pop hit since this is an app for making and sharing lip-sync videos with friends. You can add video effects – filter, fast motion, slow motion, time lapse, reverse and other 'time machine' effects – and then share videos on Instagram, Facebook, Twitter, Messenger and WhatsApp or to your camera roll.

Smiletime – www.smiletime.com (In September 2017, Smiletime rebranded as PopIn https://pop.in)

Viewers can up-vote your broadcast in the hopes of catching your attention; you can show comments on the screen along with other images through a simple drag-and-drop system; invite a viewer to appear on the screen with you, and run live polls; simulcast your video on Smiletime and Facebook (but comments do not sync, and viewers on Facebook will not be able to participate in your interactive features on Smiletime).

Stre.am – https://stream.live/

"Stream is the fastest, easiest way to watch and stream live video from your iOS device. Stream live video from your phone to the world; monetise your content, or tip your favourite streamer."

Stringwire – www.stringwire.com/

"Share your world in real-time! Stringwire lets you lets you easily capture, share and discover live video as it happens. Instantly stream video and notify followers and friends.

Viewers can chat and search through video to find out what's happening live. Help break news and report events. Be credited for video that you stream to Stringwire. Collaborate with other Stringers to capture multiple perspectives of the same event."

Twitch – www.twitch.tv/

Twitch, owned by Amazon, is designed to be a platform for video game-related content, including e-sports tournaments, personal streams of individual players and gaming-related talk shows.

Tumblr – http://livevideo.tumblr.com/

This platform only allows live-streaming through third-party services such as Kanvas, YouNow, Upclose and YouTube. Anyone following you will see it on their dashboard. When the live video is over, it becomes a regular video post.

Ustream – www.ustream.tv/

Instead of being a public social media channel with followers, this could be considered a paid-for video service that happens to broadcast live-streams.

"Broadcast live, upload videos and watch live video on your device. Ustream powers live interactive video that enables anyone to watch and interact with a global audience of unlimited size. Broadcast live to any number of viewers using the camera of your device. Upload pre-recorded videos into the Ustream app in original quality. Schedule and manage upcoming events on your Ustream Channels."

YouNow – www.younow.com/

YouNow hosts more than 100 million user sessions a month and 50,000 hours of live-video every day. Viewers can chat with broadcasters, buy bars to send gifts and request to guest. The on-screen 'gifts' translate to real-world money, with a percentage cut for the developers.

Using other software for a pro show

Facebook, Twitter and Periscope encourage it, opening up their API (Application Programming Interface) to allow other services to have users stream the video to their account.

▶   How to set up streaming software to work with Facebook

   www.facebook.com/help/755943624557739?helpref=search

Note that Facebook does not 'allow' you to live-stream to another app at the same time as you stream to theirs. Most of the software (some of it free) allows you to produce a better viewer experience than the straightforward Facebook Live, Twitter Go Live or Periscope, some of them enabling you to go live from a desktop and incorporate different angles. (See the information on the 'Periscope Producer' elsewhere in this book.) The software will let you add graphics, name-straps ('lower thirds'), play in pre-recorded video and so on. But beware of style over substance. It may be that your audience doesn't want 'TV-lite' and instead prefers outdoor, mobile and straightforward shows.

If you are a solo broadcaster using this software, you will have to multi-task: switching between your camera and your computer, playing in videos, talking and responding to comments. It's a bit of a juggling act, but it can be done. (After all, think of everything you have to do when you drive a car!) Having said that, it certainly helps to have a technical operator or producer.

In alphabetical order, here are some you may wish to investigate, together with a sample of some of the features they incorporate. Several of these companies offer a free trial version of their products so you can try before you buy. *(Note: some apps listed previously also have the ability to stream directly to Facebook.)*

BlueJeans' OnSocial – www.bluejeans.com/onsocial

Connect up to 100 remote participants or camera feeds; interactive layouts; a pre-event lobby; stream from a desktop; free training at www.krishna.me/2016/bluejeans-onsocial-for-facebook-live/

EasyLive – www.goeasylive.com/

"Cloud-powered video production platform. Whether it's one source or multiple sources, 4k or HD, Easy Live supports it. Drag-and-drop everything from live scoreboards to big-budget graphics on the fly. Our drag-and-drop interface means anyone can use Easy Live, no matter your skill level. Create bite-sized clips from your live stream with our real-time features. Our double ingest capability and automated output protect against dropped feeds. Easy Live natively integrates with publishers including Twitch, Facebook Live, and YouTube. It's as simple as click and play. Customise your feed with built-in or third-party TV-quality graphics and templates. Add video ads and sponsored logos to monetise your live stream."

JustBroadcaster – www.justbroadcaster.com/

Stream to Facebook using a Mac; easy set-up with ready-prepared templates; add lower-thirds (captions); add multiple cameras; mix in slides, videos and your Mac screen; cheap lifetime licence.

Live:Air Solo – http://teradek.com/pages/liveair-solo

"Now you can be the director, producer, and star of your own live show with Teradek's new Live:Air Solo. Uniquely designed for the iPhone, Live:Air Solo is packed with real-time creative tools such as graphics, overlays, transitions, and support for all of the popular live-streaming destinations. Share your adventures and events, in Full HD using Live:Air Solo. Streaming at your fingertips."

Make.TV – www.make.tv/

"Make.TV's Live Video Cloud enables broadcasters and publishers to discover, curate, manage and publish live video from any device, anywhere. Easily mix in crowd-sourced, contributor-based and live social video feeds to increase reach and revenue."

OBS[4] – Open Broadcast Software – https://obsproject.com/

Real-time video/audio capturing and mixing, with unlimited scenes; you can switch between seamlessly via custom transitions; set hotkeys for switching between scenes, starting/stopping streams or recordings and muting audio sources; filters and an audio mixer. This is open-sourced and therefore, free.

Periscope Producer – see information in the 'Periscope' chapter.

restream.io – https://restream.io/

Using Restream, you can stream games on YouTube, Twitch, Ustream, Livestream, Hitbox and many other services at the same time.

Switcher Studio – https://switcherstudio.com/

"Create professional multi-camera productions using iPhones and iPads. Supports screen sharing, seamlessly integrates with FCPX and enables streaming via Facebook Live, Periscope Producer and more."

Telescope – http://telescope.tv/livestudio/

"Live Studio's producer console enables you to instantly connect with your viewers through real-time curation and moderation of the conversation, integration of followers direct into a live stream, discovery and display of trends, and features to gauge audience feedback in real-time such as dynamic polls. All content can be published to the live-stream with a range of graphics templates and custom graphics solutions."

Wirecast – http://telestream.net/wirecast/

Capture an unlimited number of input devices from live camera feeds, iOS cameras, computer desktop, web feeds and more; add polish and professionalism to your broadcast with live switching, animated titles, transitions, lower thirds, watermarks, captions and more.

Live-stream production companies

Roker Media Live – http://rokermedia.live/

Fronted by US TV personality Al Roker, Live Fronts brings together agencies, producers and presenters to help them create and produce content for live-streaming platforms. "Using real-time data, we create compelling stories, commerce and branded-entertainment experiences native to live-streaming platforms Facebook Live, Twitter, Periscope, Twitch, YouTube, YouNow and Brandlive. We work with established publishers of online content to add live-streaming to the mix. By creating programming for these channels, we enhance revenue possibilities through social broadcasting."

Live-stream analytics companies

Delmondo.co – http://delmondo.co/facebook-live-analytics/

A Facebook Media Solutions partner for live video analytics:

▶ Measure an unlimited number of owned live-video channels simultaneously.

▶ Measure Average Minute Audience and Engagements per Minute for individual streams, or roll them up across series, channels and networks.

▶ Track consumption for live and replay viewers, audience insights like age, gender, location and viewing habits like sound on vs. sound off and more.

FullScope – www.fullscope.tv

"A complete analytics and marketing software that provides you with the most detailed insights from your Periscope and other live stream applications."

▶ NOTES

1 David Kirkpatrick, *How Marketers Can Pick the Right Platform*, www.marketingdive.com/ October 26th, 2016
2 I have not been paid or requested or been offered any inducement to mention any of these apps or companies.
3 *Kickstarter's New Feature Lets Its Users Live Stream Their Campaigns*, www.tubefilter. com/ November 1st, 2016
4 A 'How-to' Guide: www.socialmediaexaminer.com/

PART II
Live-stream themes

In this section of the book, hundreds of ideas are presented to whet your live-streaming appetite.

I have watched thousands of live-videos over the past few years and have written up notes on what the streamers did and why they worked.

On the next pages you will find superb streaming suggestions to help your broadcast go off with a bang. Simply mix and merge the tried-and-tested formats here with the ideas that you already have, to help put the 'show' into the 'showcase' of your business, brand, product or hobby.

6

Your live-stream strategy

▶ INTRODUCTION

Improvisation is great if you belong to a jazz band or are a stand-up comic. But it's probably not the best approach if you want to take live-streaming seriously.

As the saying goes: 'Proper Planning Prevents Poor Performance'. And that's particularly true for a business broadcast.

▶ SETTING THE STRATEGY

Live-streaming is a tool, not a strategy in itself. If you want to get results, you need to consider live-video as just one part of your marketing mix: live-video doesn't *replace* other aspects, *it should help fuel them.*

It's important that you think of creating a content plan in the same way that you would for any other of your marketing strategies:

- ▶ What is your *overall* goal?

- ▶ What is it about live-video that *could* help you get from here to there? How will this give cross-platform support to your other marketing strategies (live-streams may promote them for example, and vice versa)?

▶ Know what the benefit of the shows will be to your audience:

  ▷ Who are you targeting?

  ▷ What will they feel, what will they have learnt or what problem will be solved as a result of watching?

▶ Know what the benefit of the shows will be to *you*, for example:

  ▷ To boost brand recognition.

  ▷ To drive traffic to other platforms or a website.

▶ Analyse your competitors' streams:

  ▷ What is their content?

  ▷ How often are they broadcast?

  ▷ What engagement do they get?

  ▷ What could you do better or differently?

▶ What would be 'live-streaming success' for you? How will you identify that?:

  ▷ **Maximum concurrent viewership** – if so, focus on organically trending the topic on the platform, cross-promotion and producer interaction.

  ▷ **Highest engagement numbers** – in which case you will want a content strategy that relies on live audience decision-making, continual development of the story arc and built-in 'wow' factors.

  ▷ **Longest retention time or watch minutes** – concentrate on recapping to new-joiners, great forward promotion and 'what will happen?' moments, such as experiments.

Of course, some of what you decide to do may be determined by resource factors such as:

▶ Your budget

▶ Your staffing levels

▶ Your time available

▶ How soon you want to broadcast

▶ Your equipment and expertise

Think carefully about all these elements. Commit yourself to writing down your considerations and decisions. That doesn't mean you can't change your mind later, but working on a day-to-day gut feeling is not a sound digital strategy.

Your brand guidelines

When viewers see your live-stream in their feed, they have just a few seconds to decide whether to click through and watch 'constructively' (i.e. with the sound on).

What will help that click-through rate is if the viewer immediately recognises your brand and associates it with consistent, quality content.

'Consistency' is a staple of strong branding. (In radio programming, we call it 'the hot tap effect': when you tune into that station, you know that you will get a certain genre of music and particular presentation style and speech content. In the same way, when you turn on the hot tap, you expect hot water to come out, and not chicken soup.)

Your viewers will come to expect a certain content and style from your streams. That's not to say you won't on occasion surprise them, but you certainly won't shock or disgust them (unless doing so is part of your brand).

So, what elements will make your live-streams stand out as unique and be hard to imitate? Identify these specifics and add them to your brand guidelines to help ensure quality control. This list is of course not exhaustive, but will give you an idea of what to consider:

▶ **Composition** – the visuals such as artwork and logos, lighting, set design, and colours

▶ **Content** – when it's on and for how long, and the overall format. Plus the promotion before, during and after your live-stream (where will it be, how is it designed graphically and textually?)

▶ **Characters** – the hosts and their style and tone, intro and outro formats and 'brand-positioning statements' ('catchphrases'); whether it's a single or double-headed show, and who says what

▶ **Closure** – how you will ask for a sale and what other platforms you will direct people to and how

Everything about your broadcast will have a consistency consideration, and in creating relevant, quality content that your audience can come to depend on, and hopefully look forward to, you really want to dial in some consistency in every aspect of your live video broadcast.

Todd Bergin[1]

Also, consider what elements are 'definitely-not' issues. This may include changes to the set, the kind of language that should not be used, and alongside this, what to do if something goes wrong.

Good show-production quality suggests good actual-product quality. Indeed, as the volume of live-video increases, audiences will *demand* better-looking shows. However, even though higher production may help your video stand out, the best production won't make bad content good.

The production plan

Then brief your live-stream team for this production, via a written production plan:

▶ **Synopsis** – a brief summary of the above including the date of the live-stream, the specific aim of the show, the duration, its location, who needs to be where and when

▶ **Title** – what will be promoted and how will it be written? (See elsewhere for ways to make it creative and engaging.)

▶ **Hosts and guests** – who they are and how they are to be introduced

▶ **Role assignment** – the person/people who are overseeing this project, before, after and during its production. This may include:

▷ Who is 'in overall charge' while the show is on air

▷ Who is operating the camera

▷ Who is directing the pace of the show

▷ Who is monitoring comments, answering and posting branded content

▷ Who will promote the show before and after its broadcast

▶ **Location** – where the live-stream is happening and confirmation of necessary checks for access, privacy and technical issues (such as signal and Wi-Fi). If the presenters are moving around the location during the live-stream, where will they go and what will they show? And what will they say as they travel from point A to point B?

▶ **Platform and page** – where the stream is being shown and published and whether it should be shared to other pages. For example, on Facebook Live you could go live from your Personal, Business or Group page.

▶ **Presenter notes** – there won't be a script as such, but rather bullet points of what needs to be covered, including main content (divided into sub-topics and a rough time-guide), how to introduce specific content such as the introduction to the show, the call-to-action and the ending to avoid the common 'sudden stop'.

▶ **Contact numbers** – of all those involved

Quick check: *is everything still focused on helping you reach your previously stated goal?*

The crisis plan

Always have a Plan B when you are going to live-stream. In a similar way to your brand being enhanced by consistency, it will be damaged if something goes wrong. Although this is always a possibility because of the nature of the platform, do what you can to minimise risk by knowing how to recognise that something *could* go wrong or is *beginning to*, and what to do to prevent it from happening. That could be altering the original programme plan on the fly or stopping the show completely.

Here are just a few elements to consider, but you will undoubtedly have more of your own. For each situation, decide if and how you can prevent it and how to get out of it:

▶ **The presentation** – if the product is not positioned in the correct way (verbally or physically); the tone (a joke falls flat, a comment appears to be patronising or sarcastic)

▶ **The set** – a banner falls, the tripod holding the phone collapses, the presenter drops their cup of hot coffee on their lap

▶ **The language** – if a presenter or guest swears or defames a person or product

▶ **The product** – is dropped, fails to work correctly

▶ **The location** – being asked to move on, you are stream-bombed (passers-by deliberately and possibly maliciously getting into the shot, behind or in front of you); the theft of your phone while you are broadcasting from it

▶ **The tech** – a frozen stream, Wi-Fi drop-out, battery failure

▶ **The comments** – the possible queries, concerns and criticisms, or even abuse (there is more on this topic elsewhere in this book)

and the big ones:

▶ Who will decide to 'pull the plug'?

▶ What production and presentation staff need to know that the show will end?

> ▶ How will that be communicated to them in a live situation?

> ▶ What will be said on air?

> ▶ How will that be followed up on social media?

> ▶ Who will review the decision-making process and look at lessons learnt?

As part of this 'risk prevention process':

> ▶ Have a location recce (more on this elsewhere).

> ▶ Brief and debrief your programme production team.

> ▶ And watch social media reaction.

Doing this will help you identify *potential* pitfalls before you actually make them.

Measure your metrics

What you measure and how often is up to you and will depend on your previously identified goal. (See chapter 24 'Measuring Your Metrics'.) Be ready to adapt and evolve different elements of your strategy and content if you feel that something isn't right.

Finally

The main thing to remember is the reason you are about to go live. *If recording, editing and uploading the content instead would create a better user experience, then do that.* (Note I said 'user experience': the main reason for going live shouldn't be to save time for you, the broadcaster!)

So keep considering the value this live-stream offers to those who choose to watch, and think: how would I answer someone who said "Why should I watch?" and have a clear purpose or goal.

And remember: great content gets you great followers.

▶ NOTE

1 Todd Bergin, *5 Qualities People Want in Your Live Video Content*, http://divorcethework force.com/ September 6th, 2016

7

Content is king

► INTRODUCTION

Of course, you can live-stream pretty much anything you like, but if you want to grab attention, it has to be interesting. There is no skill from you or advantage to your audience if you literally just show people what you can see. The answer in most cases will be "so what?" After all, anyone can tap 'Start Broadcast'.

You have to add value, context, insight and uniqueness, and give people a reason to want to watch and 'care to share'.

> *A Scope-worthy broadcast is one that has the perfect blend of actionable tips and personal experience. If you can be transparent, passionate, creative, and authentic in your delivery, you're well on your way to making a big splash.*

Katya Hollatz[1]

Basic live-stream content

What can you do a show about?

> *70% of key Periscope users stream things they witness such as concerts; 30% stream themselves and their activities (preparing meals or demonstrating beauty products). People are likely to show off tech gadgets in the morning and afternoon. More users stream themselves cooking dinner than any other meal.[2]*

Via Siobhan O'Shea

Think of your life as live-stream content:

▶ What are you an expert on?

▶ What do you know *now* that you didn't ten years ago and could help someone else with?

▶ What is your niche?

▶ What are you knowledgeable or passionate about?

▶ What topic are you the go-to person on?

▶ What do people always want to know about what you do or sell, your business, service or product?

▶ What kind of questions are people always asking you?

And importantly:

▶ What have you already got material on?

If you talk about a topic you already know, or if you can repurpose content from a presentation or a blog that you know your readers have questions about, then some of your show prep (preparation) is already done! After all, it's more efficient for you to respond on a live-stream than to type answers to every comment on a screen. And doing this means it's a more effective means of communication for the commenters, too. (Indeed, you could write at the end of each blog post something along the lines of "I'll be answering questions about this topic at 7 pm EST on August 16th, live on Periscope. Follow me at @xxxxxxxxxx".)

You might still have to break down the topic into sub-sections for different shows and draft a few bullet points, but you won't have to research, and you will come across as fluent and authentic.

▶ PLAY TO LIVE-STREAM'S STRENGTHS

Whatever content you broadcast, however long your programme, whether it's at home or on location, through a mobile or desktop, there are some elements to always keep in mind. Doing so is likely to increase your success rate because you will be playing to the inherent strengths of what live-video is all about.

Live

It's right there in the name: 'live-streaming'. What you are showing people is ephemeral, 'right now' stuff (there's perhaps little point in showing content that would be better recorded, edited and put online).

Live:

- ▶ Is vulnerable excitement.

- ▶ Is candid, honest, authentic, urgent, unique and fresh.

- ▶ Encourages user engagement as it directs people to watch at a certain time.

So every time you start to broadcast, ask:

- ▶ Why am I using this app?

- ▶ What's so special about what I'm filming, that it works better *live*?

FOMO – The Fear of Missing Out

Take advantage of the *urgency* that live-streaming creates. Viewers are more likely to stop on live content, as they could be the first among their friends to experience it and share it. And doing that reflects well on them.

FOMO:

- ▶ Is see-it-now-or-never content, never-to-be-repeated or replicated.

- ▶ Keeps viewers engaged: anything can happen.

- ▶ Creates a sense of personal connection: we're all watching this together.

It's a much different experience watching something live and being first, versus something a day or more old and being the last to know:

- ▶ "Hey, baby Matthew is taking his first steps right now."

- ▶ "This fire just broke out down my street."

- ▶ "I need to share this thing I just discovered."

- ▶ "You won't believe what celeb just walked into my restaurant."

- ▶ "This is the new design rolling off the production line, live."

Interactivity

You have the amazing opportunity to talk to your viewers and to have them respond in real time right there on your screen. So ask questions and get those people to ask *you* questions, or make comments about what you are showing them or talking about. Help them direct the conversation, or literally direct you and where you should go and what they want you to show.

Images

Video is moving pictures. So show something moving! You staring at a camera talking out loud may not grip people for more than a few minutes. But showing them around your neighbourhood, or how to do something, might well do.

Global

You're going live to Planet Earth! Think about the huge market you have just opened up for yourself: either to show off your products or your personality. Now you really do have to think big! What are the best topics for your new potential audience? When is the best time to go live to get the most people awake in a time zone?

Live-streaming removes the barrier of selling abroad. You can now communicate with potential clients across the world in a cost-effective way.

Social

The main apps have 'double platform power'. With Facebook Live and Twitter's Go Live/Periscope, you get the in-built following that you already have on those platforms. Therefore, you have twice as much potential publicity for your shows than those using some other apps. Build this thought into your action plan.

JOE'S CODE FOR GREAT LIVE CONTENT

Give your viewers a content experience, the view, or the knowledge that they won't get anywhere else. Create content that has one or more of these winning features:

▶ **Jeopardy** – so people will watch and keep watching

▶ **Originality** – or why would you bother to do it, and why would someone bother to watch? Think of providing exclusive access to people, places and products.

▶ **Engagement** – it could be educational, entertaining or have a sense of urgency. It could certainly encourage comments and involvement. It may have a wow, LOL or cute factor.

▶ **Simplicity** – straightforward with a basic 'story arc' of a beginning, middle and end. Know what you will do, what you will say, where you will go and what you will show.

It doesn't matter what you have as the topic of your show: it could be from your small business, showing how money is spent with your non-profit, promoting an event, or giving a glimpse into your everyday life.

Your live-stream content database

So now here's the low-down of ideas to make live-streaming work for you and make your shows the very best. There are dozens of examples, but of course not one for every single business or pastime! So think about how you could apply these examples to what you do and what you want to make a show about. Test the content and the format, the duration and location until you discover what works for you in your niche.

It will take a bit of time and some trial and error to find what content works for you, at what time and what duration. But after a while, and possibly after some feedback from viewers, you will find a sweet spot that you are all happy with.

But remember: don't just point and shoot. Some preparation and imagination will help you reap the rewards.

> *Keep it simple . . . have a point instead of rambling.*

> *Make sure you stay on topic.*

> *It doesn't have to be monumental, but I should feel like I'm sharing something. Finally, keep it fun.*

> Al Roker[3]

▶ LIVE-STREAM THEME: BEHIND-THE-SCENES STREAMS

Whether it's out-of-hours access, a backstage pass or being allowed beyond the velvet rope, people love to see something exclusive. (Consider the popularity of the extras section on DVDs.)

Now you are able to give your viewers a 'sneak peek' as live-streaming video helps satisfy their expectations of voyeurism in this 'reality TV' world:

- ▶ Fly-on-the-wall content feels exclusive.
- ▶ You're letting your friends, customers and prospective clients feel as though they are there and involved. You are having a real-time conversation with them.

▶ You're letting your brand personalities shine.

▶ You are being transparent about how you work, elevating trust and generating a human connection.

▶ You're sharing aspects of your company or brand that consumers wouldn't know by just looking at your website.

▶ You can 'humanise your brand', building a relationship by showing non-business activities such as a charity day, not just 'work stuff'.

▶ You are giving viewers an authentic experience:

  ▷ Letting them see what's happening,

  ▷ Letting them see the context of the business, and

  ▷ Letting them hear what's being said.

So, go to places where the public (your customers) can't usually get to, and show them!

Live content is uniquely compelling when it offers rarity. Glimpses of life you'd never usually get, spaces you'd normally be denied access to, things that are happening in one moment that you've just got to see.

Topher Burns[4]

On the following pages, there are dozens of examples of how different businesses have made it work for them.

FIGURE 7.1 A unique view, live from the top of the tower of the 900-year-old Chichester Cathedral in England

Source: Facebook

So for business use, think: what do your audience or your clients want to know and see about you?

> *Use live-streaming and walk through your warehouse to show viewers how your manufacturing process works, how your designers come up with style ideas, or how you conduct testing on new products. Keep your narration short and snappy, and let the process you're witnessing give your video direction.*[5]
>
> Via marketingzen.com

Show viewers how your product is made; most people have no idea. This is a chance for you to show the journey from concept to product completion, from drawing board to factory to shop shelf. This level of transparency (i.e. how something is made, where it comes from, whose hands are making it) will strengthen customers' trust in your brand. And trust is paramount in marketing. If people know the background to something (whether it be a product or the reasons for a train delay), they become more understanding and, if appropriate, more likely to like (and buy) the brand.

> *There's spontaneity and intimacy about Periscope, and it can make fans feel like they are part of an inner circle if they are getting a unique live view of a personality or behind the scenes look at a business.*
>
> Ilicco Elia[6]

Don't just show off your showroom, or bang on about your business; give something of value to your fans. Give an insight into how your product is created:

▶ Your staff's hands making the handmade product

▶ The florist arranging an award-winning display

▶ The chef creating a distinctively decorative dish

Show people what you do and how actual, real people with names and faces are doing it: it's not all done by machines. After all, *people buy from people.*

DUNKIN' DONUTS

This brand used a 12-minute live-video to take viewers inside its factory on National Donut Day. There was a tour, a lesson in how to make a wedding cake out of donuts and then a giveaway:

▶ The event was scheduled in advance to fit with the day to get maximum leverage.

> ▶ The factory was described as 'top secret', adding to the feel of
>   exclusivity.
>
> ▶ There was plenty to see: donuts sizzling and then being doused in
>   icing, and the 'big reveal' of the wedding cake made from donuts.
>
> ▶ The giveaway was the call to action: all Dunkin' Donuts locations were
>   giving away donuts with a drink purchase.
>
> ▶ The stats: 31,330 views, 2,450 impressions, 919 comments and 567
>   shares

By letting people meet the staff (the faces behind the brand), you are giving your brand a human personality, and that helps build a relationship, which in turn helps build sales.

And selling is, of course, a people business. We buy from people we know, like and trust. Live-streaming is a way to connect with people faster, more intimately and more authentically.

Think, where will my audience never be allowed to go? Or where are they allowed to go but haven't yet been? And consider going live from those locations.

Here are some more case studies:

▶ One school[7] asked people to stream shows from their place of work and answer pupils' questions about what they do there.

▶ A band[8] shared their view from behind the stage, and you could do the same from behind a counter or before you present at a podium.

▶ This radio presenter[9] is live on Twitter Go Live/Periscope at the same time as his talk radio show is on.

▶ Here's a fan's-eye view[10] of a football final to show the stuff you can't see on TV.

▶ London Zoo[11] made its animals stars on Twitter Go Live/Periscope.

▶ And how about this for in-flight entertainment?[12] A live-stream from the jet-stream!

▶ There was a sneak peek at an art exhibition[13] before the tickets went on sale.

▶ The Royal Shakespeare Company[14] presented a series of short interviews giving supporters an insight into what goes on behind the scenes at the theatre, and the many roles involved in putting on a show.

▶ The British Museum[15] gave live tours of its galleries over Twitter Go Live/Periscope.

▶ Another group showed the writing process by Scoping authors[16] in a series of streams. As an author, you could explain more about the plot, the characters, the hidden meanings, and of course answer their questions and promote your book.

▶ At least one university gives campus tours on Twitter Go Live/Periscope for new students[17] (private access inside dorms and sports centres that are normally closed to the public), which significantly increased engagement. The viewers were encouraged to give feedback on which areas of campus they wanted to see, and the university had a series of simultaneous streams all over campus.

▶ Err, lobster fishing!

We were showing the entire process from a boat in Maine. Our community was able to comment, ask questions and get immediate response from Luke as he was holding a live lobster in his hand. A live tweeting experience doesn't offer half of what that experience on Periscope does.

Amanda Spurlock[18]

▶ MSNBC live-streamed a TV editorial meeting to explain the process of how they choose the news.

▶ Privacy issues permitting, school performances or assemblies could be shared with parents at the office who can't get time off.

▶ A travel-service manager could show live delays or a departure board at their station. A taxi firm could show queues, so travellers know if services are running late. What about a live-stream at a theme park to show people where the shortest queues are? Or maybe a stream of some entertainment or a Q&A, which visitors can watch as they wait in line. California's Disneyland has someone broadcasting live-streams from various rides and shows.

▶ For sports clubs: what about live-video views from the dressing rooms, the pitch, the training ground or the Chairman's box? Let viewers ask questions about what they see and maybe even direct the camera ("Can we see those trophies on the wall?" . . . "What is that equipment used for?") What about yacht racing?

It lends itself to live video because there is constant action. It's an amazing dynamic. You are actually interacting with the sports star during the event.

Jimmy Golen[19]

▶ What is the view of the stage from a box at the theatre?

▶ What is the view from the worst seat in the house?

▶ How opulent is the hotel you are marketing? (Some products or services are better marketed through an 'experiential sell' such as this, showing the experience and how the viewer would fit into that role.)

▶ What's happening poolside *right now*?

▶ What's the view from the top floor of your office block?

▶ What's it like to be in the local police cell?

EMERGENCY SERVICES

The Oklahoma Co. Sheriff's Office uses Twitter Go Live/Periscope to connect with its citizens,[20] streaming a behind-the-scenes look at the training of staff and animals, ride-alongs with officers and even during raids. In North Dakota, officers stream traffic stops.[21]

Fire Captain Garon Patrick Mosby of the St. Louis Fire Department has walked through the rubble of a house explosion,[22] describing the actions of firefighters live on streaming video. He says:

> *In a time when Hollywood shows over-romanticize the profession, and while politicians argue for the reduction of funding or resources, the general public has an unclear picture of what it is we actually do! Social media and especially Periscope allow us to speak directly with the population we serve.*

Finally, what about this extraordinary look behind-the-scenes? A few surgeons present regular streams live-video from the operating theatre, showing cosmetic surgery procedures. Dr Michael Salzhauer also answers questions while he works at the Bal Harbour Plastic Surgery Center in Miami, as does Dr Timothy Miller, an orthopaedic surgeon at the Ohio State University Wexner Medical Center.[23]

▶ LIVE-STREAM THEME: TRAINING AND EDUCATION

Demonstrate your expertise and experience with a live-streamed consultation taster session. Illustrate your knowledge by helping viewers in a show on Facebook Live, Twitter Go Live or Periscope, and then go on to sell your services to them.

After all, what's more engaging than helping people and providing a solution to their problem?

▶ Helping people solve a problem is useful content. Show your viewers what you can do, how they can learn it and how it will help them.

▶ You are probably showing people something you love doing yourself, so you'll be coming over as authentic and speaking from the heart.

▶ Such content is inspirational and has an immediate 'feel-good' factor.

▶ Showing people *how to use* your product is not a direct sell, so you come over more 'social' and less 'shark'.

▶ It is easy to write a show title for.

Let's look at the recent past and the *pre-recorded* videos on YouTube. Can we learn anything from the success of the kind of content that's on *that* platform?[24]

▶ Over 5 billion hours of beauty tutorials and explainers have been uploaded to YouTube in the past ten years.

▶ There are more than 135 million how-to videos on YouTube, addressing every question. The most popular? How to kiss, how to tie a tie and how to draw.

▶ There are more than 24 million question-related videos on YouTube, covering everything under (and including) the sun.

▶ Over 515,000 *hours* of videos featuring the infamous Diet Coke and Mentos experiment were viewed on the site in May 2015 alone.

Some people are 'auditory learners', picking up and retaining information more easily if they have heard and seen it, rather than read it. Approximately 91% of smartphone users will turn to their phone to look up how to perform tasks.[25]

> *If you focus on solving your audience's problems, they'll come back again and again – you'll create a loyal community. Start by asking your audience what topics they want you to talk about, and start developing ideas based on that information.*

> Josue Valles[26]

Think about tips and techniques, how-tos and DIY courses. This kind of content is huge on YouTube, and have you seen the self-help section of your local bookstore recently?[27]

FIGURE 7.2 Recording a beauty tutorial using the Arkon TW Broadcaster Single-Phone Desk Mount

Source: www.arkon.com

If you keep getting asked the same question at work, or online, consider presenting a live-stream about the topic to answer the question for everyone, all at once. It would be particularly effective if you could demonstrate the solution, live, and check with people that they now 'get it'.

> *Major corporations are integrating mobile apps like Periscope into their market- ing strategy to boost customer engagement.*

John Busby[28]

Tips could be related to anything you offer in your business. Consider doing one a week to help people complete the task or develop their understanding or hobby (*#TopTipTuesday*):

- ▶ A car garage could give advice on winter driving or saving fuel.

- ▶ If you work in a hair salon, you could teach a styling technique to hundreds of people all at once.

- ▶ Beauticians could give make-up tips, hair hacks, and lip trends.

- ▶ If in fashion, then show how you make (and then sell!) your designs.

- ▶ Fitness instructors[29] can demonstrate the exercises viewers need to do to get a six-pack: it'll be easier than writing a blog about it.

Some of these events could be sponsored by the product company or shot inside their store or salon.

IN THE CLASSROOM

Maybe you are a teacher and set some homework for the class. What about doing a 'top up' refresher lesson during the evening to remind your students of how to do their course work, or to give help if they are stuck? Perhaps construct the work so your help is only of use once they have got so far in the schedule.

> Using Periscope, teachers can invite students to keep their questions in textable form, something that helps teachers control how questions get addressed. Periscope is also more guided than Google Hangouts because there's a clear leader in the session, and that person controls the chat.

Mary Jo Madda[30]

When students are on study leave for exams, a regular live-video show could give them encouragement and inspiration to keep on going. If they are off ill, they could still follow a seminar. Parents could watch, too, to see what is being taught and how.

Could *tests* be done on these platforms? Live-stream a problem and students submit a written answer (on another platform, such as email, so other students can't see!). Imagine having your students watch a classroom in another part of the country learning the same thing? Or go on a 'digital field trip'.[31]

More resources:

▶ *Top 10 EdTech Tips: Connecting With Periscope*: www.gpb.org/

▶ *Periscope for Awesome Classroom Sharing*: http://blogs.edweek.org/

▶ *Why Periscope Is Not Perfect For Schools:* https://guildway.com/

▶ Jerry Blumengarten, a retired New York City teacher who collects and shares information about ed-tech resources online as Cybrary Man, has created a web page devoted to Periscope's use in education: http://cybraryman.com/periscope.html

FIGURE 7.3 **Live-streaming from the classroom using the Arkon Tablet Floor Stand**

Source: www.arkon.com

▶ Maybe you can teach people to play the guitar. One person who did this set up two Periscope accounts: one with a camera on his fret hand and the other camera on his strumming hand, so viewers could choose which stream to watch.

▶ Or a chef giving technique tips for creating a meal from scratch.

▶ Or a mentor, advisor or coach giving help and encouragement from a parked car while travelling between clients. (Live, unscripted video is a very quick way to market your business on the go!)

▶ One photographer does ad-hoc Periscopes while on location, explaining where they are, why they have chosen a particular angle and then discussing lenses, speeds and light. Later, back at the studio in another broadcast, they show their photos and ask viewers to choose their favourites and also discuss the challenges of each shot, the framing, settings and so on.

▶ Maybe give away a prize to the couple who present the best public live-stream while staying at your hotel,[32] or while they are on your adventure holiday.

With viewers in multiple locations, whether individually or within a company, live-streaming training means:

▶ You can reach all of them immediately.

▶ Viewers can be at their home or office.

- ▶ There are no webinar programs to download.

- ▶ There are no costs of travel.

- ▶ That speeds the delivery of information on new products or initiatives.

- ▶ Everyone can get the same message at the same time, so aiding a timely marketing plan.

You don't have to script anything – this is not a lecture or a Hollywood production! Play to the strengths of live-video: after all, being informal can be much more engaging.

You don't have to have formal content, such as a step-by-step process, either. Set a topic, have an introduction and then invite comments and questions that you can discuss with your viewers.

Give great content first, so:

- ▶ You are honest – you don't tease them with "my tenth tip is the best, stick around for that", just so that you get more emojis or hearts.

- ▶ The viewers are so blown away, they share immediately.

Use a small tripod to hold your phone as it points down at your notes on a desk, or as you write notes on a flip chart or whiteboard. If you need to show a close-up from a whiteboard, just grab the phone off the tripod. Remember, what you say may be a little 'off-mic' if you are not directly on-screen yourself.

Encourage viewers to take a screenshot of your notes during your presentation and encourage them to respond in real-time: "let me know if you'd like me to show you that again. . .".

If people want to learn something, they will expect to be taken on a journey. So make sure you don't leave them stranded: in other words, schedule shows on a regular basis so people know their knowledge is being extended, leading to a final goal.

Use feedback mechanisms (such as Periscope's hearts) as a barometer of understanding.

Your viewers could even present a live-stream themselves, showing their progress and asking for some more help or advice. ("Am I hitting this golf ball right? Take a look!")

▶ LIVE-STREAM THEME: E-COMMERCE

Humanise the shopping experience in a way that most online stores can't do, with engaging, authentic live-video of your product.

A tweet is one thing, but with a live show you can:

- ▶ Drive people to action there and then.
- ▶ See how many people have joined you.
- ▶ See *the names* of those who have joined you.
- ▶ And immediately ask them to tell their friends to watch as well.

Stats from www.brandlive.com's "Shoppers at Brandlive Powered Events" say that:

- ▶ 90% of them say a video is helpful in the decision-making process.
- ▶ 80% are more likely to purchase with live-video.
- ▶ 57% are more confident in their purchase.

And according to a report from Cisco,[33] people are 144% more likely to purchase a product after seeing a video about it.

You've probably been onto Amazon and seen video clips of products. So why not do something similar live through *live* video, where viewers can ask you questions about its design, use, availability, price and ordering, there and then? Seeing something demonstrated on video is the closest thing there is to having it in your hand. It is far more intimate than seeing a still picture. So why not stream and show your stuff in action all in real time? Especially if you are an eBay seller,[34] let the product sell itself.

By using presenters who are knowledgeable about the item, you can have your own 'shopping channel' showcasing your products, live and in context:

- ▶ Introduce a new product, and unbox, assemble and explain it.
- ▶ Have an interactive demonstration of it within the lifestyle setting of the brand – so a top-end coffee maker is shown in a glossy, expensive kitchen and luxury bedding is depicted in a warm and inviting bedroom.
- ▶ Show real-life applications of your product.
- ▶ Tell its story: the journey from inception to completion.

- ▶ Answer customer questions.

- ▶ Explain technical details in real time.

- ▶ Clarify features.

- ▶ Reduce buying objections.

- ▶ Gather feedback on the current model.

- ▶ Gather suggestions for future designs or brand extensions.

- ▶ Hold a flash sale so viewers can buy immediately.

Video is a great tool for product demos, because many people may want to refer to the recording several times to see your product in action before making a buying decision. You could use a webinar service (which will let you save your session), but that may well cost you. Live-streaming is pretty much free and easy to use: there are no email links to website addresses and log-in codes needed. And no one needs to download extra software!

> People want to connect with a person like them, not a logo. That's because they can relate to 'you' in a way that they can't relate to a building or business.
>
> Why do you think so many brands create a character for their business? (e.g. Ronald McDonald, Aunt Bessie, Mrs Crimble, Captain BirdsEye, Mr Kipling) or promote one *real* person to be the figurehead (e.g. Mark Zuckerberg, Steve Jobs, John Legere). It's so customers have someone personal and tangible to relate to.
>
> We all have stronger relationships with people, not businesses.

I want brands to become more 'real'. None of this Photoshopped, unrealistic view of life that is punted out all day, every day. Sometimes the over-dramatic adverts do work, but I'd be more impressed with a brand if they live-streamed an organic, unedited and raw experience, flaws and all.

Beverley Klein[35]

Part of your sales pitch may be around a special offer or a 'first chance to buy': exclusive, limited-time deals, bonuses and promos only available through the show. Consider putting a code word in broadcasts such as these with the advice to "say it in store to get money off". Or limit the offer to "the time we are on-air – call now".

All this adds to the FOMO of live-streaming: the Fear of Missing Out. Many people will want to watch a show when it is live, so they are the first to know about, and don't miss out on, a deal or new product announcement:

▶ You could live-stream a product launch and build a buzz of excitement as everyone turns on at the same time to see what it is (this seems to work pretty well for Apple!). Indeed, consider live-streaming all of your brand's important occasions and major milestones.

▶ Retailers could present their own streams of staff taking delivery and stocking shelves to promote the launch of a product and build a groundswell of interest.

▶ The owner of a smaller store could have a live-video each day of their 'daily deal' items or special offers.

▶ For a publisher, bookseller or author, show a delivery of a new book, its cover, a flick through one of the copies highlighting certain pages or illustrations, a launch date and a way for viewers to order the book, perhaps with discounts and giveaways.

▶ Think about having a weekly or monthly show where your stream is the only place your audience can get certain information on new releases or sales dates. People respond well to 'limited-time offers' when they can own something and get one over on their friends who missed out.

▶ Every Saturday morning, a car dealer could present a show 'live from the lot', with the 'Deal of the Week', or the car with the biggest discount, or the new arrivals, with a walk-around and showing the vehicles inside and out and answering questions along the way (e.g. "What's the finance on that?", "Is that the newer model?", "I don't want to pay out for new tyres, give me a closer look at them").

▶ One car dealership has a Periscope button built into each page of its website. Potential customers looking online for autos for sale click to send a 'view this car on Periscope' request to the salesperson, who goes out to the forecourt with their phone and presents a live show direct to the client.

▶ On a smaller scale, a musician could earn money through impromptu performances, perhaps through an app, which has a payment system built into it.

▶ Consider making any 'exclusive sale' deals for a limited time, maybe the duration of the live-stream, with a countdown clock ticking (similar to how they sell on the shopping channels). That'll help to ensure people look out for your shows and then watch them live.

Creating short windows of exclusivity actually prevents you from diluting the perceived value of the content. You wouldn't sell a Rolex or a MacBook in a convenience store; the value of social content to the millennial masses is being able to be in the moment, and permanence cheapens that.

Jay Hawkinson[36]

Create a dedicated landing page and promote that URL exclusively in your live-video so you can track people who use it, and its success.

Explain where the link will take them and what they will have to do as people like to know what to expect. So say:

▶ This is where to go.

▶ This is what you'll see.

▶ This is where you'll need to click.

Ask your audience to put your website or sales address in the comments. A lot will do so, and not only is this added endorsement, but it's also increased exposure to your link. The viewers will do this to help you (so thank them) and to help themselves: they achieve 'credibility by association' and you are recognised and verified to other viewers.

It's great to have your fans to do some of the heavy lifting: showing their support in your streams and in streams of their own about your product. They will watch out for your 'exclusive' messages, jump in and watch and then tell their friends to come and join them.

Companies that really connect with their Periscope audience correctly will build an army of promoters. Would a beverage company see a better return from a primetime TV commercial or thousands of consumers live-streaming to millions

FIGURE 7.4 A musician making money and raising their profile by live-streaming their original composition

Source: IK Multimedia Production SRL www.ikmultimedia.com

of viewers with said beverage in the shot? Marketing executives should be drooling right now.

Jonathan Long[37]

You have the potential to reach millions of viewers with this tactic. Then reward your Superfans, perhaps with a live private show, like NBC's "The Voice" did with a special programme hosted by the show's contestants.[38]

> *It's much more effective to focus on creating strong relationships with your evangelists and then let them introduce you to their own audiences. Focus your energy on the few, and you'll get the most out of the masses. It's a smarter approach to social media.*

Josue Valles[39]

The best way to make a 'trusted' sale (where the customer avoids 'buyer's remorse') is to build up a relationship before anyone needs the product or service that you are offering. That relationship of credibility, trust and respect will take time to build, but it will be what you have over your competitors. And live-video is here to help you.

Don't use live-streaming like a speed-dating service: you will not build an instant relationship with people you meet through your show. You have to help them learn to know you, like you and trust you. You do that by:

▶ Showing up regularly

▶ Having good content

▶ Helping them on air and off

▶ Being authentic

▶ Not wasting their time or their data

▶ Not going straight in with the hard-sell

That last point is a 'one-night stand' approach. And we're trying to help you build a long-term relationship.

So:

▶ If you are a plumber, electrician or builder, present regular shows about topics such as how to stop a leak, wire a plug and put up a shelf.

▶ If you run a garage, show topics could perhaps be around basic car maintenance or saving fuel while you drive.

▶ A restaurant chef may teach how to make basic family meals or how to use up leftovers.

Yes. *You give away great material.* But by doing this:

▶ You attract more shares and follows.

▶ You get a more loyal audience who come back for more.

▶ You get more sales.

Providing useful free information, help and advice helps you form a deeper bond with potential customers and adds value to their lives. You come over as welcoming, generous and unique: all great qualities for a business to have. And you now have an opportunity to relate to your viewers, interest them and entertain them. Talk about your passion for the firm, why you set it up and tell a few anecdotes, and you become a *person* rather than a *business. And people buy from people.*

> *By uploading videos with tips and strategies, businesses can not only get attention but also provide help and value to customers, which will build respect. Tips and how-tos are a great way to develop your company as an expert on the topic."*

AJ Agrawal[40]

Now when one of your viewers needs a wall built, or a location for a family party, where do you think they're more likely to go? Probably to the person they already know, like and trust.

> *Engagement and financial return are two different things. While every social interaction may not lead to an immediate financial return, the interactions can be part of a broader force that leads to an impact downstream.*

Deborah Weinstein[41]

Live-streaming gives you the ability to show things 'in the moment' and make a personal connection with people. Every time you do that, you reinforce yourself in their mind, and you reinforce what you stand for and all that they've learnt from you and all the benefit they got from you with your other content.

At a time when more and more people are buying things online, from faceless multi-national warehouse stores, isn't live-video a great opportunity to help connect with potential customers, personally?

A live-stream through Periscope supports the idea of personalisation. It generates a more intimate marketing experience, and creates a personal bond with the consumer. The stronger the connection consumers have to the brand or collection, the more likely they are to purchase with them.[42]

Why do all of this?

▶ You can directly connect potential consumers to your product and story.

▶ Promotions and contests are a great way to boost your brand's visibility.

▶ Fun and free stuff are attributes that encourage your viewers to share your content, giving your brand exposure to a new audience.

▶ It increases the 'talkability' of your show and your brand.

▶ It makes your show and brand more memorable.

Brands can forge a more personal relationship with consumers by using Periscope to give them real-time access to moments that matter, from big announcements to fashion shows to sponsored events.

Twitter.com

▶ LIVE-STREAM THEME: COLLABORATION

A great way to grow your audience is to work with other live-streamers who have a complementary product or service to yours. By cross-promoting each other's businesses, you will help each other and both groups of viewers. Note that is *complementary business*, not a *competing* business: you want to collaborate so everybody wins.

Follow my eight points, and you could increase your influence exponentially by working with other people who are:

In the same niche – for example, if you are a photographer in York, England, why not work with a photographer in New York, USA? Your skills are similar, but you are not in competition because of your location. You could promote each other's shows, swap photographic tips within each of your shows and so on.

In a complementary geographic niche – someone who Periscopes street tours in Sydney could join with someone who reviews restaurants in the same city.

In a complementary topic niche – if your show coaches people in social media marketing, then perhaps link up with someone who could offer insights into *brand* marketing.

Up and down the chain – a pottery-maker could join with the person who designs her crockery or the store which sells them. A trainer on the technicalities of Instagram could join with a photographer who could advise on contents, lighting and angles for those original pictures.

These kinds of partnerships:

Increase knowledge – of your new viewers, but also of you when you watch and share information with your new colleague.

May increase your followers and viewers – as you are being recommended by someone who already has their own family of fans.

Are built on trust – the followers of your new partner are more likely to watch you because you have been recommended by someone they are already fans of. And, of course, that works the other way with the people you recommend your followers to watch.

Support other live-streamers – 'send the lift back down' and support, comment, follow and encourage those streamers or businesses who haven't quite made it yet.

▶ LIVE-STREAM THEME: DYNAMIC RESEARCH

Welcome to crowdsourcing of feedback, via live-streaming. All marketers want a direct connection with an audience of possible customers, and live-streaming is the quickest way to get it. It's market research or an informal focus group by any other name (albeit from a self-selecting group).

You can ask potential purchasers their thoughts about your products and customer service, and viewers can ask *you* about design and delivery dates:

- ▶ Doing things this way could save costly mistakes and provide an entirely new collaborative or community feel.

- ▶ Involving your fans in your decision-making process boosts their loyalty to your products.

- ▶ Answering customer queries live and publicly gives transparency.

- ▶ It helps explain any confusion.

- ▶ And it gives another opportunity to engage and relate.

Reviews that are made over live video come across as much more genuine than text reviews published on a webpage, which is why we expect to see many brands using Periscope to solicit customer feedback in the near future.

Tim Jacquet[43]

▶ If you run a plumbing repair or roofing business,[44] you could save time and money by seeing the problem before you leave your base. Ask the householder to show you what the fault is and troubleshoot at a distance, so you send the right technician with the right part from the start.

▶ If you, the plumber, arrive and still can't work out the solution to the problem, do a live-stream to a colleague for more advice.

▶ Ask for help from people in a similar job as you. Say you're a farmer and want a second opinion on a kind of mould on a crop, you could live-stream a video to show other farmers and get their help in working out what it is and how to treat it.

▶ You could be an artist or filmmaker.

[Periscope could be] a really useful tool for location scouting, setting up shots with a second unit, or any of the other production tasks where quick feedback on a visual feed is useful in a distributed workflow and people are spread about all over the place.[45]

Via redsharknews.com

▶ Or a designer who wants to show their followers what they have created so far, and ask for feedback or suggestions to take the project further.

Let's take that idea away from business and make it personal:

▶ If you wonder whether it's worth joining your friends at a party, ask them to live-stream it to you so you can take a look and decide.

▶ Want to know the dress code, or see whether someone's wearing the same outfit? Again, ask your friends to help so you can take a sneak peek. Periscope a crowdsourcing question: "Should I buy these shoes?" or ". . . this car?" Do a tour of the car on live-video and get an expert to view live from somewhere else and give advice.

▶ Show off your holiday hotel to jealous friends back home. Live-stream your reaction to a first date. And ask whether you should kiss . . . or run!

▶ One viral live-stream featured a man whose wife was away. He asked viewers for help in what clothes to wear that day. . .

Imagine if a company fired up a Periscope live-broadcast in the middle of a board meeting to get some instant feedback on a new idea? Innovative brands will be all over this. It is far too convenient and powerful to avoid.[46]

▶ If you are in customer care, you could do a private walk-through of a product with a customer to find the fault they have complained about, or a public stream if there's a general issue that needs to be explained. Social media's penetration onto smartphones (its ubiquity and integrated video capabilities) makes Facebook Live and Twitter's Go Live/Periscope ideal platforms for interactive customer service. And, of course, videos can be saved for customers to replay later for references, which in a customer service setting is a feature you can't afford to miss.

▶ LIVE-STREAM THEME: Q&AS

(Otherwise known as AMAs – 'Ask Me Anything' – or 'Honest Hours')

Formal webinars take time and trouble to arrange. You have to sign up and download software. But using live-stream video, you can do things in a fraction of the time – and engage, live. (Live-streaming is 'one *with* many' instead of 'one *to* many'.)

It's all so simple: for a set period, people can ask questions of people at the business who are in the know, from the CEO to the shop-floor worker, and get their answers back immediately.

These kinds of events are usually very successful:

- ▶ They are a way of letting you hear what your fans are thinking and saying about you and your product: you get to know their needs, their suggestions and their concerns.

- ▶ It'll show bosses, who may be shielded from the 'coal face', what the actual perception of the company or product is and get some front-line feedback, ideas and suggestions for developments.

- ▶ You show your human face, reacting live to real questions from people who want to engage, humanising your brand.

- ▶ Q&As are raw and honest without room for 'spin'.

- ▶ You will be doing them when your competitors aren't, creating a point of difference in a crowded marketplace.

- ▶ They increase customer engagement with viewers feeling as though they have a personal relationship with the guest.

- ▶ It's a para-social relationship (almost a one-to-one experience) as the celeb looks at the fan (through the screen), calls them by their name and answers their question.

- ▶ Q&As can become 'gamified' with a hint of jeopardy of what questions will be asked, making the stream more interesting for the viewer and the guest.

You could talk your audience through developments related to your industry and give reactions as they occur. For example, lawyers explaining regulation changes, accountants giving tax advice at Budget time, political commentary around elections, etc. Mobile streaming can supplement other channels when you want more spontaneous interaction with your audience.

Anthony Lingwood[47]

▶ Maybe you're an expert in something, and people are coming to you for advice. Use these kinds of events to show off what you know and to help someone: they may come back and buy your product in the future.

▶ Maybe you don't run a business, but you are a sport or music star. Or perhaps you are an author, actress, celebrity chef or scientist. Great! Now you can talk live with your fans *all over the world* in real time. With just a few taps of a phone.

▶ See how these skateboarders[48] used Periscope, with a great explainer on their website and a schedule too.

When a brand's product experts and advocates appear on live video, their passion shines through and makes a strong, authentic and emotional connection with the audience. Pre-recorded video has a polished sheen, but one that savvy viewers can often see right through . . . they desire a more genuine, conversational experience.

Fritz Brumder[49]

▶ One celebrity invited their viewers to message them A-or-B-type questions that he answered in rapid succession: Indian or Chinese takeaway? Home or away? A place in the sun or a week away skiing?

▶ When Def Leppard[50] released their new studio album in October 2015, Joe Elliott and Phil Collen took part in a Q&A session with fans on Periscope.

▶ JC Penney used Periscope when actress Eva Longoria did a Q&A session with her fans for the department store.[51]

You won't be able to answer *all* of the comments (hopefully there will be lots of them, coming thick and fast), but do try to respond to half-a-dozen, so those who are watching feel as though they are being listened to.

You only have a few seconds to come up with an answer. This is how to avoid the awkward ones:

▶ Create a list of possible topics before the show, so you have some prepared answers for awkward questions.

▶ Focus the conversation and invite questions on a certain topic, so it's not all-encompassing, and you have some information prepared.

▶ Have someone with you to help answer the questions, fill for time and rescue you if necessary.

▶ Have other things to say and show so you can overlook the questions you don't want to acknowledge, and you are not left looking desperate if no questions are asked.

▶ Remember that sensitive questions can be ignored more easily on a live-stream than on a written, permanent thread or through a hashtag.

▶ You don't have to answer *every* question: say you'll do some on-air and others you will post in the chat later. You could also send a video answer or ask someone to contact you in another way.

▶ If a viewer brings up a great topic, say you'll devote a whole show to it another time.

▶ Don't let just a few people dominate the conversation.

▶ Say if you don't know, and that you'll find out and get back to them. Be honest.

▶ Have a producer who can filter comments and hand them to you, together with some possible answers.

▶ Thank the viewer for what they say.

▶ LIVE-STREAM THEME: SPYING ON RIVALS

Now you have another way to monitor what your competition is up to: simply watch their live-stream videos.

▶ Follow their accounts.

▶ Analyse their content, duration and regularity.

▶ Identify any weaknesses in their programmes or products.

▶ Create content that fills the gaps to better serve the audience.

Then, target those other people who watched your competitors' shows. Follow them as a way of giving them a nudge that you exist, and they will hopefully follow back. Later, on Twitter, invite them (politely) to watch your show "Hi (name). I saw we both watched (title). I'm planning a similar show soon. Shall I let you know when it's scheduled?"

But:

> *If you're spending more time on coming up with clever ideas for Periscope stream-ing than you are on more tried-and-true inbound marketing techniques, you're likely to find that the juice isn't worth the squeeze. You're going to experience a diminishing return on investment.*

John E Lincoln[52]

▶ LIVE-STREAM THEME: STAFF EVENTS

Employees who feel valued are more likely to be engaged in their work and feel sat-isfied and motivated. And you can use some live-streaming to help show them that you appreciate them:

- ▶ Have real-time business meetings with people from different time zones.

- ▶ Have a live-streamed staff meeting perhaps going over the high points and progress. Perhaps have a manager or customer give thanks to a member of staff.

- ▶ Using an app's private feature, you could hold an internal staff meeting for your employees, wherever they are in the world, all at the same time.

- ▶ Help people apply for a job at your place of work: give tips or explain what you do and what your ethos is.

> *People want to know exactly who it is that they might become professionally involved with. Furthermore, the presentation of company culture needn't only be limited to the front desk and water cooler. Business trips, sales calls, office tours and employee bios are all attractive access points for B2B interactions.*

Lucas Miller[53]

- ▶ Got new joiners at several locations? You could stream a private overview of the company, describe workplace essentials and what other departments do.

- ▶ If you have a person who is running another department remotely, they can take a virtual tour to see what happens and who their colleagues are, and so better understand their place in the system.

- ▶ Have an 'Employee of the Month' and follow them around during their day at work and explain what they do and why. It helps everyone understand

FIGURE 7.5 Use www.belive.tv to live-stream from several cameras at the same time. In this case, it's a talk show, but you could also use the same app to connect staff at several locations

Source: Jeff Adams, www.belive.tv, Facebook

and appreciate each other's part in the business. Why use your own staff to present from your streams? Because they are the real deal. They know what they are talking about and showing. A genuine colleague will help with the engagement and trust you seek. And if they don't want to speak on camera, that's fine. Perhaps they can show something, and another person can explain the process.

▶ If you have a big charity day at offices across the world, live-stream what is happening at each venue to maximise engagement and sense of community.

Tell your story, so people better connect with you:

▶ **Your back-story** – why you decided to do what you are doing and how you got to here

▶ **Your current story** – what it is that you are trying to do

▶ **Your future story** – where you want to go, why and how

▶ **Your progression** – keep your viewers updated on how you get from A to B

▶ LIVE-STREAM THEME: TAKEOVERS

This is when you give temporary access to your account to someone else, possibly an expert or celebrity, so they can stream directly from their location and interact with fans of your joint brands. They have the power to say and do anything, so you need to have complete trust in them.

They could maybe do a tour or a Q&A and have viewers connect directly with their hero. Or have them do a point-of-view live-stream from on stage.

Consumers are accustomed to seeing influencers and celebrities in commercials, movies, and television shows. What if they're able to see that same influencer via a live stream – raw, uncut, and unscripted.

Juntae Delane[54]

▶ LIVE-STREAM THEME: VLOGGING

What could be easier than holding the phone in front of you, pressing a couple of buttons and then talking out loud about what's on your mind? Within seconds you can be talking to the world and sharing your thoughts, feelings and views.

Whether it's an off-the-cuff rant or a more considered presentation, you'll have friends, followers and fans looking into your eyes, hearing your conviction and making a connection. Then they'll reply in real time, further strengthening the rapport.

These informal chats can be streamed from anywhere and will show there is a person behind the brand and not a faceless machine. And whether it's a basic live-video 'hold the phone and moan' or something a bit more thought-out, with direct live-video you have the opportunity to present more compelling, more effectively-engaging messages.

So grab that opportunity!

Many times I will engage with viewers by showing them how I'm cooking something at home that I demoed on 'Today'. The viewer gets another chance to connect and they get a glimpse of my personal life.

Al Roker[55]

▶ You can appear on live-video, streaming what would normally have been your *written* content: now you have a live blog post during which people can interact with you asking questions and passing on comments. We speak roughly 10,000 words an hour. Think about how long it would take you to write all that material.

▶ Don't wait for speaking engagements to come to you; create your own opportunities. Mari Smith advises that you set up notifications in other social media platforms to let you know that there's breaking news in your areas of expertise:

Then when something happens, you can go live immediately and share it with your audience . . . and also add your own thoughts and opinions. Doing videos like these helps you establish your expertise. Remember, journalists, other influencers and potential clients could be watching.[56]

▶ Live vlogs simply take the place of, or are extra to, your *text* blog, giving another level of engagement as fans ask you questions about what you have written or just presented.

▶ On live-video, people can get to see you sound-off about something, hear the tone of your voice, see the thing you are talking about and of course comment and question in real time, continuing the conversation and giving feedback.

You are hit with a brilliant thought that you'd love to share. Rather than coming up with an outline, writing out your post, formatting it, adding pretty pictures and making it ready for publication. . . . You pull out your smartphone, open up the app, click on the start broadcast button.

Leslie Samuel[57]

▶ As a brand, you will show you have more about you than simply putting text on a website (which of course you could do as well).

▶ Supplement your blog posts. If one is getting a lot of hits and comments, instead of writing a follow-up, jump on a live-stream.

You could even make announcements of social media news, on a live-video on social media. It makes sense, doesn't it?

▶ LIVE-STREAM THEME: REVIEWS AND TESTIMONIALS

We have seen how *you* can show off your product, but what about live-videos from your customers demonstrating how they use it? Let's call this 'activating your advocates'!

Testimonials from people who paid good money for something are more valuable than a live-stream show from *you* about it. That's because psychologically, people are more likely to believe someone like them than they are a business.

▶ If you have a company where a Superfan regularly supports your product, consider inviting them into your office or factory and go live with them to talk about how they use your product and how it's been of use.

▶ *You* could also review other items that could be used alongside yours, in a similar way to how food manufacturers use other ingredients for their recipe suggestions. So if you sell crockery, then review tablecloths, silverware, glasses and table decorations. If you run a beauty channel, then consider linking in with those presenting shows on fitness tips, or fitness equipment or fitness clothes.

▶ Or you could do a live review of the restaurant you're at. Or straight after seeing the latest movie release or play, approach people leaving the theatre to get their instant reaction.

FIGURE 7.6 Anthony Lenzo regularly presents shows of 'unboxings' and reviews on his channel

Source: Anthony Lenzo, Carlos Phoenix at www.livestreamingmaster.com, Facebook

▶ Which leads us to fashion unboxing. These are hugely popular on YouTube: instant reaction to the opening of a just-bought item. As a producer, you could show the factory-fresh new lines as you open the box. Perhaps have a customer there with you who can give viewers their instant review as the product is put through its paces.

▶ Here's a live-streamed unboxing of a new series of Lego[58] characters.

▶ LIVE-STREAM THEME: 'ME TV'

Fed up with not getting your point-of-view across, or news releases not being reported by the mainstream media? Is there a sport that you are passionate about that doesn't get the coverage you feel it deserves? Here's your chance to talk directly to the people you represent, or who are your fans.

Live-video has urgency and spontaneity, just right for news channels and 'personal press conferences'. Now's the chance for you to control your name and your brand, the rumours, news and controversy.

Periscope enables marketers to place a brand's perspective on breaking news in front of journalists, bloggers, industry influencers and the general public as quickly as you can pull your smart phone from your pocket.

John Hayes[59]

▶ A council could refute political accusations with a live-stream after telling local media to tune in. Indeed, they could have regular presentations to local residents on topics of interest and importance: explain why a long-term road closure is necessary; what happens to fat and oil when it's poured down the drain; home

FIGURE 7.7 Greenpeace Executive Director, Annie Leonard, speaks on the Greenpeace Facebook page, moments after being arrested

Source: Greenpeace, Facebook; www.facebook.com/greenpeaceusa/videos/10154201114629684/

security tips; or more time-sensitive issues such as updates to a flood situation or where pupils from a fire-damaged school need to attend. (One council did a live-stream from the opening of a 100-year-old time capsule!)[60]

▶ Now, company news can be shared with your colleagues and customers *at the same time*. Perhaps have regular broadcasts about what is going on in your business or your industry.

▶ Monsanto, the agrochemical and agricultural biotechnology, presented a series of live-streams giving updates on their crops. The shows provided good visuals, a chance to explain and answer questions from their followers (farmers, agriculturalists, scientists, employees and students) and gave a developing story arc over the series of shows.

To be relevant, you have to show up and create compelling content. Facebook Live enables us to share real-time stories . . . a peek into what our customers are dealing with – a behind-the-scenes look in which anything can happen and high production elements are stripped away, creating an exciting, authentic experience.

Nick Weber[61]

▶ A sports team could announce their new signing live (Adidas used Periscope to show fans the soccer player James Rodriguez signing a contract extension), showing the star putting their name on the dotted line on the contract and then being taken around the dressing room.

If you are going to do breaking 'corporate' news, make sure you prepare:

- ▶ Know your message and practice delivering it. If it's serious, then you need to be fluent and confident.

- ▶ Be like a TV reporter: start the stream and have a press officer introduce themselves and explain what is going to happen, who will be talking and (if appropriate) whether questions will be taken afterwards.

- ▶ Have the camera near the podium, so the sound and picture are clear, and stream the press conference live.

- ▶ If you have two mics, you could have one on the main speaker and another for the press officer. They could chip in and give a commentary, such as explaining who the speaker is, repeating questions from the floor that may not have been picked up by the mics and reminding viewers what is going on.

- ▶ Take the main speaker (e.g. the mayor, chief executive, fire officer or whoever) aside at the end of the main podium presentation to ask them a few supplementary questions, including those posted on the screen by the viewers. If the main speaker doesn't co-operate, then maybe one colleague can 'interview' another to cover the main issues.

▶ LIVE-STREAM THEME: INTERVIEWS

You don't fancy being the one answering the questions? What about *asking* them instead? Or at least asking some of them and then getting viewers to submit more of their own.

Having a guest will:

- ▶ Attract more viewers as the guest will bring with them *their own* followers.

- ▶ Help boost your credibility and authority while providing value to your audience.

- ▶ Share a personal side of your brand.

- ▶ Make you appear more natural: you are in conversation with another person rather than talking one-way to the camera lens.

- ▶ Give more variety to the show, with another voice.

Get a guest, an industry leader or commentator, an expert or blogger in the field to meet you and go through a Q&A. (You may need to coach them a bit in some camera technique: do you want them to address you or the camera, for example?)

Simply sketch out a rough plan of the areas to talk about that you know your general audience will appreciate and then go for it, keeping it natural and relaxed and authoritative.

You could have the guest in the room with you, or use the dual-presenter mode in Facebook Live. An alternative may be to set up a Skype, Facetime or Google Hangout and simply play the audio from a screen that you stand in front of, or are shown on. Or have a phone-in. You appear on camera and viewers dial a separate handset of yours and are heard on the live-stream via the speaker.

You come out looking great as you have provided the expert guest. They come out of it looking great as they are perceived as the thought leader. Your audience gets a 'toofer': a two-for-one broadcast with a double-value view, of the expert and you. And then after the show, put it all on YouTube and/or your own website page.

Or why not risk things and go 'naked'?! Try out some spur-of-the-moment interviews on the street. Just take your phone and approach people, explain what you are doing

FIGURE 7.8 Charles Hodgson of *View News*, **Australia interviewing local election candidate Ted O'Brien on a live-stream**

Source: @CharlesRHodgson and @viewnews on Facebook, Twitter and other social media; www.facebook.com/viewnews/videos/vb.104798568714/10153700816263715/?type=3&theater

and that they are live and ask them for their opinion on a certain topic: a live focus group. Or maybe a taste test. Or a challenge. . .

▶ LIVE-STREAM THEME: CITY TOURS

Present a tour around a building or a city, such as the Periscopes @ClaireWad and @EuroMaestro host in Paris and @PenguinSix introduces in Hong Kong, and have viewers ask you questions about the sights as you pass them.

Be a 'virtual tour guide', perhaps looking at a different part of the city or destination each week. Interview locals, show the best places to shop and get sponsorship from restaurants you feature. Such tours have the factors of:

- ▶ Discovery
- ▶ Education
- ▶ Surprise

As a viewer, it's the pleasure of travelling without the hassle of airport queues! – and as near to the teleportation that Periscope developer Kayvon Beykpour anticipated as there is likely to be.

FIGURE 7.9 Viewers commenting on a Periscope tour of Paris presented by Claire Waddington

Source: @ClaireWad, Periscope

▶ LIVE-STREAM THEME: PRIVATE CONTENT

By this, I don't mean XXX-rated 'adult' content (which will be against the terms and conditions of any app!)

Make your shows exclusive, and either have viewers *pay* to watch or give individuals access as part of a prize or bonus. Such exclusivity creates a FOMO factor: people will want to be part of the 'special group' or 'inner circle' to be able to see what goes on, what guests you have or what you show.

In both Facebook Live and Twitter's Go Live/Periscope, there are settings so you can choose which Groups will be given the 'entry ticket' to your broadcast.

▶ LIVE-STREAM THEME: CROSS-PLATFORM CONTENT

Use live-streaming to either enhance or promote what is happening *on another platform*.

'Enhancement coverage' could be along the lines of a 'watch party' for people who surf on their phones while watching a programme on their main TV. So, while say *Game of Thrones* is on, or maybe a sports final or political debate, present a show based on *reactions to it*. The content is your comment on the main TV show, stats and back-story, hidden trivia, suggested plot development and so on, all mixed with the thoughts of those watching both screens (their TV and mobile), with you.

This would work particularly well if yours was a brand that complemented the main event, something that people were likely to be using such as a drinks or snacks company, or a political group during a debate, or a brand of tissues to wipe away tears during the finale of a drama series. Also consider building in a call-to-action sale at the end of your show, such as a code if used within the next hour. Alternatively, use live-streaming as a way to *publicise* and *support* an event or promotion of your own.

In 2016 the UK TV station Alibi presented what it called "the world's first interactive escape room murder mystery" on Facebook Live, to launch a new season of the crime drama *Crossing Lines* (which started on TV just as the live-stream ended). The hour-long interactive murder mystery focused on a security guard at an exclusive art gallery who was trapped in a room with a dead body. The guard was wearing a head-mounted camera for the stream and had 30 minutes to piece together what happened before he was framed for the crime himself. Viewers were encouraged to debate clues in the on-screen comments and were asked to vote using Facebook's reactions emoticons. Moderators went through the comments to pick out the answers that would help the guard progress through the story.

French phone company @OrangeTelecom set up an interactive TV ad campaign, driven by Periscope. The TV commercial[62] featured teenager Victor flirting with Chloe, the girl next door, who eventually agrees to go on a date with him. The company used Twitter and Periscope to ask viewers what Victor should wear for his date and where they should go.

And Netflix previewed a new season of *Narcos*[63] on Facebook Live, with 150,000 views and 3,000 interactions.

▶ LIVE-STREAM THEME: SLOW TV

Some of the most successful live-video shows have been those which got out of the 'live-stream jet-stream' and were presented at a much slower pace. Such 'slow TV' can be, as Mashable said,[64] boring and gripping at the same time.

Slow TV originated in Norway, where networked broadcasts showed events such as train rides and knitting. These were devoid of commentary with just an occasional caption to highlight, say, places that the train was passing through. It was later picked up on by the BBC and Netflix, the former showing a reindeer ride through Lapland and the journey of the Flying Scotsman steam train. Now the idea has spread to live-streaming, with some success:

- ▶ **The Drummond Puddle Watch**[65] – In 2016, thousands of people were engrossed as pedestrians tried to negotiate a large puddle[66] across a pavement in Newcastle, UK. The stream (!) continued for six hours.

- ▶ **The Watermelon Challenge**[67] – BuzzFeed streamed footage of staff wrapping a watermelon in elastic bands until it exploded. At its peak, more than 800,000 people watched the stunt live, and replays have brought the total up to 11 million.

- ▶ **The sunrise over Pearl Harbor**[68] – This, on the 75th anniversary of the December 7th 1941 Japanese attack when more than 2,400 Americans lost their lives, was shown by CNN.

- ▶ **Holographic streamers**[69] – They mesmerised visitors to Los Angeles's Pershing Square and were streamed by NPR.

- ▶ **Jellyfish at the National Aquarium**[70] – another stream by NPR

- ▶ **SendMeToSleep** – As part of World Sleep Day, consumer electronics brand Philips actively tried to create content so boring it was capable of sending their audiences straight to sleep. They broadcast what they claim to be the world's longest Periscope stream: 41 hours straight of splashes of paint being added to a canvas. They say that more than 6,000 people tuned in to watch paint dry.

On a smaller scale, you could set up a live feed of:

▶ A typical day in your office as a way of letting people see behind the scenes of your restaurant, tailors, factory line. . . (Don't forget to put a notice up telling people that they may be caught on camera!)

▶ A developing storm from the window

▶ Drivers negotiating a new one-way system around your town

These work because:

▶ The idea is basic. People can join at almost any time and know what is going on.

▶ There is still a sense of suspense and jeopardy. That worked well with an experiment such as the 'Watermelon Challenge': when will it explode and what will that look like?

▶ Stickability. As viewers don't know when it will end, they are dissuaded from leaving.

▶ There is a developing story: even with a train ride, viewers will watch the ever-changing countryside.

▶ They may not need audio, which means viewers can watch anywhere where otherwise that might be a problem (such as at work or on public transport).

▶ LIVE-STREAM THEME: CREATIVITY

People want a bit of fun in their lives, and you need to grab their attention. That might be through the sheer wit and verve of your personality, or it may be by doing something a little bit more creatively than the other broadcasters.

Before live-streaming, brands who *spent* most would get the most engagement. Now the playing field is a little more level, and creativity can help win the day.

▶ Maybe it's a challenge ("Watch me as I attempt to . . .") or something with a bit more jeopardy or mystery: "This is my fridge. If I get 100 viewers, I'll smash the eggs with my bare hands".

▶ Ask the audience to decide what happens next: "Should I turn left or right?"[71] (It's a bit like a remote control or the *Choose Your Own Adventure*[72] books in the

1980s and 1990s, in which the reader could determine how a story developed by choosing options and then turning to a particular page.) Get immediate reaction to the question "What do you think about this person, place or product?" Or maybe the question is "Red . . . or Black. . . ?" A live-stream of a roulette table, experiencing the thrill and excitement of what will happen and asking the audience what to do next.

With a live-stream, a marketer knows that the audience is actively engaged. . . . The broadcaster can see live reaction and adjust to what the audience wants in real time. This tactic would allow for a more organic marketing approach where action and reaction drive the broadcast.

Geoffrey Dion and Devon Rauth[73]

▶ What about a skit, parody or take-off? Perhaps get an improvisation team in? This kind of content production could add personality to your brand. But don't forget that all this is live, and even though that adds a frisson of excitement to your super-creative show, you will need to rehearse: when it's live, it's live!

▶ Consider a series of weekly instalments like a soap opera: your viewers could suggest (in a freeze-frame moment) what happens next. A series of linked shows is a good idea for engagement and to subtly reinforce a message.

▶ Be ready to react to another (fun) story in the news. Can you make mileage out of it in your next stream? Doing this will get you much more traction and publicity, if it's quick off the mark and well-executed.

FIGURE 7.10 "The church is open, would you like me to show you inside. . . ?"

▶ You could live-stream a treasure hunt (have different people with the log-in details for a single account, and send streams from different places giving clues to their location).

▶ Schools have held games where pupils connect with another school[74] somewhere in the world, and ask questions to find out where each other is located.

▶ One travel company[75] did a 24-hour Periscope of different locations around the world. The campaign involved 19 travel bloggers sharing travel tips and knowledge of their country to people tuning in.

▶ This airline[76] Scoped from the cockpit of the plane as it flew from Turkey to the US.

Is one of your customers having a birthday? Did they just get a big promotion? Become a parent? Gather all the employees in your department (or your entire office), invite the client on to a private Periscope session and shout "Hip-Hip-Hooray" and give them a standing ovation.

www.dontheideaguy.com

▶ During the taping of a TV show, several people were positioned in different parts of the studio to give Periscope viewers alternative angles[77] from which to watch what was happening.

▶ The restaurant Applebee's had Scopers at every single one of their restaurants[78] in the US, with people showing a free food giveaway, and hosts in 'Applebee HQ' linking all the shows together.

▶ Those who want to be professional actors, TV presenters or musicians use the apps to showcase their talents, presenting live-streams from backstage, parties and announcements, giving tutorials and interviewing fellow cast members.

FIGURE 7.11 A live-stream 'audition' and raising their profile by live-streaming an original composition

Source: iKlip Grip Pro from IK Multimedia Production SRL www.ikmultimedia.com

▶ TV anchor Jason Carr started streaming from his vehicle[79] as he said he would in his last TV broadcast, but didn't tell viewers where he was going. The suspense built until he arrived, at his new job at rival station WDIV!

▶ AT&T presented a stream in which Mrs Claus and a group of elves prepared for Christmas with Santa.[80] Via Facebook Live, he read out names of 200 children who had been more nice than naughty, after parents sent in their kid's name. The company let parents know when to tune in to hear their child's name being read out. The audience was able to interact with Santa by commenting in real time, and personalised videos captured by camera crews of Santa reading the kids' stories were sent to each family as a keepsake.

Think creative! Think **BIG**!

▶ LIVE-STREAM THEME: CONTESTS

Anyone likes winning, and if you are creative enough you can use your live-stream channel to have a giveaway that helps highlight your brand credentials.

▶ *Oh Polly*[81] boasted 23,000 views on its video, which showed the brand popping numbered balloons to reveal prizes for commenters.

▶ *Chain Reaction Cycles*[82] simply asked who would like a high-tech toolkit. They received nearly 10,000 interactions.

▶ Airline *Monarch* ran a competition with 7,000 answers. (They later posted[83] on their Facebook page that "As the video is not live anymore, the prize draw is now closed". Remember to do something similar for any contest you run, as viewers can still comment/enter well after the closing date.)

▶ It can be tricky keeping up with replies and entries, as *HolidayPirates.com*[84] realised: "We can't believe how many comments you sent! We actually weren't able to keep up. So Matthew wasn't even the first person to give us the correct number! Not to worry though because we've decided to give out TWO prizes! One to the first person who guessed the right answer, and one to the amazing Matthew Hallesy! Cheers!"

▶ *SilkFred.com* ran a Wheel of Dresses[85] competition. "Welcome to 'Wheel of Dresses'! Comment on this video, we'll spin and you win the outfit it lands on. Let's go!" they had 95,000 views and 3,000 comments.

▶ *Myprotein*[86] simply showed a live-stream of a shaker bottle: "First person to find and neck this shaker gets £50 cash."

▶ At a much more basic level, you could simply have viewers identify something you walked past two minutes earlier.

▶ LIVE-STREAM THEME: EXTREME STREAMS

This section covers how using additional tech such as drones, 360-degree and action-cameras can help show places and perspectives people won't have seen before.

Being a bit more creative will have a more visual impact and help lure people into watching (and *keep* watching) them. However, always consider whether your use of such tech really does help bring someone closer to the action and better explain a situation, or is merely a gimmick. You can sync these wearable and aerial devices to your live-stream account to achieve some dynamic and creative content, such as sports action and spectacular bird's-eye views to create more visually engaging content to enhance your communication and storytelling:

- ▶ Surfing and skiing views
- ▶ From hot air balloon or underwater
- ▶ Streaming from a skateboard or car
- ▶ Have a camera on your helmet as you bungee
- ▶ A view from the conveyor belt in your factory
- ▶ A puppy-view as a shelter dog meets its new owners
- ▶ An athlete's view as they train
- ▶ An aerial view of your building site or festival
- ▶ News reporters are better able to show a protest with a drone or from a natural disaster area such as a flood with a GoPro.

Note: not all phones support these two features, and not all GoPros or DJIs are compatible with the phones.

Note: some regions have restrictions on where, when and who can operate a drone.

360 Cameras

Showing an all-round view of a scene can be more engaging and memorable for the viewer:

- ▶ It is more *immersive* as they can experience more of the location.
- ▶ Encourages viewer *interaction* as they can see what they want to see.

▶ Tells a better story as it puts a location in perspective.

▶ And that increases the time that they spend within your live-stream.

In other words, live, unedited, reality from the thick of the action. TV can't do that!

Possible uses of such cameras include:

▶ **Great on-location views** where there is a lot happening – such as tourism views of a city centre.

▶ **Emotional streaming** where such cameras help you capture a mood or feeling – such as a wreath-laying, or a concert.

▶ **Interactive streaming** – when you can ask viewers to direct you, or to spot an item at the location.

▶ **Better story-telling** – for example, to more clearly show a factory production line or a radio studio (so you can see the presenter *and the guests*, who are usually sitting opposite each other) or explain the layout of, say, where a gunman struck.

▶ **Immersive streaming** – to give a better feeling of 'being there' such as inside a cathedral or at the bottom of a canyon, or, in 2017 President Obama's 'farewell' speech. (Links to how that last example was managed.[87])

▶ **To add a sense of jeopardy** – where viewers can be part of a developing situation and experience something even before the broadcaster. ("Is that a rhino over there in the bushes?")

FIGURE 7.12 The world's first ever Periscope using a 360 camera

Source: Alex Pettitt, Periscope

How is your story spherical, not linear? Do the shots make me feel anxious, like I'm missing something behind me while focusing on something in front of me?

Jenna Pirog[88]

CONSIDERATIONS FOR 360

Don't think about where to *point* the camera, because everyone can see everything. Instead, think of where to *position* it. Treat the camera as a person. Where would the viewer want to be and look around?:

▶ Have the camera at eye level to give a more realistic viewing angle.

▶ Take the viewer to the heart of the action immediately. In other words, don't walk into the scene or do a pre-amble piece-to-camera first.

▶ Get in the *middle of the action* to give a raw and natural perspective with something to look at in every direction. That may be a different location from a TV camera whose crew is more likely to be standing back and *giving an overview*. At a concert, a TV camera may be behind the audience giving a view of the orchestra on stage. A 360 camera might be within the orchestra, showing the musicians, the conductor and the audience looking on – or between two people having a conversation. So consider an angle where you can show the most variety.

▶ Have your camera positioned so the best images are about 1–6 metres away. Too close or too far away and the image is distorted or blurred. The best distance for an interviewee to stand is about 1 metre away.

▶ The cameras work by stitching together views from two or more wide-angled lenses. So position guests or key subjects away from where the 'join' will be (usually 90 degrees to the direction of the lens).

▶ Keep the camera steady and limit quick movement. You can't move the camera too fast in a forward direction, because viewers may still be scrolling in a left-right direction at the same time. (Technically it's possible, but it may add to disorientation.) Movement therefore can induce motion sickness in the viewer. Have an eye on the horizon so you keep the camera generally level.

▶ Consider a mount or tripod for your 360 camera – the slimmer, the better. Otherwise, viewers will have part of the view obscured by a close-up of you, with a giant thumb holding the phone.

- ▶ If you don't want to be in the shot, run from the camera or blend in with the scene (hide behind a tree!), and beware of thieves while you leave the camera alone.

- ▶ Try and avoid extremes of light, including the sun, although that is difficult as you have to consider all angles.

As for narration:

- ▶ Provide context to guide your viewers through the experience.

- ▶ Find a balance between giving your audience direction and letting them explore the scene themselves (they may have FOMO, while you are directing them one way, they are wondering what's happening elsewhere).

- ▶ You don't know where any viewer is looking at any one time, so it's difficult to explain a view or direct them:

  - ▷ Broadcaster: "You see over there by the clock. . . ?" / Viewer thinks: "Hold on, where's the clock. . . ?"

- ▶ . . . or to handle comments:

  - ▷ Viewer comments: "What's that green thing?" / Broadcaster thinks: "What green thing? Where?!"

  - ▷ Viewer comments: "Go left!" / Broadcaster thinks: "Where's left?!"

- ▶ The viewers may see something that you didn't in the recce, that may not be appropriate. Or they may see something that's behind you that you don't notice.

You will need to have a special camera to present live all-round video in Facebook Live and Twitter's Go Live/Periscope, such as an Insta360 Nano, Ricoh Theta, Giroptic's iO or Samsung's Gear 360 (several more are available). Some of these are standalone cameras and others plug directly into the phone and are approved by Facebook, so you will have a seamless stream.

To watch:

- ▶ On the desktop, viewers can click and drag around the screen to rotate the camera (or at least their view of what the camera is picking up).

- ▶ On mobile, they turn their phone to change the 'immersive perspective'.

On Periscope: When broadcasting in 360, you can double-tap the screen to flip the preview you see 180 degrees. It won't change the angle your viewers see, just your preview.

Although these were not Lives, check out these recommended 360 videos:

▶ GoPro went deep beneath the ocean to swim with sharks (www.facebook. com/gopro/videos/10154003742876919/)

▶ The *New York Times* followed Usain Bolt's 100-metre sprint as he broke the world record (www.facebook.com/nytimes/videos/10150867985079999/)

▶ Take a cruise of the New York harbour with ABC News and learn a little more about the city's history (www.facebook.com/ABCNews/ videos/10154667673943812/)

Other points:

▶ You can go live in 360 from all Facebook Profiles and Pages.

▶ Anyone can watch a Facebook 360 on their phone (Android from 2012 and OS 4.3; iOS 8 and newer). Viewers on older phones will see a regular 'flat' video.

▶ You can't embed a 360 video or view one on a TV.

Drones

(Also, see the section on drones in the 'legal' chapter.)

(Only some apps have the capability of taking a feed from a drone, only some drones are compatible with the apps, and the feed may not necessarily work on iOS and Android devices.)

FIGURE 7.13 A bird's-eye view of the Australian coast; Periscoping with a drone

Source: Dan Moore, Periscope. Instagram: @DANandMOORE

Drones let you stream aerial pictures right to apps such as Twitter's Go Live/Periscope – so not so much 'behind the scenes' as *above* them! It takes live-streaming to a whole new level.

> For five days (and 30 streams) in July 2015, General Electric flew drones over and into five of their most remote testing facilities to give audiences a never-before-seen look at where GE builds jet engines, locomotives, wind turbines and industrial machinery.
>
> Using Periscope, the drone also showed off a 47-acre site and views from the top of a wind turbine. Staff on another account were able to field questions from the audience while the drone was in flight.
>
> Compilation video here:[89] YouTube search "GE #DRONEWEEK"
>
> More information: *GE Use Drones, Periscope In 5-Day Campaign Blitz* www.mediapost.com/

You can only broadcast live from certain drones, as they have to have a wireless link with your phone. You monitor the flight path on your phone's screen (which is usually in a cradle alongside the drone's joysticks).

You may (depending on the app you use) be able to give a running commentary to your viewers through the mic on your phone. Don't forget to interact with those who are watching and reply to their questions (likely to be along the lines of "where is this?" and asking to be shown certain scenes). When the drone is up, you can use the sketch feature on Facebook Live and Periscope to draw on the screen to highlight any points of interest. You may also like to bring the camera down to your level once in a while so your viewers can see you, and show you are not just a disembodied voice. You certainly have to be multi-skilled!

Lots of practical advice on drone flying can be found here: http://dronesafe.uk/.

Action cams

Your favourite live-stream app may also support external action-cameras, such as some of the GoPro series, so 'extreme footage' can be broadcast live via a device-to-phone Wi-Fi connection.

> ▶ Perfect for thrill-seekers who want to make the live-stream more immersive.

- ▶ You get an extra-wide field of view from an action-cam that you may not get from your phone's in-built camera.

- ▶ The image sensor on one of these devices is so good that it can gather more light in darker conditions.

- ▶ Action-cams are rugged and waterproof. (You could get a rubberised waterproof case, but these cameras are built for the job in hand.)

- ▶ Such devices are more readily attached to other items, thereby not limiting you to broadcasting from a phone-on-a-selfie-stick.

- ▶ There is less likelihood of damaging an expensive phone (and losing contacts, photos and so on), if the action-cam is the device 'in danger' on a car bonnet, or attached to a ship's mast, and your phone is safety in your rucksack in 'lock screen' mode. (You need to keep both devices within range of each other.)

- ▶ The audio can be taken from your phone so you can give a running commentary of what you are showing your viewers.

- ▶ You can swap between your outside source and the phone during your broadcast, with a GoPro it will continue to record the footage even if you are not broadcasting it.

- ▶ You can use the 'sketch' feature to highlight on the screen parts of the view you want the audience to note particularly.

Possible scenarios:

- ▶ Mount an action-camera to a skateboard,

- ▶ Or on a helmet to catch extreme PoVs (point of views),

- ▶ While snorkelling or in a hot-air balloon, or

- ▶ While walking through snowy streets or trekking a canyon, to give a wide-view without the intrinsic logistical issues of using a 360 camera. (Action-cams are small, don't need a tripod, are rugged, and sometimes showing something in 360 is just not necessary.)

- ▶ You can literally live-stream from a stream, or a river, or white-water rapids.

Disadvantages:

- ▶ There's less opportunity for interaction during the stream, as your phone is likely to be away for safety and you are probably involved in the sports activity.

- ▶ Your device and phone need to be nearby for them to remain tethered over the Wi-Fi connection.

Broadcaster features:

▶ You can still see, for example, the comments and hearts in the Periscope app while using a GoPro.

▶ The video (minus those interactions) will be saved to your camera's SD card.

▶ You can switch between the camera and the phone during the stream.

▶ Tap a button on the screen to lock the phone, so you can stream directly from the camera and put the phone away without accidently ending the broadcast.

For great how-to guides from Periscope, go to https://help.periscope.tv/ and search for 'GoPro' or 'DJI'.

Auto-edit cameras

The Mevo camera can help you create a professional-looking TV-type show into Facebook Live, Twitter Go Live and Periscope, by providing multiple-shot options from the single device. Using a wide-angled lens, facial recognition and smart microphone, the camera automatically pans, zooms and cuts to show whoever is talking. Alternatively, you can control these features manually.

The audio of the built-in mic of the Mevo is a bit poor, although you can plug in an external mic. And even though (at the time of writing) it has a 4K sensor, it doesn't

FIGURE 7.14 Periscope's first underwater live 360 broadcast

Source: @MitchOates, Periscope

shoot in 4K: it needs the sensor for cropping, so what you actually get is a default resolution of 480p, although you can change this in 'settings' to 720p.

▶ NOTES

1 Quoted by Anna Jasinski in *Bloggers: Why Periscope Is a Game Changer for Your Blog and Your Brand*, mediablog.prnewswire.com October 1st, 2015

2 Quoted by Siobhan O'Shea in Periscope, *It's Just . . . Stuff*, www.siobhanoshea.com/ July 24th, 2015

3 Al Roker, *Al Roker's Top Tip on How to Improve Your Brand*, www.prweek.com/ July 29th, 2015

4 Topher Burns in *As Social Platforms and Brands Turn to Live Video, Will Viewers Keep Tuning In?*, by Marty Swant, www.adweek.com/ December 4th, 2016

5 *10 Ways to Amplify Your Brand Reach With Live Streaming*, http://marketingzen.com/ October 13th, 2016

6 Sean Burrows, *Loyalty Marketing Tool: Live Streaming*, https://seanburrows.com/ (no publication date)

7 Mary Jo Madda, *A Peek at Periscope's Potential—and Privacy Concerns—in the Class-room*, www.edsurge.com/ June 11th, 2015

8 Jon Blistein, *Bonnaroo, Twitter Partner for New 'Wish Granting' Service*, www.rollingstone.com/ June 11th, 2015

9 www.periscope.tv/iainlee

10 www.mediaupdate.co.za/79061/heineken-south-africa-takes-uefa-champions-league-finals-to-the-next-level-with-periscope

11 Zoe Craig, *London Zoo Animals Are Periscope's Newest Stars*, https://londonist.com/ 13th July, 2015

12 Aden Hepburn, *The World's First Periscope Flight*, www.digitalbuzzblog.com/ July 15th, 2015

13 Sally Perry, *Live Sneaky Peek*, https://onthewight.com/ April 24th, 2015

14 Emily, *The Royal Shakespeare Company on Periscope*, www.socialmedia-trainingcourses.com/ May 6th, 2015

15 Matt Brian, *British Museum To Give Live Tours Over Periscope*, www.engadget.com/ May 28th, 2015

16 *Behind The Scenes Of the Writing Process*, www.artshub.co.uk/ June 3rd, 2015

17 *Behind The Scenes Of the Writing Process*, www.artshub.co.uk/ June 3rd, 2015

18 Bruna Camargo, *How Zagat Is Brilliantly Using Periscope*, www.ignitesocialmedia.com/ October 30th, 2016

19 *Periscope Goes Back to the Sea in Around-the-World Race*, www.espn.com/ May 13th, 2015

20 Ariana Garza, *Sheriff's Office Using Periscope App*, www.koco.com/ April 13th, 2015

21 Erik Ortiz, *Police Using Periscope App To Stream Traffic Stops*, www.nbcnews.com/ August 21st, 2015

22 *Live Report From House Explosion*, www.statter911.com/ July 22nd, 2015

23 Neil Versel, *Ohio State Surgeon Streams Operation On Periscope*, http://medcitynews.com/ June 27th, 2015

24 http://youtube-trends.blogspot.co.uk/

25 David Mogenson, *Want-to-Do Moments: From Home to Beauty*, www.thinkwithgoogle.com May 2015

26 Josue Valles, *The Marketer's Guide to Periscope*, https://blog.kissmetrics.com/ (no publication date)

27 See: Jayson DeMers, *Why The 'How-to' Boom in Content Marketing Is Still Growing*, www.forbes.com June 1st, 2015

28 *Unlock Mobile Advertising by Measuring the Real World*, www.marketingprofs.com/ October 16th, 2015

29 *Periscope Offers Impromptu Exercise Class*, http://print.thefinancialexpress-bd.com/2015/10/23/113235 October 23rd, 2015

30 Mary Jo Madda, *A Peek at Periscope's Potential*, www.edsurge.com/ June 11th, 2015

31 Coo, *Schools*, www.abc57.com/ May 14th, 2015

32 *Global Day of Discovery With Periscope*, www.eturbonews.com/ June 5th, 2015

33 White Papers, www.cisco.com/c/en/us/solutions/collateral/service-provider/visual-networking-index-vni/complete-white-paper-c11-481360.html June 1st, 2016

34 Kathy Terrill, *The Secret of Periscope for Ebay*, http://ilovetobeselling.com/ August 29th, 2015

35 Beverley Klein, *Why Periscope Is the Future for Brands*, www.bizcommunity.com/Article/196/82/129055.html May 29th, 2015

36 *Why Live Streaming Is the Water Cooler of the Future*, www.adweek.com/ October 15th, 2015

37 Lucas Miller, *Present, Promote and Publish: The 3 Ps of Effective Periscope Marketing*, www.socialmediatoday.com/ June 22nd, 2015

38 *The Voice Viewing Party*, http://vast-media.com/the-voice-on-periscope/ April 2nd, 2015

39 Josue Valles, *The Marketer's Guide to Periscope*, https://blog.kissmetrics.com/

40 AJ Agrawal, *3 Reasons Why You Should Be Marketing on YouTube and Periscope*, www.forbes.com/ January 3rd, 2016

41 Deborah Weinstein, *Hints From the Pros: Social Media Done Well Requires Risk*, www.mmm-online.com/ May 13th, 2015

42 Brielle Jaekel, *Target Gets Personal on Periscope to Tease Eddie Borgo Collaboration*, www.mobilecommercedaily.com/ May 22nd, 2015

43 Eric Siu, *25 Brand-Building Ways to Use Periscope – Twitter's New Live Streaming Video, Apps*, www.singlegrain.com/ (no publication date)

44 *Periscope For Roofers*, http://blog.hailstrike.com/periscope-for-roofers-live-video-for-roofing-marketing/ July 20th, 2015

45 Andy Stout, *Periscope, Meerkat and What Live-Streaming Apps Can Do for You*, www.redsharknews.com/ May 21st, 2015

46 Jonathan Long, *How Brands Can Utilize Periscope in Direct Marketing Efforts*, www.huffingtonpost.com/ April 1st, 2015

47 *Periscope v Meerkat: How to Use Live Mobile Streaming for Business*, www.zero21.ie/ (no publication date)

48 *Live Streaming Via Periscope*, www.wheelbasemag.com/live-streaming-via-periscope-catalina-island-classic-iv/ May 1st, 2015

49 Fritz Brumder, *Why Live, Online Video Should Be PR Firms' Next Big Land Grab*, www.prdaily.com May 28th, 2015

50 *Album Release Day*, www.youtube.com/watch?v=-Zyk2ZRzVqg#action=share

51 Tanya Dua, *JC Penney Joins Retailers Taking On Periscope*, https://digiday.com/ April 24th, 2015

52 John Lincoln, *Should Twitter Periscope Be Part of Your Social Media Strategy?*, https://ignitevisibility.com/ August 4th, 2015

53 Lucas Miller, *Present, Promote and Publish: The 3 Ps of Effective Periscope Marketing*, www.socialmediatoday.com/ June 22nd, 2015

54 http://juntaedelane.com/ (Exact source unknown)

55 Al Roker, *Top Tip on How to Improve Your Brand*, www.prweek.com/ July 29th, 2015

56 Mari Smith, *Facebook Live: What Marketers Need to Know*, www.socialmediaexaminer.com/ January 4th, 2016

57 Leslie Samuel, *220 Periscope for Bloggers: Why and How to Embrace This New Trend*, www.becomeablogger.com/ June 17th, 2015

58 James Zahn, *31 Days of Halloween*, www.therockfather.com/ October 7th, 2015

59 John W Hayes, *6 Tips for Your Next Periscope Broadcast and How to Increase Viewers via Email Marketing*, www.business2community.com/ October 26th, 2016

60 *Capitol Time Capsule*, www.therolladailynews.com/ June 17th, 2015

61 Nick Weber, *Tips for Using Facebook Live From Monsanto's Team*, www.prdaily.com/ *(and elsewhere)* December 21st, 2016

62 @Orange_France, https://twitter.com/ May 18th, 2015

63 Netflix, www.facebook.com/NetflixUK/ August 25th, 2016

64 Johnny Lieu, *Slow TV Finds Life Online*, http://mashable.com/ October 26th, 2016

65 Andrea Romano, *Stop What You Are Doing and Watch a Live Stream of This Puddle*, http://mashable.com/ January 6th, 2016

66 Elena Cresci and Josh Halliday, *How a Puddle in Newcastle Became A National Talking Point*, www.theguardian.com/ January 6th, 2016

67 Chelsea Marshall et al, *This Is What Happens When Two Buzzfeed Employees Explode A Watermelon*, www.buzzfeed.com/ April 8th, 2016

68 www.facebook.com/cnn/ December 7th, 2016

69 www.facebook.com/NPR/ August 9th, 2016

70 www.facebook.com/NPR/ September 14th, 2016

71 Ann-Christine Diaz, *BMW Debuts an Interactive Live Action Adventure*, http://creativity-online.com/ October 28th, 2015

72 https://en.wikipedia.org/wiki/Choose_Your_Own_Adventure

73 Geoffrey Dion, *Gaining a New Marketing Perspective With Periscope*, https://marketing-discussions.wordpress.com September 28th, 2015

74 Mary Jo Madda, *A Peek At Periscope's Potential*, www.edsurge.com/ June 11th, 2015

75 www.marketingmag.com.au/news-c/skyscanner-uses-new-live-streaming-app-periscope-24-hour-global-broadc (Link no longer available)

76 Phil Davies, *Turkish Airlines Claim Aviation First*, www.travolution.com/ July 21st, 2015

77 Sandra Gonzalez, *You Can Watch The Action of Tonight's @Midnight From Basically Every Angle*, http://mashable.com/ August 4th, 2015

78 Brent Schlenker, *Is Live Mobile Streaming the Future of Learning?*, www.litmos.com/ July 28th, 2015

79 Jason Carr, www.facebook.com/ May 23rd, 2016

80 AT&T, www.facebook.com/events/1812610649026456/, December 23rd, 2016

81 Oh Polly, www.facebook.com/ohpollyfashion/ November 25th, 2016

82 Chain Reaction Cycles, www.facebook.com/ChainReactionCycles/ October 14th, 2016

83 Monarch, www.facebook.com/Monarch/ September 14th, 2016

84 Holiday Pirates, www.facebook.com/Holidaypiratescom/ July 15th, 2016

85 Silk Fred, www.facebook.com/SilkFred/ November 25th, 2016

86 My Protein UK, www.facebook.com/MyproteinUK/ October 11th, 2016

87 Eric Chevalier, *How We Live Streamed President Obama in 360*, http://vrscout.com/projects/ January 2017

88 Jenna Pirog, *How to Pitch a 360 Video to the New York Times*, https://medium.com/journalism360 January 12th, 2017

89 GE #DroneWeek, www.youtube.com/watch?v=X57vJYRt35Y July 31st, 2015

8

Focus on...

After running through the different types of live-stream formats, with dozens of examples, in this chapter I am going to dig a little deeper.

In the following pages I will look closely at how specific groups and businesses have integrated live-streaming into their 'marketing mix'. By reading these more-detailed case studies, you should clearly see how live-video could be used in your field.

▶ FOCUS ON ... JOURNALISM[1]

One of the fastest take-ups of mobile live-streaming has been in the media community. After all, reporters are trained storytellers and professional presenters, so these apps have extended what they have already been doing. Video being (arguably) more accessible and emotional than text, it may be able to help reporters reach those who may not read an article.

The caveat for professional reporters is: remember your priorities. It may be fun to fire up Facebook or power up Periscope and talk to 500 people, but your priority is to your employer and the 5,000 or 5 million who may potentially watch on the TV. Is it a productive use of your time to live-stream, or would it be better spent taking photos, recording video and tweeting? Do your viewers really want or need to see it live, or would they prefer the edited highlights that will be quicker for them to watch and easier to understand. Are you giving a unique view that surprises and gives context, or one that is confusing and unfocused?

As journalists, (we) have some responsibility to help the public make sense of the information we're presenting.

Mark Frankel[2]

Live-streaming offers transparency in reporting, audiences value the raw, unfiltered content. Many feel that live-streaming is the only way to get an unbiased account of current events. It can feel as though the use of live-streaming is an alternative to actually reporting.[3]

Via http://ufsocial.jou.ufl.edu/

Professional news users[4]

Live-streaming is a way to get a story out immediately when a traditional news programme is not actually on the air. Although doing this may tip off other media, it is extra content for viewers that a few years ago would not have been possible to provide.

For radio and print journalists, it's a whole new medium they can use to tell a story: *showing* the land that the new estate will be built on, *hearing* the emotion in the voices of those whose houses may be razed to make way for it, all in real time.

With these apps, you can quickly and cheaply:

▶ Produce tailor-made content for niche-interest groups.

▶ Tell stories for hyper-local communities that otherwise may not have been covered.

As live-streams can be pretty much open-ended, and can be as easy as 'point and shoot', they are a straightforward way to explain what matters to a community by providing content and *context*. But what are the benefits of broadcasting?

▶ **Visual** – Are you taking the viewer somewhere?

▶ **Interactive** – Can the audience participate? Are you able to respond?

▶ **Intimate** – Is there a connection between you and them?

▶ **Developing** – Is the story moving? Are there changing facts?

And remember, even though you may be using similar skills to when you are live on TV, you need a more relaxed style for this more intimate and more interactive social platform.

One of the things we don't want to do on Facebook Live is it to be TV-lite. We do TV really well – on TV. We want Facebook Live to be something different.

Samantha Barry[5]

You will not be on a huge screen on the other side of the living room, but on a small screen in someone's hand, a foot or two from their face. You don't have to break through the clutter of what else is happening in their lives, as they have *chosen* to watch you. Yes, you need to engage them, but you can reduce excitement in your voice and the pace of your presentation. For radio and print reporters particularly, using moving pictures to tell a story may be quite new. Remember to *show* rather than *tell*.

Breaking news

People love to see an unexpected event unfold in real time, and being able to go live with a story as it happens is also the stuff of dreams for a journalist. Now with these apps, it is easier than ever before to give your viewers a front-row seat to an unfolding event, with no need for a sat truck, clunky camera and a mile of cables.

It is, of course, quite unlikely that you will be just where a news story explodes (sometimes quite literally. . .), although in 2016 Richard Gutjahr, reporter for German national broadcaster ARD found himself at both the Bastille Day lorry killings in Nice (14th July) and the fatal shootings in a Munich shopping centre (22nd July).[6] He presented live-streams as well as audio reports for 12 hours non-stop from the France attacks. At a previous incident in the same country, Sky News's Kay Burley hid under a table in the aftermath of the Bataclan shootings in Paris in November 2015; her view from a restaurant floor during the safety scare was put live to air.[7]

The BBC's Nick Garnett presented Periscope reports from locations affected by Nepal's 2015 earthquake. He was able to get to a remote village near Sindupalchok before TV crews as he'd had less luggage to pack, collect at Kathmandu airport and then carry.[8]

Facebook quoted the TV company Univision, who live-streamed their coverage of the death of musician Juan Gabriel and his funeral procession. It gave his millions of fans around the world, who may not otherwise have had access to the footage, a way to see what was happening. The live-video had 3 million views and 36,000 comments.

In each of these stories, the reporter was experiencing what was happening at the same time as the viewer, and that shared experience helps strengthen relationships. In effect, the viewer is 'out on the job' with the journalist.

FIGURE 8.1 A live-stream in an earthquake zone by the BBC's Nick Garnett

Source: @NickGarnettBBC, Periscope

Consider what you are offering that's different from other news-streamers at the same event. Do you have a better vantage point or a more inciteful commentary? Are you able to provide something extra, such as a Q&A with an expert?

Anticipation news

Stream when you anticipate doing something a little unusual. A great example of democratisation is to live-stream events such as news conferences: the full speech by the outgoing chief executive, a revealing report by the head of an inquiry, an appeal from a grieving mother. There is always the jeopardy of a possible loss of temper, resignation or tears.

TV stations may not have the time or space to run all this live on their network, but it's easy, honest, straight-to-air newsgathering.

Precede the conference (and fill for time as you wait for the speakers to gather at the top table) with the background to the event, why you have been invited and where, who will speak and what they are expected to say. Afterwards, present a summary of what was said and possibly take questions from the audience, or seek out one of the speakers to interview live.

Fire up a live-stream when you know something is going to happen but with no specific time. This gives a sense of jeopardy for the audience: when will the president

FIGURE 8.2 Live-streaming from a police news conference. In this instance, a traditional TV crew had previously asked the mobile live-streamer to stand at the back as they "weren't a proper broadcaster"

Source: Facebook

leave the White House? When will the royal couple leave the hospital wing to show off the new princess?

Live videos are by their very nature unpredictable, and ones streamed at a news event are likely to be more so. Action unfolding in real time is also immensely share-able, as people want to 'watch with friends' to create a water-cooler moment.

In August 2016, a man climbed the outside of Trump Tower in New York City. Facebook says around 80 live-streams were created from the event, with a total viewership of around 14 million around the world. CNN's stream was shared 55,000 times.

Immersive news

Using live-streaming can enhance your news coverage in ways like never before. Because phones are so ubiquitous and small, and data so cheap, you can take viewers directly to the heart of a story without raising suspicion or high costs.

In 2015 Bild reporter Paul Ronzheimer travelled with a group of Syrian refugees from the Greek island of Kos across Europe to their ultimate destination of Germany, live-streaming on Periscope as he went. He says that the unedited nature of the videos made the migrants' stories more authentic, and the comments feature meant that viewers could ask questions and get direct answers:

> *For the refugee story, the personalisation is very important. It's not just showing lots of refugees walking on a road: you can ask them how they feel.*[9]

This was truly behind-the-scenes content with real, raw stories. Not only would the logistics have been nearly impossible with a TV crew (the number of staff and amount of equipment), but safety may have been compromised (think of the reaction to overt filming in sensitive areas such as land borders).

Using a compact and discreet smartphone allowed Paul to get close to the action and reduce the chance that people would change their behaviour. The migrants were likely to be more open, engaging and authentic talking to a mobile phone than they might be to a TV camera.

As for post-production, Bild took the footage and turned it into a 16-minute documentary for its website.

More controversially, Facebook was used by Al Jazeera and Channel 4 News in the UK to live-stream the 2016 Battle for Mosul in Iraq in what was perhaps a first for wartime media coverage. There was much debate about the broadcast: several people

FIGURE 8.3 A March 2017 Periscope by Paul Ronzheimer showing devastation in Mosul

Source: @Ronzheimer, Periscope

questioned the ethics of showing war (albeit from a distance) as 'entertainment' complete with floating emojis.

> *We wanted to bring one of the most significant stories of our time to our viewers as it happened. Given the nature of conflict – we are cautious and vigilant that the material is appropriate at all times and have measures in place to stop the stream when necessary.*[10]

Jon Laurence

What can't be disputed is that streaming the coverage on Facebook gave the audience a forum on which they could discuss the operation as well as the coverage itself, which may not have previously been possible.

On a smaller scale, in the Euro 2016 tournament, ex-footballer and now commentator Stan Collymore used Periscope to live-stream a report from the middle of a riot.[11]

Interactive news

Live-video creates a different relationship with your audience from the traditional 'network broadcasting'. This book talks elsewhere about the value of comments in strengthening the bond between presenter and public, and this is a revelation to those from a background in one-way communication. For them, the change has been from talking *at* people to taking *with* them, and viewers have gone from being passive consumers to active participants: viewers with a voice.

And those viewers can ask journalists and their guests questions directly to drill down into their knowledge or to take the conversation in another direction. And that

FIGURE 8.4 Ahead of the UK EU referendum in 2016, the then Prime Minister, David Cameron, was grilled by audiences in the studio and online

Source: BuzzFeed, Facebook

'need to know' data from the audience is valuable to the broadcaster who can use it to produce more targeted content in future.

A reporter can provide updates to viewers wherever they are, in a solo presentation, or interviewing another reporter or guest either on location or in the newsroom.[12] Such a connection helps them tell and explain their stories and gives viewers an opportunity to interact with them, and can help a news organisation discover what viewers want or need to know about a story, and so help shape their future coverage.

> *In live interactive journalism, what's happening on the screen is affected by the audience in real time. This is as much about the audience as it is about the journalism.*
>
> Louise Story[13]

You could also try more light-hearted interaction: the *New York Times* tries to solve its crossword by 'mass participation', and other organisations have tried quizzes of the week's news.

Exclusive news

We have already suggested that a great use of live-streaming apps is to show behind-the-scenes coverage at a location or event. And all this is as true for a journalist in a newsroom as it might be for someone in a factory or at an historic castle.

So show places that your followers have heard about but never seen: celebrities, events and locations that we take for granted but our viewers and listeners don't. Consider a live-stream from behind the scenes at locations you find yourself at in the course of your work. After all, a field reporter gets to see many places that the 'average' person doesn't, so fire up your phone and take them where you have been given special access:

▶ At a refugee camp

▶ Behind the scenes at the stadium before the big match

▶ At the top of the cathedral tower as they carry out construction work

▶ As reporters gather for a news conference

Consider taking your phone into a news production meeting as the possible stories for a newspaper or bulletin are discussed and decided. Explain what that process was, the story order, the length of each piece, possible interviewees and story 'treatments' (e.g. the different elements, the 'angle', clips and so on that make up the final item).

Creating creative content

If videos have more traction and engagement with audiences, then making an appeal for help or information in a live-video may be more effective than a similar text-only version. That is particularly likely to be the case if there is something visual to show.

A good example is when *New York Times* journalist Deborah Acosta came across a bag full of photographs from an old slide projector on a Manhattan street. She went live to show the slides and to appeal for help to find out the back-story of where they were of and who they came from.[14]

And as discussed elsewhere in this book, you could use 360 cameras, action-cams or drones[15] to be more creative, more immersive and give the viewers more perspective of a story:

- ▶ A 360-degree camera could show the devastation from an earthquake zone, allowing the viewer to see all around them at ground level.

- ▶ The BBC used a drone to show the Syrian[16] city of Aleppo while it was under siege and the results of its continued bombardment (although this was not live-streamed).

- ▶ A GoPro action-camera linked to Periscope and attached in a prominent place could show an approaching storm minute-by-minute with a meteorologist answering questions along the way. The Weather Channel did something similar when Hurricane Hermine approached Florida in 2016. The result: 3 million views and 23,000 comments.

In-house news

There are many examples of news organisations using these apps to live-stream extra content which supports their established services. The biggest potential use is around TV or radio stations' outside broadcasts/remotes where they can provide 'added value': a behind-the-scenes experience that is live, interactive and simple to film.

For example, stations or publishers could present a daily show or column, looking at news events from a particular geographical area or area of content, giving insight or answering questions about it.

User-generated content

We have already seen how a great live-stream may include:

- ▶ Sights that people rarely see

▶ A sense of jeopardy

▶ In-the-moment, raw, emotional and engaging footage

And, sadly, these are all attributes of great footage from the scene of natural or man-made devastation.

Now more than ever, live-streamers are truly eyewitnesses: what they have seen and recorded gives the opportunity for others to (to use Periscope's slogan) see the world through the eyes of somebody else. Today, established news organisations are increasingly relying on crowdsourcing video coverage of news events.

As soon as a story breaks, staff in newsrooms will clarify information from various sources, including first-hand accounts of those at the scene.

Such content, especially moving images:

▶ Gives broadcast TV journalists and their viewers (potentially) authentic views from where an event is unfolding.

▶ Gives a newsroom journalist first-hand accounts of what has happened, from 'real people' (that is, not 'officials'). These can add to the (possible) authenticity and accuracy of the storytelling and a more real experience for the viewer who sees 'someone like me'.

▶ As well as helping editors decide *what* the story is, live-streams can also help them decide *where* the story is and so, how to deploy their own staff.

▶ Enables journalists to contact eyewitnesses directly, perhaps to clarify information or to interview them on another platform (maybe on network TV).

Journalists are not just creating their own content with live-streaming apps, but also producing reports using videos created by other people: so-called user-generated content. This footage is invaluable. In the past, if the event was recorded at all, it would have to be found, bought and sent back to the newsroom, by deploying reporters on the ground who'd negotiate face-to-face. Now, those images are live-streamed straight to an editor's desktop and with the cameraperson's contact details right there on the screen.

Searching and monitoring

Discovering the best streams first is a race against time for a producer, and a complex one. If a news story has broken at a busy location, then dozens or hundreds of people may have taken to Facebook Live or Twitter's Go Live/Periscope to stream the unfolding events. Each will have their own literal point-of-view (being in the right place at the 'wrong time'), with varying levels of camera work, natural sound or commentary. It is, of course, almost impossible to monitor all of those incoming streams of live-video at the same time, on at least two different platforms, and even more time-consuming to review content after a live-stream has ended.

The two map features of the apps are the best way for fast discovery of streams:

Facebook Live – www.facebook.com/live (desktop only)

▶ The blue dots on the zoomable map show all public, live videos: the larger the dot, the more viewers there are for that video. Lines emanating from the dots show where people are watching, and each dot disappears when that live broadcast ends. (Material adapted from https://firstdraftnews.com/.)

You can *search* by a map reference of a location. So, if there has been an incident in, say, Dealey Plaza, Dallas and you wanted to see live-video from that location:

▶ Go to Google Maps and put 'Dealey Plaza, Dallas' into the search box.

▶ When the map has reloaded, copy the co-ordinates from the address bar (32.7788184,-96.810488) and into the www.facebook.com/live address bar between the @ sign and the final comma.

▶ Adjust the number after that final comma to 10 (which is the maximum zoom on the map).

▶ 'Enter' to have the map refresh to your chosen location, from where you can view the available live-streams.

Alternatively, you can find videos on Facebook by searching what keywords broadcasters have put as their titles:

▶ Put a keyword in the search box, and then click 'all results'.

FIGURE 8.5 The Facebook Live map

Source: Facebook

> ▶ On the left-hand side, you can narrow your search by source, location and date range.

> ▶ You can also search photos and videos. Although the filters aren't normally available for this content, here's the hack:

>> ▷ Follow the first two steps (above).

>> ▷ Then, in the resulting search bar, delete the word 'top' and replace it with the word 'photos' or 'videos' (no inverted commas).

To easily monitor several live-streams:

> ▶ Click on a dot to open the video from that location, then click the video's timestamp at the top of the text box that also appears.

> ▶ This will give a near full-screen view of the video and also (importantly) the unique URL for that video, which you can bookmark or paste to another tab.

> ▶ Do this several times for different tabs so you can quickly and easily monitor various broadcasts.

Periscope

> ▶ Use the map feature (not available for Twitter Go Live and only available for Periscope on the mobile app) to zoom into a location and see which videos are being live-streamed at that moment (or ones which have recently ended).

Additionally, create a feed of user-generated content from citizen reporters:

> ▶ Set up a 'breaking news' filter column on TweetDeck.

> ▶ Use geotags such as 'near:Dallas'.

> ▶ Turn on the option to show only tweets with photos or videos.

Verification

Is what you see in a stream true? There are some basic elements that you can check initially:

> ▶ Profile:

>> ▷ First, do basic 'common-sense' checks on what the broadcaster has made public elsewhere.

▷ Does their profile suggest they are likely to be at that location?

▷ Do their recent posts on Twitter and Facebook suggest that they are where they claim to be?

▷ Do the kind of people *they* follow, and who follow *them*, suggest that they can be trusted, or do they have an 'agenda'?

▶ Location:

▷ Rather than a live-stream on-location, is the stream actually a pre-recorded video from another day and place?

▷ Contact the streamer and talk to them. Ask them to stream from where they are *right now* with the location feature on, and see if it is the same location as their recent stream.

▷ Remember that so-called fake location apps can show the streamer to be at a location other than where they actually are.

▷ Does what they're streaming have a similarity with that from other sources (particularly trusted ones)?

And what is 'truth' anyway? The content of a stream may be 'one person's truth' or their 'perspective'. Is the presenter an activist for an organisation? (Even aid-workers will have some kind of agenda as they stream to their supporters and fundraisers.) Or it could be an exaggeration, downright lie or deliberate hoax. Maybe a 'professional' journalist might be needed to view different streams from the same scene, to scrutinise and weigh them and select what they consider to be the 'best bits' to broadcast on traditional TV. And perhaps a 'professional' is useful to 'join the dots': if they see lots of similar small stories from several places, they may realise a larger event is in play.

Citizen and accidental reporters

To misquote Mark Twain: "Amateur video streams will go around the world while the traditional broadcasters are still putting their boots on". Now anyone with a mobile phone can be a reporter in their own right, whether they seek out news stories or find themselves at the scene of one.

With on-the-spot, in-the-moment reporting, live-streamers are media's 'first responders', their eyes and ears on the ground. These citizens can illuminate immediately, and possibly with an authenticity of voice (describing the aftermath of a bomb blast, or a flooded home) in an emotional way that a 'professional' is trained not to.

And, of course, there are simply a greater number of citizens than newspeople, all telling their own stories from their own perspective, creating a diversity of voices and adding a depth and context to what's happened.

> *Facebook effectively has one and a half billion news bureaux to capture news.*

Jonathan Klein[17]

First responders

Of course, eyewitness footage is not new: the famous footage of the JFK assassination was, in effect, 'user-generated content'.

Periscope had an impact on its very first day in March 2015. After an explosion in New York City, dozens of local people started streaming their eyewitness views.[18] And in November 2015, dozens of people streamed live-video of the aftermath of the Bataclan terrorist attacks from their phones to the world, well before TV crews arrived. The streams showed crowds in closed-off streets and racing emergency vehicles. One man showed his view while crouched behind a police car after gunshots were heard; another interviewed eyewitnesses.

There is, of course, no way traditional broadcasters can compete with the speed of eyewitnesses who have 'a TV station in their pocket'.

Hyper-local journalism

Live-streaming platforms are increasing the *range* of stories that are being told, from people and places that previously were ignored by 'network news'.

View News (viewnews.com.au) is a network of journalists and content creators in Queensland, Australia who use mobile devices to "tell stories and engage with their audience, over social media platforms". As well as producing pre-recorded videos of local news and events, they also regularly use live-streams to tell the local communities of events that are happening nearby.

Similar small-scale, often voluntary groups are around the world: they see the use of live-streaming as a way to run a TV-like station at minimal expense. They can run breaking news, scheduled interview programmes and, once saved and edited, they can produce shorter bite-sized nuggets for easy distribution on other social media channels.

FIGURE 8.6 Broadcasting a major local story, that of an agreement of airport expansion, live and direct on Facebook

Source: @CharlesRHodgson and @viewnews on Facebook, Twitter and other social media. www.facebook.com/viewnews/videos/vb.104798568714/10154303710598715/?type=3&theater, Facebook

Jeanette Maynes and Jannean Dean campaigned for the live-streaming of Fraser Coast Council meetings in Queensland, Australia for two years before getting the go-ahead. In a blog,[19] Jannean wrote:

Live-streaming will:

▶ *Generate a bigger audience.*

▶ *Provide the ability for online interaction.*

▶ *Open opportunities for new revenue.*

▶ *Providing live-video recordings of council proceedings, grants the community immediate access to the chamber without having to leave the comfort of their living room. It encourages a greater number of people to get involved: parents can follow a full council meeting while getting the dinner on, while those working long hours can catch up with proceedings on their tablet or smartphone.*

> ▶ Critics might argue that an army of under-informed armchair activists is the last thing that local government needs facing a crisis and the thorny question of what councils should and shouldn't do. This rudely underestimates the intelligence of residents and is an age-old excuse for conducting the business of local government in the dark. It would be great to see our Council like others across Queensland who are working in the full gaze of the public eye.
>
> ▶ Visual recordings won't be edited in a way that could lead to misinterpretation of the proceedings as Council has full control.
>
> ▶ Live-streaming Council meetings so more people can see how decisions are made. Understanding how local government operates is the first step to getting more people involved on a practical level, whether lobbying councillors, taking part in community groups or considering standing for office themselves.
>
> ▶ Few people have the time or inclination to attend meetings like this in person. But many will join in or observe the debate if you make it accessible to them, in a way that better suits their lifestyles. Being able to submit a question online and then sit back and see it answered from your sofa has to be a positive thing for transparency and local democracy.
>
> ▶ Public participation is important so the community know what problems we face in our region and can support the causes that need change.

Social activism

Live-video has impact. And because it is eminently shareable, it's an effective way of getting information out to a wider audience and into the collective consciousness, and so helps democratise society:

> With no skill or ability to edit, no special permission or high-cost technology, any of the 3 billion humans in the world with access to a networked camera can show what they are actually experiencing, right now, and anyone else in the world can experience it with them.
>
> Matt Hackett[20]

Issues about which people hold strong views will create authentic, emotional footage that is likely to be more engaging than that which has been pre-recorded and produced.

That was certainly true at the Standing Rock Sioux Indian Reservation in North Dakota in November 2016, where Native Americans and environmentalists fought against the construction of a controversial Dakota Access Pipeline, using the power of live-streaming. Video of clashes with police was streamed from the remote location by E'sha Hoferer, a member of the Walker River Paiute Tribe, to viewers around the world.

> *Hoferer was broadcasting live on Facebook on October 27 when the Morton County Sheriff's Department forcibly removed hundreds of demonstrators from their camp in the track of the pipeline's construction. . . . Hoferer's Facebook Live carried an audience of more than 30,000 people then and had been watched more than 200,000 times by Saturday morning.*[21]

And during a kayak protest in Seattle against oil drilling in the Arctic, protesters and journalists were able to make their cause interesting to people who might not sit and read an article about Shell's Polar Pioneer drilling rig.

Pressure and social-movement groups, such as Black Lives Matter in the United States, regularly use live-streaming to show what they see happening on the streets of their neighbourhoods. They say it evens things up with law enforcers who themselves wear body cameras. Their main aim is to expose what they claim to be police brutality. The secondary one, that broadcasting live may embarrass officers into changing their behaviour, hasn't necessarily worked. [22]

The calm 10-minute Facebook Live video, broadcast by Diamond 'Lavish' Reynolds immediately after her boyfriend Philando Castile was shot by a police officer in Minnesota in July 2016, was thought to be a game-changer.

> *Watching Mr Castile take his final breaths (in real time) was so compelling, the raw footage so unforgettable, and Ms Reynolds' pain and terror so palpable, that the unjust death of a single citizen was transformed from a local tragedy into a national moment of reflection.*
>
> Tarun Wadhwa[23]

It showed his moment of death, as officers frantically tried to regain control of the situation.[24]

> *I wanted to put it on Facebook to go viral so that the people could see. . . . I wanted the people to determine who was right and who was wrong. . . . I wanted the people to be the testimony here.*
>
> Diamond Reynolds[25]

FIGURE 8.7 Democracy in action. Candidates for a local election were invited to discuss their policies and answer voters' questions on a live-stream. This was actually held in the broadcaster's kitchen.

Source: @CharlesRHodgson and @viewnews on Facebook, Twitter and other social media; www.facebook.com/viewnews/videos/vb.104798568714/10153678968323715/?type=3&theater

These examples suggest that after years of accepting a 'police narrative', increasingly now it's witnesses who can tell their story first. And live.

Evidence gathering

Live-streams could be valuable in evidence-gathering for authorities, as was the case after the bombing of the Boston marathon[26] in 2013. Then, as in other cases, police requested recorded and live-video and still images to help piece together timelines and who was where, when.

Safety and security

Be careful you don't literally walk into danger. There are obvious safety concerns for those live-streaming from the scene of a breaking story: one man in Paris after the Bataclan attacks told his Periscope viewers: "I've heard the gunman is up this street, so that's where I'm going . . ." He was caught up in the moment, but was that wise?

Streamers could also unwittingly broadcast sensitive information such as a SWAT team preparing to move in or snipers taking position on a roof.

And it's claimed that:

> *During Occupy, people with cameras and live-streams were more likely to be arrested.*[27] *Journalists, often toting smartphones with Internet-connected photo and video capability, have been subject to arrest or abuse while covering events like Ferguson and riots in Baltimore.*[28][29]

Always consider what may still be private property: many sports clubs will not only stop you from live-streaming a match but also anything from the stands, entrances or forecourt too.

And individuals are allowed their privacy (particularly if they are on private property), so check with those who are featured significantly that they know that you are broadcasting live.

Sending and selling your stream

If you have some newsworthy video, you could either offer it to a news channel, website or other publishing media, or they may approach you directly.[30] Indeed, you may be deluged by a bombardment of requests to use your footage, but should you sell it and, if so, to whom?

First, let's take a look at those requests. They may come in thick and fast but only for a limited time. One would hope that, after you have experienced an unexpected and possibly traumatic event, any message (probably via Facebook or Twitter) will start with an introduction of who is contacting you and a check that you are okay. They will probably then praise your footage ("great video!") and ask you if they can use it. They may suggest a credit, either your real name or your username, which they won't use if it is inappropriate (after all, @sexyfluffybunny would not be an appropriate name alongside footage of the attempted assassination of the president). You may not want your name publicised for personal reasons such as safety.

Only the larger news companies or those who desperately want your video will start offering money at this stage: like anyone, they will try and get your stream for free, first. Others may simply use it without asking or telling and, if there's any on-screen credit at all, it may be very small.[31]

Morally, you may consider whether you should make money from a video of someone else's misfortune, a death, a flooded house, a light plane crash and so on. But if you don't, and if the video is powerful enough, someone else will.

That's because whoever you let use your material may sell it on to another organisation, put a pre-roll advert at the start of it, or have it on a website page where there are other adverts. Other companies or individuals may just download and use your video without asking, without a credit and without paying you. So you may want to charge, and then if you feel uncomfortable, donate that money to charity.

Any organisation that pays you for your content will want to have exclusive rights to use it, to sell it on and use it in any way. That may include putting their logo on your video.

Note that there are a lot of companies around who may promise to pay you for your footage and to keep your name on the screen while it is played, but do neither. Apart from seeking money via a solicitor, which will be expensive, there's not much you can do. And they know that. They also know that your video has a very short lifespan.

There are some agencies who will act as the 'middle man' in negotiations to get you more money and protect your rights. If you are interested in this route, Verifeye Media may be worth a look: www.verifeyemedia.com. They don't just deal with live-streams, so you could also send them another video that you record through their app. Their website says:

▶ *Shoot* – You shoot your breaking news using our iPhone camera app. While you film, our app gathers time, date and location info which allows us to verify the footage. You will need an iPhone 4S or newer running iOS 8.

▶ *Send* – You upload your video or photo directly from our app. We encrypt all information to protect our contributors working in dangerous areas or under repressive regimes, and all contributors remain anonymous to our clients.

▶ *Sell* – We verify, curate, market, license and distribute your videos and photos to our clients, and we share the revenue with you on a 50/50 basis, paying into your PayPal® account within 7 days of sale.

Editorial and ethical considerations

Live-streaming can:

Disrupt and devalue journalism by relaying troubling images devoid of context and insight and hosting comments based on conspiracy theories, prejudice and lies.

Mark Frankel[32]

THE FIVE C'S OF BEST PRACTICE FOR JOURNALISTS

Consent – get agreement before you start.

Compliance – only go live with the knowledge of a senior editor.

Community management – know how to manage offensive material or individuals.

Care – be assured that contributors understand that they are live; be under no pressure to stream, stay at a scene or answer viewers' questions if you are not comfortable.

Courtesy – remember taste, decency and impartiality are still the basics.

Broadcasters and individuals risk reputational damage if something goes wrong, or if a viewer takes offence.

For reporters:

▶ Do you need to do a live-stream at all? Don't just do it because you can. How will it reflect on you or your organisation? At a dramatic and traumatic event, *recorded* video and *still* images might be more ethically considerate. Think about whether posting a picture or video *immediately after you have taken it* defeats much of the object of not actually going 'live'.

▶ Consider the platform. You will know whether it is best to stream from Facebook or Twitter/Periscope depending on the communities you have at each of those sites and who you don't mind seeing and commenting on what you are about to show.

▶ On Periscope, consider turning the ability for people to comment to 'off'. Don't be persuaded to show something, just because commenters have asked you to, to get more hearts (on Periscope) or views.

▶ If you anticipate that the situation could be traumatic, then make regular announcements on the stream, warning viewers that "anything could happen".

▶ Be careful what you say or allow other people to say. In the UK there may be a defence of 'live defamation' if someone speaks a little too liberally. If you don't know what 'defamation' or the 'live defence' is, then that may be an indication that you shouldn't go live in an emotionally charged situation.

▶ If you talk to someone else on camera, do they appreciate that what they say is being broadcast live to 'everyone' and not merely being recorded on your phone?

▶ In a potentially dangerous breaking-news situation, try and have a colleague with you to 'watch your back'.

▶ In a potentially traumatic situation, try and use some peripheral vision to see what it is that you are about to screen next.

▶ You should try to give context on what has happened. Although the situation may be confused, you may be able to reassure in some way by what you are able to show.

▶ Think before you show what may seem to be 'exciting and exclusive' scenes such as police preparing to raid a building, as it could tip off those inside and put lives at risk.[33] It will almost certainly give an attacker the 'oxygen of publicity' that they crave. Always assume 'the baddie' is one of your viewers.

▶ If you want to cover an event but are concerned that you may show too much sensitive detail, or people's faces, consider a wider or longer shot from across the street to stream the *situation* but not the detail.

▶ Consider how social media can spread news of an event and that someone may discover that a family member has been caught up or killed by seeing it on a live-stream. Indeed, your coverage (say, of violence and danger) may add to the distress and vicarious trauma of people who know that a loved one is in the area, although that person may, in fact, be okay.

▶ Going live could encourage you to get carried away, get closer to the action and find yourself in an unfamiliar situation which could be dangerous. Your presence may hinder the work of the emergency services, whether that is having to clear you from an area or help you if you are injured.

▶ Once you end your live-stream, take a moment to consider its content and whether you will post the recording or delete it from your feed. This decision may be taken together with an editor who was not at the scene and so has a more objective view.

For editors:

▶ To what extent will live-streaming disrupt the editorial process? Does taking recordings of one, two or more live-streams from eyewitnesses really tell an accurate story of what happened? Is there proper context when you have no 'trusted' source?

▶ Taking a live-stream direct to air is risky: you may not know who is holding the phone, and you will certainly not know what will happen next. Eyewitnesses, unlike trained professionals, don't 'self-edit'; they just hit 'Go Live'. You have no control of where they are, what they will say or what comments will appear. You could consider just taking a soundtrack or putting the feed into a delay before you show it on TV.

▶ If you use material from a dangerous situation, the implication is that your organisation has sanctioned the streamer being there, that maybe you commissioned it and are knowingly putting them in danger.

▶ Can a well-recorded stream look 'too good'? A handheld, jerky video looks raw and authentic, gritty and dramatic. But some enthusiastic amateurs and professionals have equipment and experience that makes footage look slick and possibly staged.

▶ Paying a contributor who provides dramatic eyewitness video may encourage them to get into a more dangerous situation in the future.

▶ Consider the trauma that your reporter might experience by being in this situation, seeing and showing disturbing events. There will be added pressure on them as the video was live: a pressure (possibly self-inflicted) to keep talking, keep showing and keep streaming. They may feel guilt for streaming rather than helping. Also think of the vicarious trauma of the viewers: those who may see things that they can't 'unsee'.

WHAT ARE YOUR LIVE-STREAMING 'LINES IN THE SAND'?

What would and wouldn't you show on your show? Where is your 'moral compass' when it comes to dignity, humanity, integrity and compassion? Where is the fulcrum between 'privacy' and 'newsworthiness'? What are the reasons you would show any or all of the scenarios below?

▶ A house fire? The fire engines? What if there was someone inside, would you show a rescue, or them at a window or on a ledge? What if they fell? Would you trace their fall live on air? Would you show their body on the ground? Would you give any verbal warning to your audience? What would you say and how often? How would you feel about Periscope hearts floating up the screen as you streamed this? Are those viewers sending love and sympathy to those affected, or loving the dramatic scene that you are showing them? How do you know?

▶ If there's a car crash and you were first on the scene, would you fire up your phone to call for help or to live-stream? What if you were the fourth or fifth person on the scene? Would you show a rescue attempt? How close to the cars would you go? After all, cars and number plates are pretty identifiable to families who may be watching. What if you were filming a passenger being taken to an ambulance on a stretcher, and as you did so the crew put a blanket over the victim's face?

▶ If there was an explosion at any airport you were travelling through, would you show the aftermath, the rubble and the panic? Why? Would you point your phone at the severely walking wounded? What about wounded children? What about the wounded on the ground? How do you know they are 'wounded' and not dying? How close to them actually dying would you continue to film them? What if they opened their eyes and looked at you as you did so? What if they asked for help? Would you show body parts on the ground? Are you familiar with what they may look like to be quick enough to avoid them? What if a (presumed) terrorist makes an announcement on the loudspeaker, would you live-stream that? If one of the gang grabs a tourist and threatens to behead them, would you live-stream that? And if you spotted troops gathering on the concrete for a possible rescue attempt. . . ? Are you aware of terms such as 'news blackouts' and 'D-Notices' and why they are sometimes put into place?

▶ Are you prepared to witness any or all of the above in real life? Would you help or call for help from others? Would you consider the potential trauma caused to you or your viewers? If you did film, would you let your mother see it? Or your children?

LIVE-STREAMING BREAKING NEWS

There is a degree of 'rough and ready' with a live-video at a breaking-news event: people accept that because of the situation, it won't be as slick as TV news, but it does have to have some degree of professionalism. Here are some top tips to help you get it:

▶ Rewrite your biography in the live-streaming app so you can be easily contacted if a broadcaster wants to use your video or interview you as an eyewitness.

▶ If you are attached to a news organisation, have colleagues use their on-air programmes to promote your stream. This is a valuable platform that other live-streamers don't have, so take advantage of it.

▶ Keep your phone charged. Have a spare battery pack: live-streaming eats power and your data allowance. Remember, at a mass event you may have trouble getting a signal because of the multitude of other phones also using the network.

▶ Have plenty of storage on your phone to avoid losing what you have filmed.

▶ Consider whether in Periscope you use the location feature. Switch on the location feature for discoverability (so you appear on the app's map, which is what reporters will search to find people streaming where news is breaking). Having it off gives you greater safety and security.

▶ When writing the title of your stream, use a recognised hashtag for the event – certainly key words such as 'Paris', 'explosion' and so on.

▶ Get noticed by putting Twitter @names in your title (Periscope titles can be automatically tweeted as soon as you go live).

▶ Film in landscape to show more of the scene and to fit the dimensions of broadcast TV. Video streamed in landscape orientation not only looks better on a mobile phone (and when seen on a widescreen TV), but it also stands a better chance of being picked up by TV news channels.

▶ Move the camera phone slowly and steadily, and look out for shots of events that will only happen once.

▶ Don't feel the need to talk constantly, particularly if it's obvious what's on screen. Often the natural pictures and sound are better than what you can add. If you do talk, short, simple sentences are fine.

▶ Have an external mic so you don't have to shout: that will reduce background noise and allow you to be more discreet if necessary.

▶ Don't forget to describe elements the camera can't pick up, such as the mood of the crowd, the smells, etc. Give context if you know it – the location or the immediate lead-up.

▶ If people are hurt or vulnerable, showing a wide view gives more privacy and dignity.

▶ If nothing much is changing at the scene, change your location. The same scene from a different perspective (the other end of the street, or from a building) will keep interest. Getting up higher is usually very useful. Don't merely provide what amounts to live surveillance footage.

▶ Remember respect: being 'first' is not always 'fair'. Do the families of those affected want this to be the way they hear what's happened?

▶ Only say what you *know* or can see. Don't speculate or presume.

▶ Don't obstruct those who are trying to help or investigate. Obey the authorities. Keep your cool. Keep your distance. Don't lose your temper. Know your rights: it's okay to film in a public place. You may *not* have to stop if they tell you to (although pressure from other bystanders may persuade you to).

> ▶ After you stop your broadcast, talk to other eyewitnesses and try to gather more details about what happened.
>
> ▶ Immediately after the stream, alert the media to it. Think in advance who would be best to tell.

It's more important than ever to share what you're feeling and thinking so we can understand each other better. When we see more people doing that, and we bring live video to more of Twitter's surfaces, that will encourage others to take part in the conversation.

Sara Haider [34]

▶ FOCUS ON . . . CONFERENCES, EVENTS AND SHOWS

Streaming simply *is* live-video, so go to a *live* event such as a trade show, summit or seminar and show your viewers what is happening there. Your followers are likely to be interested in the same topics as you are, so this could be a perfect synergy and help you expand your digital reach to those people who can't be there with you in person.

Explain:

▶ Where you are and why

▶ What your participation is (are you a speaker?)

▶ What you hope to get out of the event

▶ How often they will hear from you

At a show, why not be a 'roving reporter' who can tour the displays and talk to the exhibitors, get a view of their products and reactions from passers-by:

▶ Live-stream the opening or ribbon cutting, the flow of people rushing to booths.

▶ Show your stand and your staff.

▶ Talk to organisers.

▶ Show who the other delegates and speakers are.

▶ Show their stands and what is on display or for sale.

▶ Interview brand associates from other companies who you work alongside.

FIGURE 8.8 Screenshot of a live-streamed interview at a trade exhibition

Source: David McClelland, www.davidmcclelland.co.uk; Angela Nicholson, www.camerajabber.com, Facebook

▶ Show new products and discuss new ideas.

▶ Talk to attendees and delegates.

▶ Speaking at a conference yourself? Raise your profile by getting a colleague to live-stream your presentation, and then when you leave the stage, respond to questions from your viewers.

In short, do what your viewers would do had they been there, and be their eyes and ears. This kind of 'value by video' will help make you memorable and build stronger relationships and rapport. This may attract more viewers to your brand, platform or page:

▶ Those from other stands at the event

▶ Other attendees who didn't know about you

But if you intend to do live-video at a conference, don't just hold a phone up to the platform. Why?

▶ It'll make for dull viewing.

▶ There'll be a dozen other people sitting near you doing the same thing.

▶ You won't be able to respond to any of the comments.

▶ The sound will be bad (viewers will hear a nearby cough, louder than they will the voices of those on stage).

▶ You will get a tired arm!

So you have to give *added value*. Think about the event from a *delegate's perspective*. Or more specifically, from the perspective of a *wannabe-delegate*:

▶ What would they want to see before, during and after events that they couldn't otherwise experience on their own?

▶ Give your thoughts and experiences to the camera on what's going on, maybe a short recap at the end of each day on the highlights and what you have learnt.

▶ Talk to other attendees about why they have attended and what they've heard and learnt.

▶ Interview the speakers before they go on stage, or once they step off.

In other words, *don't add to the noise, but add unique insights*. Then, non-attendees may better understand the event and be more likely to buy tickets next time.

DON'T BE MEAN IN YOUR LIVE-STREAM

▶ Check that no one minds you streaming at an event:

▷ The other *attendees* may be peeved: they paid big bucks for a ticket, and you are broadcasting the keynote speech for free.

▷ The *organisers* will be put out: maybe they didn't sell as many tickets as they could have done because people are free-streaming content. (Even if the event was free to attend, organisers may be gathering data from attendees such as email addresses, that they can't get from viewers of a live-stream.)

▷ And the *speaker* may feel frustrated as they may not be able to give their presentation to another similar group. Oh, and you may have broken their intellectual copyright on their content by redistributing it.

▶ If you are live-streaming from the delegate area, tell people that's what you're doing: it's courteous, because some people don't like to be filmed, and you'll avoid accidentally broadcasting private conversations. Consider posting a notice in the area or making an announcement before the event.

If you are organising an event

Promote your conference on a live-stream before it happens:

▶ Explain your thinking about its shape and content.

▶ Crowdsource ideas about topics and talkers, the location and decorations.

▶ Live-stream views of hotel or conference centre options and have viewers vote for their favourite, to feel involved and build anticipation.

▶ Explain what it takes to organise an event and therefore justify the cost of attending. Viewers will get exclusive content and extra appreciation of the work behind the scenes and what they'll be getting for their ticket price.

▶ Show the city where the event is being held, so delegates know how to use the metro ticket machines, where to go for a night out or the top tourist must-sees.

Ask speakers to live-stream their journey to the event:

▶ Writing their script

▶ Packing bags

▶ At the airport and hotel, then at the conference centre

All these, in a series of shows, will help promote your event and convey their expertise.

Before the day, you could have encouraged attendees to live-stream about how they were looking forward to going along to the event, and on the day have your reporter outside speaking to people waiting in line about their anticipation. Present an overview of the exhibition so people know where to go and what the layout is, which could be a great help for those who are coming to Day 2 or Day 3 of the event.

> *Speakers could very easily continue the session with a Q&A broadcast a few days after the event: 'Why don't you try these tips at the office Monday, and I'll be on Periscope at 4 that afternoon for a brief follow-up.'*

Leyton Rasco[35]

Technical considerations

You could cover this kind of event by yourself, but it may be preferable to have a cameraperson/producer with you.

▶ Plan where to go and what to show:

▷ You might do one general tour around the exhibition space and then a series of shorter streams from a variety of stands.

▷ With the general tour, work out the best route to see the booths which are most appropriate to your audience. Prepare a few words to say about what is on display to whet the appetite of viewers of your later shows. Have a note of who is on the stands so you can identify them to your viewers as you pass: that way it will show them that everyone is a valued contact.

▷ Consider using a handheld stabiliser, to smooth out the stream as you walk.

▷ Some people may not realise they will be shown live on video, so make sure you explain that clearly. Perhaps have a leaflet explaining what is happening and where it will be shown so they can promote the broadcast to their fans and followers. (You could even wear a branded shirt with a notice in the back: "Filming Live for Facebook.com/xxxx. Watch and follow us now!")

▶ Consider the connections:

▷ Despite dry runs where everything seems fine, it is difficult to predict whether the Wi-Fi will crash due to the number of people on it at a trade or exhibition centre. So, you may need to access a private or office network at an event.

▶ Make audio plans:

▷ If in an auditorium and there's an event on stage, get close to the PA speaker, or get a line-out from the microphone control desk that feeds the speakers.

▷ If a 'roving reporter', use a directional wired or wireless mic, rather than the in-built one on the phone. The hall is likely to be noisy and with an echo, so an external mic will help viewers hear what is happening.

▶ FOCUS ON . . . NON-PROFITS

Charity groups should be all over live-streaming: free, global exposure . . . what's not to like? It has, perhaps, more impact than an article and still images in a quarterly newsletter (it certainly *adds* to that impact). With live-streaming, volunteers and donors witness first-hand and immediately the impact that their support has made. So if this is your niche, use live-streaming to:

▶ Connect personally with your supporters.

▶ Show you are confident in being transparent about your work and where the money goes.

▶ Build trust in the group that is asking for donations of time or money.

Many non-profits will inevitably have to turn to live-streaming as a way to help broadcast their work, and meet their younger audiences where they are, in an effort to educate, advocate, and build the next pipeline of donors and supporters. The power of live-streaming is that it also has great potential for increasing organizational transparency. . . . Live-streaming . . . has the power to make non-profits communicate their work in a more engaging, frequent, and visual way. Non-profit videos, often created less frequently due to lack of resources and budget constraints, will have new life as mobile live-streaming opens the door to an affordable, engaging and powerful visual tool. Periscope and other mobile live-streaming apps will continue to shine a light on social injustices around the world, giving us access and unprecedented leverage that will help put pressure on governments, who will have a much more difficult time turning a blind eye to the injustices around them.

Caroline Avakian, Managing Partner, Socialbrite, www.socialbrite.org @ CarolineAvakian[36]

Live on location

Show your donors where their money goes and the benefits it gives to people by sharing some great human-interest stories. Or *why* their money is needed and appeal for more of it. These 'from the field' broadcasts may be:

▶ The view from inside the air ambulance

▶ A tour around a refugee's camp abroad

▶ The new kitchen built in the homeless shelter down the road

▶ The look on the child's face when they come to pick up their rescue puppy from the animal shelter (Indeed, daily live-streams of the dogs and cats looking for new homes could be a winner.)

▶ Even a behind-the-scenes look at the charity's office or walking the trickiest hole on the course where you will hold your upcoming charity event

These are all moments that might previously have gone unshown and unknown.

Q&As

Give your supporters a chance to quiz those they give money to. That might be:

▶ Directors who decide where the money goes and who can explain where it is spent, and why

▶ Admin staff and experts who can answer questions about the issues that members have, perhaps with diet or disability, funding, form-filling, or changes to regulations

▶ Maybe it's an awareness week, and you want to explain the basics of what you do, and at the end of the show give a website for more information, or through which people can donate.

▶ Consider regular 'ask an expert' sessions or presentations

▶ Those who work in the field who can talk about their experiences

▶ Other fundraisers like themselves who can pass on tips for reaching new donors

▶ Volunteers usually have great heart-rending reasons for why they give their support and time. It might be a family connection, a personal experience or a deep-seated ethical or moral stance. All these can provide great stories to emotionally connect with your viewers.

▶ Celebrity supporters, maybe in a private live-stream for significant fundraisers

Events broadcasting

With live-streaming, your supporters can attend an event (e.g. a gala dinner, a conference) that previously they may not have had access to.

> *How great would it be to have a staff or volunteer correspondent at your next benefit, fundraiser or conference, in charge of showing viewers around and chatting with honourees and guests? It's a fantastic way to share these exclusive events with your Facebook community.*[37]

Live-stream anything from a ball, fun run or fete. You could show and describe items given for the charity auction, so people who can't be there can still bid. And then save and edit the show and put it on YouTube or your website, to help promote what you do.

Fundraiser streaming

It's not just the charity itself which can present live-video. Fundraisers could show weekly instalments on their journey to raise money: the hours in between getting pledges and actually doing the event, say a charity run:

▶ Getting advice and help

▶ The start of training

- ▶ The practice runs

- ▶ The fitness scare

- ▶ Setting off on the big day

- ▶ The pre-race jitters

- ▶ The run . . . the win . . . the relief

- ▶ Where the money went

While a charity walk wouldn't be broadcast anywhere else on earth, on Facebook, to the friends and supporters of the people walking, it is highly relevant.

Dave Wieneke[38]

Facebook live donations tab

The app allows verified pages and organisations to start a personal fundraiser, within a live-stream. So, you can have a direct call to action – asking people to tap a Donate button – while presenting a show related to the cause.

Me TV

We saw elsewhere in this book the value of having your own 'TV channel'. Charitable groups can use this to their advantage to make announcements such as:

- ▶ Extra funding achieved or needed

- ▶ Plans for a new programme

- ▶ Praise or criticism of a new government initiative

- ▶ Reaction to an event in the news that links with your charity

- ▶ Setting the record straight on an issue with which you have experience and expertise

▶ FOCUS ON . . . PROPERTY SALES

Do you sell houses or other property? Then live-streaming could make your job so much easier.

Not only is your safety assured – no one is physically in the home with you – but the homeowners don't have to worry about theft or damage. You no longer have to sit around wasting time. . . . Anyone . . . can still view your narrated tour when it's most convenient for them.

Nadine Larder[39]

Other advantages of live-streamed house viewings and open days:

▶ Let people see the property before they travel to see it in person (especially true if the house and potential buyer are in different countries).

▶ Potential purchasers can direct the camera and ask to see specific views, such as how big that cupboard is, or the view from the end of the garden.

▶ Viewers can ask the kinds of questions that may be tricky to do face-to-face.

▶ Friends and family of the prospective purchaser can view the property at the same time, and chip in with their thoughts and suggestions.

▶ And don't forget the value of 'private broadcasts', so you know exactly who you are talking with. That deters time-wasters, nosey parkers or potential thieves.

▶ And, extreme-stream alert! If the property is even moderately large, why not launch a drone-stream? Then you can better show the swimming pool and grounds and so on. And if you use a 360-degree camera as you walk through the house, viewers can virtually be in the property with you.

So, could live-streaming spark the end of the traditional open house?

It definitely seems like it could make a big impact. I don't know if it will signal completely the end of the real estate agent, but it may make a dent in that.

Dr Eric Levy, Judge Business School, Cambridge[40]

Planning your property stream

Carefully plan your tour through the house. Note where you will go and what you will show. What will you say in each room, and what will you say as you walk *between* the rooms? Any property agent will know that the best tour may not be simply starting at the front door and then viewing each room on the ground floor in turn, and then upstairs. More successful sales often come from describing a story, tapping into the aspiration of a buyer and their needs. Grabbing viewers with a tour of the superb cinema room, for example, before showing the room that maybe needs a little bit of work.

So on your 'recce' (reconnaissance) trip, work out who would want to buy a property like this, and point out the features that will entice them to bite. That might be the

FIGURE 8.9 Clare Dube regularly presents live house tours

Source: Clare Dube, Carlos Phoenix at www.livestreamingmaster.com, Facebook

height of the ceilings, the size of the garden or that no extra work needs to be done in the living areas.

Another reason for the recce is to work out *where you will stand* in each room as you give the tour. The best angle for light may not show the best parts of the room, so you may need to re-arrange furniture, draw curtains slightly, have an external light on your camera frame and so on. These are issues that would not need to be considered prior to a regular house tour!

Attach a wide-angled lens to your phone. That way you will be able to get more of each room within a shot. And wear a lapel mic: as I mentioned elsewhere, when you use the back camera (as you will be in a typical house tour), the phone will use the back microphone, and that will mean that you will sound distant. Plugging in another mic means that you will be heard clearly. If you have a colleague holding the phone and you are the presenter, invest in a wireless lapel mic kit, so you can move around freely. Also worth considering is the purchase of a stabiliser, so when you move between rooms, and especially when you go upstairs, the shots are as smooth as possible and have that 'Hollywood feel'.

Pay attention to the visuals, so concentrate on the newly fitted windows, the grain of the real wooden floors, demonstrate the soft-close kitchen cabinets, the power of that shower, the hand-carved bannister rail and so on.

But being a real estate agent is more than selling a *property*; you are also selling a *location*. And you are not just promoting your business to those coming into the area to buy; you are also promoting yourself to those already here, who may one day want to *sell*. So with that in mind, consider pitching yourself as a 'local authority' presenting live-streams showing prospective clients what the area is like. To do this well, think of the places that a tourist would want to see, show off the area and give background information:

- ▶ **Provide local tours** – present shows from the high street, the local park or near the stadium to give viewers a feel and flavour of what could be their new neighbourhood. Answer questions before they are asked: the distance to the beach, how close the nearest Starbucks is and so on.

- ▶ **Talk about local need-to-know issues** – the quality of the local schools, community arts and sports events, big construction and improvement projects. And as well as talking, *show them*! Stand by the building site and describe what will be there this time next year, walk the route to the train station to show how close it is and so on.

- ▶ **Chat with local people** – maybe entrepreneurs, shopkeepers and voluntary groups and promote their work.

- ▶ **Stream from local entertainment and leisure businesses** – the restaurants, the nearby views, countryside, race tracks, etc.

And in a series of business-related streams:

- ▶ Interview satisfied customers you have helped previously.

- ▶ Discuss house-buying trends, property prices and mortgage deals with experts.

- ▶ Give property advice to home *sellers*, such as tips on making a home more desirable, or basic DIY, to make their home more sellable. Also consider helping with tips such as what to look for in their next home or how to choose another agency at the 'other end' of the chain.

- ▶ Give *financial advice* to home sellers, such as money-saving tips, checking their credit score, how to apply for a mortgage, advice for first-time buyers, or the system of conveyancing.

- ▶ Consider holding open Q&As with an expert on any of these topics. Run a contest within such shows with a prize of a free home-viewing, free valuation or a preferential rate.

After each show, upload the video to your website or YouTube to increase the viewing numbers for weeks to come, and hence the chance of a sale.

Before uploading, consider some edits. There are many advantages to live-streaming, as we have seen already, but there are also advantages to short, dynamic, edited videos, too. With basic software, free-to-use music and eye-catching graphics, you can enhance your video for the post-live audience.

And you can re-purpose some of the content time and again. The live-stream from the community summer fair can become stock footage to insert into another video on 'summer events' or 'events in this park'.

> *The smarter the technology you use, the more you tell your clients that you are smart. To the casual observer, real estate agents can all seem rather the same –*
> *but not after they've seen your video! . . . Your video makes you look more human.*

Roxana Baiceanu[41]

▶ FOCUS ON . . . RELIGION AND MUSEUMS

Religion

As long ago as the mid-1980s, I would record the services at my local church onto cassette tapes, which I would then distribute to the housebound, so they could still feel part of the community. Now tech has come on leaps and bounds: services can be shown live on video.

Content suggestions:[42]

- ▶ Church/temple/mosque services for the local housebound, the unwell, those with children or members of the congregation travelling on business or vacation. Or for those deciding which church to join without committing themselves.

- ▶ Maybe mid-week prayer meetings or a daily morning devotional. Perhaps preview the Sunday sermon and ask for hymn suggestions. One church is delivering the 'Alpha' course (discussions on faith) on Periscope, and the Archbishop of Canterbury presents 'Facebook Live Bible Studies'.[43]

- ▶ Interviews with local faith leaders and visiting speakers, or members of staff or the congregation at the church about why they believe what they do.

- ▶ Show the inside of the church building and explain to newcomers what happens, where they park, where the crèche is and so on, to make a first visit less daunting.

- ▶ Outside the confines of the building, reflect the local community and show the work of local volunteer groups. Indeed, why not be a 'town TV' station reflecting all sorts of aspects of where the church is, and being at the heart of the local area.

- ▶ This Periscope[44] covered a two-hour farewell service of Bishop Richard leaving St Paul's Cathedral in London.

- ▶ Live-stream a wedding,[45] Bar or Bat Mitzvah and so on for family members who can't be there.

▶ Or a funeral: Around one-fifth of Britain's 281 crematoriums offer a live-streaming service, according to a recent survey,[46] while 61% of funeral directors had received requests for services to be live-streamed.

▶ This site[47] suggested Muslims "use the Periscope app to live-stream their observations on Ramadan" to help others in the same situation.

One concern church elders might have is whether a live-stream may lead to a decline in the number of people in pews:

> *Some pastors . . . have us "blackout" the availability for people . . . within 50 miles of a church campus. (But) by giving people an opportunity to stay connected with you in real time when they cannot be there in person, live-streaming actually helps increase rather than decrease your church attendance.*

Alan Riley[48]

The tech:

▶ Use a basic phone, although you may have problems with the picture and the sound, as you are unlikely to be able to get close to the preacher without spoiling the experience for those in the congregation. An additional problem with the sound will be the one voice of the speaker in one part of the service, and the mass voices of the singing at other times. And all that in what is likely to be a large and echoey building.

▶ Best to attach a wide-angle lens so you can get the preacher and congregation or choir in the same shot, and take a feed of the church microphones from their PA system.

▶ Consider using several phones linked through one app, such as Switcher Studio, whose feeds are mixed before being broadcast via Facebook Live. That way you can have views of the speaker, choir, Bible, congregation and so on that you can cut between.

▶ Look at some of the API apps and programs mentioned earlier in the book, so you can link different devices and microphones, and mix the shots and balance the audio before streaming to your Facebook Live page.

Museums

In May 2015, the British Museum used Periscope for a 30-minute tour of its exhibition, *Defining Beauty: The Body in Ancient Greek Art*, hosted by British historian and broadcaster, Dan Snow.[49] This was a great advert for the exhibition and to attract more people in to visit it. Indeed, in the stream viewers were told of an exclusive code to use for discounted tickets.

Once the live-stream was over, Museum staff completed the circle by re-versioning the Scope for another audience.

Museum staff say they:

▶ Shot the stream on a smartphone camera.

▶ Customised the phone with a basic universal wide-angle lens that clipped straight onto the phone to give a better view of the artwork on display.

▶ Decided to shoot in landscape to fit a lot more into the frame: "The exhibition was designed to put these incredible sculptures in conversation with one another, so we agreed that landscape was the best way to capture this."[50]

▶ Mounted the smartphone to a handheld Lanparte gimble (like a Steadicam) (www.lanparte.com around £200), which smoothed out the camera movement.

▶ Connected a Sennheiser wireless clip-on mic (http://en-uk.sennheiser.com around £400) with the iRig XLR to minijack adapter (www.ikmultimedia. com/products/irigpre/ around £50).

▶ Swapped to a boom mic to capture the conversation between Dan and his guest.

The Australian Museum use it [live-streaming] when some of their experts are giving talks to museum visitors. This is a great way to amplify your content without having to spend time or budget on producing it. The experts were giving these talks to museum visitors anyway.

Damian Madden[51]

FIGURE 8.10 Another museum that regularly hosts successful Facebook Live video tours of its exhibits is The J. Paul Getty Museum in California. Here, curator Bryan C. Keene hosts "The Shimmer of Gold" Facebook Live exhibition walk-through

Source: © 2017 J. Paul Getty Trust. Work pictured: *The Branchini Madonna*, 1427, Giovanni di Paolo. Tempera and gold leaf on panel. The Norton Simon Foundation.

▶ FOCUS ON . . . MAKING MONEY FROM LIVE-STREAMS

Some people do live-streaming for fun, others for fame. But inevitably you may want to produce a show as a means to making a fortune. In China, where live-streaming is huge, broadcasters are potentially earning thousands of pounds/dollars per month. But the reality elsewhere is a bit different.

You have to build an audience before you have anyone to sell to. You do this by providing great content that fits with the brand or product that you are representing (like the product-reveal presented by Harley Davison[52] in August 2015).

> *Live-streaming enables you to cut through all the noise or competition. If your content is solid, it will get shares and more people in the stream. The more attention you can create for yourself and your brand, the more opportunities you have in business.*

Austin Iuliano[53]

And how do you tell people about the content if you are just starting out on your live-streaming production? You leverage your relationship on other platforms, such as your Facebook page, Twitter account and other places where you and your customers and potential customers already live:

> *This will give you an audience you can market your live-streaming video sessions to. . . . It will also give people social outlets to connect with your business once the live-streaming sessions are over. That way, even if they aren't ready to buy, they will continue to follow you.*

Kristi Hines[54]

What you can do to earn

▶ Products or services:

▷ Demonstrate what you have and mention your website. Perhaps include a discount code in your live-video, or perhaps sit in front of a banner with your website address on, or a sign of latest offers.

▷ Maybe you host a daily or weekly demonstration of your product. A garage could live-stream a walk around the cars for sale on the forecourt each day, with views inside each one and a commentary about its features and price.

▶ Yourself:

▷ From free to *fee*, you could provide basic information on a course in a live-stream and then if people have questions or want more in-depth training, they can pay (through PayPal and so on) to join a closed group.

▷ Do a training session on live-stream and then make the replay private and sell access to it through the YouTube Monetization system. (*https://support. google.com/youtube/answer/72857?hl=en-GB0*)

▷ Share ideas to show your expertise, and then get hired in real life.

If your business can teach others how to do something better, this is the perfect platform! Teach some of what you have and create an environment where you leave them wanting the rest! Remember, content that shows you are an expert will attract the right people to you!

Lisa Balthaser[55]

▷ Use the map feature to connect with local people. For example, on Periscope, zoom into the area where you live or work and pitch to them. So, if you are a plumber in a suburb of Madrid, pinch to see who is Periscoping in your neighbourhood and drop those people a line in their Scopes, or on Twitter, introducing yourself and explaining how they can get in touch if they need you.

▶ Collaborate:

▷ Once you have built a loyal legion of fans, sell those pairs of eyes to an advertiser. That could be the sponsor of the show, for example (giving you cash or product to review).

▷ Wear branded merchandise (yours, or those from a sponsor) during your show.

▷ Tips – There are some live-streaming apps, which link to a payment site and through which you can sell items directly to your viewers. Other apps have incorporated ways to 'tip' the presenter of your favourite show, and reward them for their content. This is a fast-moving area of the apps' development, but at the time of writing:

▷ Twitch viewers can earn, purchase and spend virtual currency to reward streamers or bet on the outcome of a game they are watching.

▷ YouNow says it processes payments of over $1.5 million a month, 50% going to the hosts of the shows.

YouNow users can purchase virtual gifts for their favourite broadcasters such as hearts, thumbs up and gold bars. A package of 6500 gold bars costs US$49.99, with broadcasters who have been accepted into YouNow's partner program getting a percentage based on how many people are watching.[56]

▷ Live.ly also shares payments 50/50 with broadcasters.

"You can make a living on this," Live.ly star Bart Baker told *Variety*. "When people see me drinking a Starbucks on Live.ly, they go to Starbucks and order the same drink." Baker claims to have earned as much as $30,000 in revenue from about a dozen live-streams.[57]

Those systems are currently not available to the users of the two main apps Facebook Live and Twitter's Go Live/Periscope, but something similar was built into the now-dead Meerkat app.

> *On Meerkat, a button appears after a broadcast that allows viewers to give money to the artist or get more information about the topic. At the conclusion of Madonna's 'Ghosttown' music video premiere, users could click a button that would send them to iTunes if they wanted her album.*
>
> Diana Tolockaite[58]

Simply have your PayPal account details on the screen while you present your fantastic information or sing your new song so people can donate.

Facebook Live ads

There is an option to run short ad breaks within Facebook Live videos. You are prompted to play the commercial within your show, and any income generated from the advertiser is split with Facebook.

Yes, you can make money this way, but you may not be helping your viewers, just selling their attention to another company. Consider how this may affect their perception of your brand.

The soft sell

Sell your product before people need it. In other words, if you build a relationship with your audience first (so they know, like and trust you), they will then be much more 'amenable' to buying from you when they need your product later. Become a 'go-to guy' now, by:

- ▶ Giving away information and help, before you start to sell

- ▶ Engaging with your viewers, followers and commenters: answer their questions, thank them and help them

> *Make your videos a point for interaction by encouraging people to comment, asking people what they thought, asking people to share it forward, and so on. And anyone who does respond to you in any way becomes a potential relationship.[59]*

You want to build a long-lasting relationship with customers, both current and future – not have a one-night stand of 'sell, sell, sell'. Conversation builds relationships, and relationships drive sales. And yes, you can build it with LUCK:

- ▶ L – the viewers learn to like the business.
- ▶ U – they understand the product.
- ▶ C – they care about the people who work there.
- ▶ K – they know the story of what you are doing and why.

'Person' is one of the P's in the basic 'Marketing Mix' (https://en.wikipedia.org/wiki/Marketing_mix), which also includes Product, Place and Price. So think of the Person and less of the immediate Promotion.

Let's put it another way that is familiar to marketers when they talk about consumer behaviour: you have to consider AIDA:

- ▶ **A – Awareness** of you, and of the product. You have to be on their radar. You have no way of selling anything to anyone, however much they may want it (or however much they may pay for it) if they don't know you exist!
- ▶ **I – Interest**. You have to create interest in the mind of the potential customer, in you, what you're talking about and then what the product is.
- ▶ **D – Desire**. Convince people that they want and desire the product or service . . . and that it will satisfy their needs, solve a problem, help them in their job, earn them more money, or save them time.
- ▶ **A – Action**. What you need to do to lead people to become customers and buying from you.

How the apps make money from you

We have already seen how tips or micro-payments sent to a broadcaster are split between them and the app developers. And, of course, Facebook already makes money from you, by using the information that it has about your watching and reading habits. Although you are not paying them directly, they track what information you find most interesting (what you click to watch and read, what you like and comment on, how long you spend on any particular page), and use that data to place appropriate ads on those pages. Any click-throughs to those external sites by you trigger a micro-payment to Facebook from the owner of that site.

There is another way they, and Periscope, could go:

> *The easiest path will be to place very short/Vine-length ads just before the play-back of archived broadcasts. The archived video playback alone will generate incredible cash-flow in addition to being perfect for search results and a huge honeypot for attracting new users.*

Chris Sacca[60]

To conclude:

▶ Get in now, grab your niche, build your audience, make mistakes.

▶ Be first and get the competitive advantage.

▶ Be an authority – show your personality and knowledge.

▶ People buy from people they know, like and trust.

▶ Don't go in hard: build long-term relationships, not a one-night stand.

▶ Follow through on Twitter and watch comments and give help off the air.

Learning how to do live-video is a marathon, not a sprint. It will take time, effort and patience.

▶ NOTES

1 I recommend the following article: Nicole Dahmen, *Facebook Live, Journalism and the Public*, https://nicoledahmen.wordpress.com/ February 15th, 2017

2 Mark Frankel, *News Journalism and Live-Streaming on Social Media*, https://medium.com/@markfrankel29/ December 20th, 2016

3 Alicia Slate, *Live Streaming: A Myth or a Bust?*, http://ufsocial.jou.ufl.edu/ September 21st, 2016

4 I realise that there is a constant shift in terminology, but I have used the term 'journalist' to cover those who are 'trained and paid', who weigh up facts from various sources and work for an established news company. The term 'reporter' I have used for those who are mainly 'members of the public' who either seek out news events or find themselves involved in them, and whose personal testimony and experiences are also invaluable in telling and explaining a news event.

5 Liam Corcoran, *Best Facebook Live Publishers of 2016*, www.newswhip.com/ December 15th, 2016

6 Caroline Scott, *How One Reporter Covered the Attacks in Nice and Munich With a Mobile Phone*, www.journalism.co.uk July 25th, 2016

7 Charlotte Krol, *Paris Attacks: Sky News Presenter Kay Burley Reports From Cafe During Panic From False Alarm*, www.telegraph.co.uk/ November 16th, 2016

 8 Cathy Loughran, *Nick Garnett's Solo Mission to Nepal*, www.bbc.co.uk/ariel/32622544 May 7th, 2015

 9 Stuart Dredge, *How Live Video on Periscope Helped 'Get Inside' the Syrian Refugees Story*, www.theguardian.com/ September 13th, 2015

10 Jon Laurence quoted in Jane Martinson's article, *Channel 4 News Defends Facebook Live Stream of Battle for Mosul*, www.theguardian.com/ See the footage on Facebook, here: www.facebook.com/Channel4News/videos/10154155702846939/ October 18th, 2016

11 www.periscope.tv/w/1djGXwbMNXVKZ

12 More ideas and links to live-streams from NPR here: Kara Frame, http://training.npr.org/ social-media/nprs-guide-to-facebook-live/ June 2nd, 2017

13 Louise Story quoted in Abigail Edge's article, *How Newsrooms Are Using Facebook Live to Engage Viewers*, http://blog.wan-ifra.org/ September 19th, 2016

14 See the full story *Fragments of a Life: A Curbside Mystery*, at www.nytimes.com/

15 The Professional Society of Drone Journalists, www.dronejournalism.org

16 www.bbc.co.uk/news/world-middle-east-38294748

17 Jonathan Klein, former president CNN in Farhad Manjoo's article *Live Streaming Breaks Through, and Cable News Has Much to Fear*, www.nytimes.com/ July 13th, 2016

18 Ben Popper, *There Was an Explosion in New York City, and Seconds Later I Was Watching It Live on Periscope*, www.theverge.com/ March 26th, 2015

19 Jannean Dean, *Council Meetings are Now Live*, http://janneandean.com.au/ green-light-live-streaming/

20 Matt Hackett, *Live Video: It's Not About the Content*, https://medium.com June 23rd, 2016

21 Chiara A Sotile, *Dakota Access Pipeline Fight Watched on Facebook Live Around World*, www.nbcnews.com/ November 5th, 2016

22 Citizen reporters who want to record video evidence in police interactions and other situations can use apps that increase their security in the field (Sam Dubberley, *Apps that Increase Your Security In The Field*, https://firstdraftnews.com/), the ACLU's Mobile Justice app (www.aclu.org/feature/aclu-apps-record-police-conduct) or Stop and Frisk (www.nyclu.org/app), and refer to WITNESS's *Field Guide to Collecting Video as Evidence* (www.mediafire.com/view/aa6uxaj6fc7ljzr/VaE_BasicPractices_v1_0.pdf) to help them do so safely and ensure their footage will be usable by officials and news media. (Both links via https://firstdraftnews.com/)

23 Tarun Wadhwa, *2016 Is the Year Live Streaming Came of Age*, www.forbes.com/ December 9th, 2016

24 Claire Wardle, *How Did News Organisations Handle the Philando Castile Facebook Live Video?*, https://firstdraftnews.com August 5th, 2016

25 Tilia Tequila, Facebook Live stream, www.facebook.com/ July 7th, 2016

26 Kate Dailey, *The Boston Marathon Bomber*, www.bbc.co.uk/news/magazine-22191029 April 18th, 2013

27 Josh Stearns, *One Year of Occupy: One Year of Journalist Arrests*, https://storify.com/ jcstearns/ September 17th, 2012

28 Kevin Rector, *Photojournalists 'Taken Down,' Detained by Police in Baltimore Protests*, www.baltimoresun.com/ April 26th, 2015

29 Ted Fickes, *Handheld Devices Put Livestreaming to Work on Campaigns*, www.mobilisationlab.org/ June 22nd, 2015

30 *Why Eyewitness Media Is Central to the Future of the News Industry*, https://medium.com/1st-draft/ October 26th, 2015

31 A video I produced for my employers was used on the website of a national newspaper without permission being granted. See if you can spot the credit: www.dailymail.co.uk/news/article-4155324/Bodies-man-woman-child-Surrey-cottage.html

32 Mark Frankel, *News Journalism and Live-Streaming on Social Media*, https://medium.com/@markfrankel29/ December 20th, 2016

33 One of the surviving hostages of the January 2015 terror attacks in Paris sued several French media outlets for broadcasting information about his whereabouts during the siege, which he claimed put his life in direct danger. www.thelocal.fr/

34 Casey Newton, *You Can Now Broadcast Live Video From the Twitter App*, www.theverge.com/ December 14th, 2016

35 Layton Rasco, *No, Not That Periscope! The Live-Streaming App*, http://planyourmeetings.com/ June 28th, 2015

36 Grateful thanks to the author for permission to use this longer quote.

37 Caroline Avakian, *Facebook Live Video for Nonprofits*, www.huffingtonpost.com/ February 3rd, 2016

38 Beth Snyder Bulik, *Facebook Live for Pharma?*, www.fiercepharma.com/ December 13th, 2016

39 Nadine Larder, *Tired of Traditional Open Houses? Use Periscope Instead*, http://activerain.com/ August 3rd, 2015

40 *Periscope House Viewings 'Changing Estate Agent Image'*, www.bbc.co.uk/ May 28th, 2015

41 Roxana Baiceanu, *73 Tips for Real Estate Video Marketing*, www.point2homes.com/ February 8th, 2016 *More General Social-Media Advice for Estate Sales*, http://thatinterviewguy.com/

42 Resources: *Twitter Teams Up With Church to Broadcast Live Services on Periscope App*, https://uk.news.yahoo.com/

   ▶ Carey Nieuwhof, *8 Ways Church Leaders Can Use Periscope to Aid Your Mission*, http://careynieuwhof.com

   ▶ *The Periscope Episode*, www.churchmarketingsucks.com/

43 www.facebook.com/archbishopofcanterbury/videos/vb.164961400224681/101

44 www.periscope.tv/RonWaxman/1MnxnrwrgkExO

45 www.adweek.com/lostremote/vh1-turns-to-periscope-for-love-hip-hop-wedding-red-carpet-livestream/52365 (article no longer available)

46 Charlotte England, *Funeral Live-Streaming Might Encourage 'Lazy Mourners'*, www.independent.co.uk/ October 2nd, 2016

47 Folarin Okunola, *How to Use Twitter During the Ramadan*, http://pulse.ng

48 Alan Riley, *Does Live Streaming Your Service Hurt Church Attendance?*, www.pikselfaith.com/ October 11th, 2016

49 On YouTube, search for *British Museum Live on Periscope*.

50 *Defining Beauty: The Body in Ancient Greek Art*, www.britishmuseum.org/

51 Damian Madden, *How to Use Snapchat and Periscope in Your Content Marketing*, www.damianmadden.com/ March 10th, 2016

52 Karl Greenberg, *Harley Davidson Raises Twitter Periscope For Global Product Reveal*, www.mediapost.com/ August 24th, 2015

53 Austin Iuliano, *How to Use Live Streaming for Content Marketing*, https://smallbiztrends.com/ August 16th, 2015

54 Kristi Hines, *How to Determine If Your Business Needs Periscope or Meerkat*, www.hiveage.com/ June 27th, 2015

55 Lisa Balthaser, *7 Important Lessons I Learned About Periscope*, www.fleurdelisasolutions.com/ July 29th, 2015

56 Claire Brownell, *For Generation Z, It's All About Live Video*, http://business.financialpost.com/ October 16th, 2015

57 Todd Spangler, *Live-Streaming Stars Are Earning Thousands of Dollars From Adoring Fans*, http://variety.com/ October 31st, 2016

58 Diana Tolockaite, *The Rise of Live Streaming Apps: What You Need to Know*, http://digital marketingmagazine.co.uk/ June 4th, 2015

59 *Networking With Video for B2Bs*, www.qumu.com/ June 25th, 2015

60 Alexei Oreskovic, *Here's How Twitter Could Make Money From Its Periscope Acquisition*, www.businessinsider.com.au/ June 4th, 2015

PART III
Pre-show production

In this part, more need-to-know material before you go live. There are consider-ations to make about where and when you broadcast. Will you present a show from your home or business or outdoors, and what about the best duration to get the optimum viewers?

Plus, you might need some additional kit – mics and lights and so on – so I break down the dos and don'ts before you splash too much cash.

And there's the matter of safety. Whether you are trolled on screen or followed in real life because of a 'fan', I explain what to do to protect you and your family.

9

How long and
when it's on

▶ INTRODUCTION

You may be used to producing *pre-recorded video*, and with *that* format, some of the most successful shows are around one minute. With *live* video, the consideration is, what is the tipping point between 'being interesting and worthwhile' and 'being live long enough to get a good audience'?

Of course, a lot of live-streaming is about being spontaneous and in-the-moment. That's great when you want to show people the view from your holiday hotel in Dubai or the harbour-side in Monaco: you can fire up your phone and stream away for as long as you want.

When considering a lengthy live-stream, remember:

- ▶ Battery life
- ▶ A decent Internet connection
- ▶ Your phone might not have enough space for the video to save to your Camera Roll afterwards!

But if you are using the platform for business, it will pay dividends to be more strategic. Timing is everything if you want to create expectation and anticipation.

▶ **HOW LONG?**

An often-quoted story is of Abraham Lincoln, who was asked by a small boy, "How long should my legs be?" To which Lincoln reportedly replied, "Long enough to reach the ground".

So how long should a programme run? Long enough to hit your objective. Say just as much as you *need* to say, and then stop.

But how do you know what you *need* to say? This in part will be determined by:

▶ **Your planning** – you will have made notes and structured your show, so you have a beginning, a middle and an end. You know what you want to say and how you are going to say it. You will know the point you want to make and how you are going to get there. You may even have had a short run-through, and you will get some sense of how long it is all going to be.

▶ **Your content** – if you are giving two top tips, or streaming the moment when 90-year-old grandad blows out his birthday candles, then obviously, the show will be quite short. If you are interviewing someone or teaching a new skill, it may be longer. If you are presenting a real-time cookery show, then it will inevitably be longer still. If it's a tour of a location and the scenery and content keep changing, then again it could be another duration.

We tried a Scope where we couldn't show much, and once viewers figured they'd seen everything, they dropped off. However . . . we showed the Infinite Corridor[1] and since the scenery was changing . . . we had many more people stay on the Scope for longer.

Stephanie Hatch Leishman[2]

▶ **Your intended viewer** – who are you targeting, what do they want to get from the show (a full discussion, or a top tip?) and how much time do they have to spare? Will they have background knowledge already, in which case your duration may be shorter, or will you have to set the context for the show before you deliver its main content? Do you have to give the main content at all? Perhaps the aim of your show is to give some great, free ideas and then a 'call to action' to visit your website or blog or paid-for course, for more.

Watching a whole concert, sermon or game on Periscope would be awful. Periscope is designed around a taste. Something quick and then over. . . . Periscope is not a full content delivery system; it's a content interest generator.

Pastor Landon Macdonald[3]

Understand your potential audience before you even get a feel for your duration.

▶ **Your interactions** – this is a bit of a variable as you don't know how many messages you are going to get and how long it may take you to read them, mention them and reply to them.

You can always break down your content into several shorter shows, either designing them that way, or by breaking off one live show and returning a few minutes later with another. Deciding on this second option may also make it easier for viewers who can perhaps more easily watch ten-minute 'mini-shows' on the same topic. And as the longer you broadcast for, the more opportunity there is for a mistake to be made, you might agree that shorter shows are safer.

The critical issue is, you want to keep your viewers from disengaging.

Do longer shows mean more viewers?

A longer show is inevitably likely to get more viewers than a shorter one, but it's not just about the sheer numbers. That's because what's important is:

▶ How long they stayed (the *'churn'* is the name given to the continuing comings-and-goings of your audience over the duration of the stream)

▶ How much they were engaged

▶ How much they loved the show, to share it to their own community

Also, remember that even though a broadcast on Facebook Live is given priority in a newsfeed and shared to more potential viewers than any other post, the longer it (or a Periscope) is on, the further it will slip down the feed of your followers and would need re-shares by viewers to stay discoverable.

Keeping track of time

Verbose is gross! Most people are time-poor and have a short attention span. You have to be fantastically creative and compelling to keep people interested for more than a few minutes. If you're creating content where there are *no* time limits, it's easy to ramble and be unfocused. So be careful to make content that truly matters.

It is very easy to lose track of time when you are presenting. Many times, you hear a presenter say at the start of a show that it will "be short", and it then ends after an hour! So have a clock near you to remind you of how long you have been speaking for.

Consider 'snack-sized shows' and have an alarm clock as *part of your show*. I presented a series on Periscope in which I said, "I'll never talk for more than 11 minutes. As soon as the alarm goes off, so do I!" On @LSInsiders, our Shows are just 30 minutes.

So a guide for show duration (and considering Facebook are themselves recommending shows are at least 5 minutes) might be between 10 and 15 minutes, with a 'sweet spot' of about 13. On Facebook Live, a show can be up to four hours long, although they also offer a feature called 'continuous live video' which lets you broadcast for up to 24 hours, although the stream cannot be shared or saved.

Facebook distributes videos (pre-recorded/'once-live'), based on how much of each one is watched: 'percent completion'. In other words, completing a longer video is a bigger commitment than completing a shorter one. So longer videos will be given a weighting in the distribution algorithm, although longer videos that people don't want to watch will not perform better.

But as they say:

> *Pages should focus on creating videos that are relevant and engaging to their audiences. The best length for a video is whatever length is required to tell a compelling story that engages people, which is likely to vary depending on the story you're telling.*

Facebook.com[4]

But again, duration doesn't really matter, as long as there is value.

HOW TO MAKE PEOPLE WATCH FOR LONGER

Throw ahead. Give them a reason to keep watching. Keep teasing:

- ▶ "That's just the first three Top Tips; I have another three to go!"
- ▶ "Coming up. . . / Still to come. . . / On the way . . ."
- ▶ "Before the end of the show, I'll tell you . . ."
- ▶ "And in a bit, I'll tease you with what's in my next show . . ."
- ▶ "And at the end of the show, I'll tell you who's won our competition . . ."

Remember – for you and your viewers – time is megs. Don't waste either!

Make sure that your shows are informative and beneficial to your viewers, but also entertaining to watch.

Give good content – concentrated.

▶ WHEN IT'S ON

Do a bit of research and find out when most of your friends or clients (or those you want to be your clients) are online and active, or indeed awake!

- ▶ On Facebook pages, look through the Insights tab.
- ▶ For Twitter's Go Live/Periscope, use analytics such as Followerwonk and Hootsuite (or go to https://analytics.twitter.com/about > Followers) to see what time zones most of your followers are in.

Then present your show on a day and at a time when they are most likely to be able to watch it. Timing needs to be at the heart of any advertising strategy. Take advantage of all the information that's just a click or two away.

One common mistake is to forget about a potential global audience, so remember the time differences (www.timeanddate.com/worldclock/) so you don't do a show that tries to engage people in Europe when they're mostly asleep! Or think you are doing a late-night/adult show when it's being seen at breakfast time somewhere else. Another way around this is to stream the same content on two separate occasions, to two different time zones. (Incidentally, the time when most people in the world are simultaneously awake is 11 am GMT/UT, 6 am ET.)[5]

In the spring and autumn/fall, consider that different parts of the world change their clocks for daylight saving purposes on different dates. So if you are broadcasting from London, a regular showtime for you may, for a week or two, be at a different time for a regular viewer in the US.

Also, you may want to try and avoid making your comments too time-specific: so consider dropping 'good morning' in favour of 'hi, how are you?'

Test and find what works best for you: after all, a show for 'mums with kids' probably won't work very well live if it's at tea-time, bath-time or picking-up-from-school time.

▶ HOW OFTEN

Don't be one of those people who broadcasts because they have nothing else to do. Only live-stream when you have something to say that has content and value. It may be that you present a-show-a-day. Much more than that and followers may become annoyed at the notifications.

Certainly, viewers may come to expect a show to a schedule:

- ▶ On certain days (whether that be several times a day or once a week)

- ▶ At certain times (within, say, an hour's window)

Having such a routine like this will help increase brand loyalty. If you don't broadcast consistently, your brand will be forgettable, and your viewing numbers, terrible. Just broadcasting 'when you feel like it' may be fun, but it won't increase your 'following figures' or boost your business. Look active, engaged and consistent.

If you get into a routine to broadcast, your viewers will get into a routine to watch.

YOUR BROADCAST SCHEDULE

To help you broadcast consistently (note: not *constantly*!), create a 'broadcast marketing schedule' of when you will go live, with what content and for how long.

This will be a content calendar, maybe linked to events such as end-of-year results, a new product line or Hallowe'en, outlining a clear communication objective to your customers.

Also include other factors that we have discussed: for example, the objective of each show, the call-to-action, the presenter/producer/tech requirements and any post-show analytics.

visibility = credibility

You can just randomly go live, but it helps if you set it up with your audience (especially if you are a brand) either by letting them know when you will appear, or set a regular time each day/week and then stick to it.

Damian Madden[6]

Creating the expectation of your show schedule helps people decide whether or not they want to Follow you. But remember, presenting a show more often may impact on the quality of content, which may damage your brand and upset your whole marketing strategy. Two buzzwords to remember when presenting: be *committed* and be *consistent*. Regular shows, done well.

> *The more regularly streams occur, the longer we see creators and brands able to sustain the audience."*
>
> Stephanie Patrick[7]

Maybe create a 'tip of the day' or comment on industry news to keep your clients or staff up to date with emerging trends. Schedule these programmes at the same time every day, so people get into the habit of watching. Promote them through Twitter and use the usual hashtags and tagged mentions of the people you're prompting to watch.

THE CONTENT PROMOTION FORMULA

Consistency from you leads to expectation from the viewer.

Experiment with your timings:

▶ When

▶ How often

▶ How long

In relation to your:

▶ Content

▶ Audience

▶ Format

Great content + Optimization + Ongoing Promotion = Ongoing Views

Or ignore all of this! And stream randomly with special deals, information and secret hacks, and create a sense of mystery around each new stream, so clients are left in anticipation wondering when the next stream will be and what it will include.

▶ NOTES

1 *The Infinite Corridor*, https://en.wikipedia.org/wiki/Infinite_Corridor
2 Stephanie Hatch Leishman, *Periscope: What We've Learned So Far*, http://connect.mit.edu/ July 30th, 2015
3 Pastor Landon Macdonald, *How to Use Periscope for Youth Ministry*, https://pastorlandonmacdonald.wordpress.com/ August 18th, 2015
4 *Updating How We Account for Video Completion Rates*, http://newsroom.fb.com/news/ January 26th, 2017
5 www.fastcodesign.com/1665437/infographic-of-the-day-what-time-is-the-internet-the-most-awake
6 Damian Madden, *How to Use Snapchat and Periscope in Your Content Marketing*, www.damianmadden.com March 10th, 2016
7 *The 5 Secrets to Livestreaming Success From the Game Theorists, YouTube's Largest Regular Livestreamers*, www.tubefilter.com/ February 8th, 2017

10
The recce

▶ INTRODUCTION

Let's be honest, being live creates many opportunities for failure. Just because it's live it doesn't mean that it can be completely raw. You have to think ahead, plan and produce your content as much as you would any other part of your marketing mix. Unfortunately, when a brand or individual fails, it's often because of a lack of planning. In fact, because you have no second chance, there is even more need to have a strategy. Rehearse and re-evaluate to set yourself up for success.

▶ YOUR LIVE-STREAM 'SET'

Where you are when you present your show says a lot about you, your brand and your professionalism. It'd be great to think that viewers will be captivated by your content, but you don't want them distracted by your surroundings.

Find a quiet but an authentic place from which to broadcast. In general, you want somewhere which 'looks the part': it fits with your presentation style and with the content of your show. Viewers may (arguably) be more likely to take legal notes from a smartly dressed presenter sitting in an office than one wearing a Hawaiian shirt on the beach.

So, think of the visuals: a show about cooking presented from a kitchen with stainless steel and boiling pans, rather than from your bedroom.

Indeed, is broadcasting from your bedroom okay, or is it better to broadcast from your *boardroom*? The former may be considered either amateurish or intimate. The latter may be professional or possibly, distant. Only you can decide.

What will be directly behind you as you present? Think televisually: reporters don't talk with a white screen or a brick wall behind them. They have something visually interesting and appropriate alongside them. (If it is a plain wall, make it a matte finish rather than gloss, to reduce glare.)

As well as the general location, also consider the immediate background:

▶ **Tidiness** – Does the background to your show look untidy? What does that say about your business or personal brand? Are the books on the shelf behind you straight? Clear surfaces rather than cluttered ones will give a more professional look. See your location with a new set of eyes: does that pile of paperwork in the in-tray give the impression of inefficiency, or does it say that you are running a busy business?

▶ **Noise** – Background noise, even (or, especially) if you can't see what's causing it, can be distracting for you as you present, and the audience. Banging doors, outbreaks of laughter, sirens, the wind on the microphone are not viewer-friendly. This includes music from a radio, which may break copyright rules, causing Facebook to stop your broadcast mid-flow, mid-show.

▶ **Background movement** – If you are presenting a show from the shop floor, an auction room or classroom, then, of course, do have *appropriate* movement. It adds to the authenticity of the presentation and will make the show better because of it. But imagine presenting a lecture-type live-stream

FIGURE 10.1 The image on the right shows the set for the Buzzfeed 2016 US Election coverage

Source: BuzzFeed, Facebook

and having people constantly walking by behind you. Even worse is if this happens when you are doing a private stream to a colleague, or an explainer show to a client.

▶ **Privacy** – Not everyone wants to be part of your programme. Consider colleagues in a busy office or members of the public who do not appreciate being caught on camera.

NOTICE OF LIVE FILMING TAKING PLACE HERE

Please be advised that [*company name*] is filming here to show [*e.g. behind the scenes at the zoo*], between the hours of [*insert hours*] on [*insert date*].

The video will be streamed live on [*www.facebook.com/_____*] and it is possible that you may appear in the background as you enjoy your day out.

If you do not wish to appear, please:

▶ [*avoid this area at these times*]

▶ [*sit at the back of the theatre/use the alternative entrance*]

More information can be obtained from: [*insert contact details*].

We thank you for your co-operation and apologise for any inconvenience.

▶ **Image** – Look again at those book titles on your shelf. Do they reflect you or the company? Is that calendar the kind usually seen in a garage workshop? Is that a staff member picking their nose?

▶ **Branding** – Consider having a pop-up banner or poster in-frame with your logo or website address on it. (Remember, with some app-and-phone combinations, this may be shown in reverse. On Facebook Live, go to the 'magic wand' icon, to be able to spin the view.) Maybe you always have the same backdrop or always stream from the same yellow sofa (where yellow is part of your brand logo). Do whatever you can to add your personal or business branding: your consistent visual identity will help aid recall.

▶ **Security** – You don't want to inadvertently compromise confidentiality. Be eagle-eyed for sales forecasts on a whiteboard or a client list on the wall.

▶ **Electronic screens** – You could have an HD TV screen alongside you (a non-HD screen will seem to flicker when shown on the camera), on which you have a graphic:

▷   Your company logo

▷   What you are talking about – the product, the location, the person

▷   Text – such as key points, your web address, the benefits of a product

These items could, if produced in a simple programme such as PowerPoint, even be moving.

In short, if a location or backdrop is incongruous with your content, it may undermine your authority.

YOUR CONSISTENT VISUAL IDENTITY

Create a look that is consistent with your brand and from video-to-video. Among the elements to bear in mind:

▶   Location

▶   Backdrop

▶   Presenter

▶   Style

▶   Format

▶   Titling

▶   Catchphrases (the way you begin and end your show)

▶   Props

▶   Clothes and makeup

▶   Use of colour

▶   Graphics

▶ TECHNICAL ISSUES

▶   **Signal strength** – Is your Wi-Fi network robust enough to have extra traffic on it from streaming content? If customers or staff also use it to stream, could it hamper your main business? At a conference or event, there may be lots of people on a Wi-Fi signal that was strong when you tested it before everyone arrived. Have a MiFi hotspot with you as a backup. Check the signal and mic in a private stream before you go live in earnest.

▶ **The phone** – Also check your battery levels and storage on your phone if you intend to keep the stream.

▶ **Extra kit –** Do you need an external microphone or can you use the in-built one on the phone? What about lights? They are probably unnecessary, unless you are in a dimly lit office, but a tripod is a must if you are to avoid your viewers feeling seasick.

▶ PRODUCTION ISSUES

When you are streaming live, you are presenter, producer, moderator and salesperson all rolled into one!

▶ Do you need someone to hold the smartphone while you walk through the office?

▶ Will you be able to see and respond to comments?

▶ How will you react to, and act on, any disparaging comments that are made in the stream?

▶ How will you start and end the show, let alone decide on what to say during it?

▶ Will there be someone to suggest that, actually, it might be time to end the show now?

11

Live-stream privacy, security and safety

▶ INTRODUCTION

I urge you not to skip over this section. It's serious, it's important and it could save you a lot of trouble.

And reputation.

And money.

And maybe your job. . .

> ▶ Radio presenter Tony Blackburn was told to stop live-streaming[1] at BBC Broadcasting House because of privacy and security implications.
>
> ▶ Marisa Mendelson, a now-*former* reporter for NBC's Tucson news station KVOA, was fired after she innocently live-streamed her sleeping dog[2] after bosses told staff not to use Periscope.
>
> ▶ Journalist Stephanie Wei lost her PGA press credentials for Periscoping some off-the-green conversations[3] with golfers.

It is important that you protect yourself when online in any situation. More so perhaps on a live-stream because it is:

▶ **Live** – you may show or say something before thinking through the consequences.

▶ **Video** – moving pictures convey more information than static ones, and of course you can move from location to location.

▶ **Global** – you don't know who is watching or where they are.

What follows can only be a rough guide. I'm not a lawyer, and I don't live in your country or state where laws on such issues as privacy, defamation and copyright may be different (the following is based on UK law and governance). But it is a heads-up so you can keep your head when you decide to go live.

Two big notes before we go further: claiming you didn't know about a law does not mean that it doesn't apply to you. And if you see someone else breaking the law, don't think it's necessarily okay for you to do the same. (Yep, even most of the 'big names' on live-video illegally stream music, fail to declare they've been paid to promote a product, or knowingly re-stream TV programmes – I've seen lots of examples.) Do your own 'due diligence'. And if you stream on behalf of a company, make sure that they have an understanding and necessary clearance of what will be shown.

In 2016, the NFL announced that teams could be fined for breaking new social media policy, which included live-video. Teams were told that they could not do live-streams inside a stadium during a game (or pre-record video and post it on social media). Fines were said to be up to a possible $100,000 for repeated offences. This was so the league maintained control of what was being produced and distributed.

Always assume that five people will see everything, and keep them in mind as you broadcast:

▶ Your best friend

▶ Your worst enemy

▶ Your boss

▶   Your mother

▶   Someone's solicitor

Then consider:

▶   *Could* they sue?

▶   *Would* they sue?

▶   Could they *win?*

▶   Would they win?

This is what Periscope has in its Terms of Service:

> *You are responsible for your use of Periscope Services, for any Content you post to Periscope, and for any consequences thereof. The Content you submit, post, or display will be able to be viewed by other users and through third party services and websites. You should only provide Content you are comfortable sharing with others under these Terms.*

▶ YOUR LOCATION

Do people have a reasonable expectation of privacy at the location where you are streaming?

▶   Your place of work

   ▷   If you own the premises, your staff and clients might not appreciate being included in live-video that you present.

   ▷   What guidelines do you have to manage 'behind-the-scenes' streams presented by your staff or clients? They may help publicise your business but also show or say something you prefer they didn't.

▶   Someone else's place of work such as an office or shop – you are not even an employee there, after all.

▶   A 'security-sensitive' location such as a government building, airport, military establishment, power facility, port or bridge. And certainly not inside a British courtroom.[4]

▶   A religious location such as a church, cathedral or mosque, graveyard or memorial.

▶   A place *you may consider to be public but is actually privately owned* such as a shopping mall,[5] whose managers have the right to refuse entry to anyone. Places such as bus garages or farmland/countryside are usually private, and unless you are there for a good reason (catching a bus, on a hike), this may be considered trespassing. A good example: in London, part of the South Bank of the Thames outside City Hall (and opposite the Tower of London and Tower Bridge) is privately owned. Politicians had to negotiate with the landowners to be interviewed by TV crews outside their own offices, and officially you are not allowed to even take a photograph there. Although a blind eye may be turned to the latter, if you set up a tripod and have a presenter with a mic, you may be asked for your permit and be moved on swiftly if you cannot produce one.

▶ Be careful with a usually public place that is *temporarily* private, such as a city park which is fenced off for an open-air theatre production and for which people have to buy tickets.

▶ Anywhere else where you have to buy tickets to get in, such as a conference or trade show. If you are at a conference, it may be against the terms and conditions of your entry ticket to stream the speakers' presentations. The speaker may object as it is an infringement of their copyright (they may lose out on future speaking engagements if their material is freely available), and the conference organisers could claim that fewer people will pay for tickets to future events if they can get the material online. And yes, that may also include a restriction on you broadcasting your own presentation.

▶ Somewhere people would have a *reasonable expectation* of privacy, such as toilet facilities, or hospital or a hospice. A general view of a beach may be one thing. Showing semi-naked sunbathers, particularly if they are children, is another. Consider whether your stream goes beyond recording to harassing or stalking, invasion of privacy, peeping and so on. Gratuitously showing nakedness, abuse, etc. is obviously not allowed.

Also, think carefully before you show the outside of a 'sensitive' building such as a police station or a military base (although you may be standing on a public street), which will inevitably arouse suspicions. The same goes if you are outside a school, or standing on a public pavement and broadcasting the faces of people going into, say, an abortion clinic.

Saying "but I pay my taxes, I 'own' that public building, so I should be able to show it", or "the shopping centre films us, so why can't I film them?" are interesting discussions for a bar, but they become less interesting (and more expensive) in a police interview room, a security guard's office or a court of law.

If you get verbal permission to live-stream from a private place, get it in *writing*, too (or have the permission-giver stay with you while you stream). It's not good to be stopped, questioned and ejected from a building live on air. Neither is it good to think all's gone well and then, later on, receive a letter from a solicitor.

Even if you have permission to broadcast from a private location, consider the 'footfall' of the area and any written notice you may have to give employees or members of the public at that location that you are 'live', and if they walk past their image may be shown. (There's the suggested wording of a sign that you can put up at the location, in the chapter on doing a recce.)

SHARING YOUR LOCATION

On Facebook Live you control whether your location is shared, just as you do with any post. If you have Location Services on, you can tag the location of your broadcast before you start. If you don't want your location shared, do not add your location to your broadcast before you go live. The Live Map (www. facebook.com/livemap) is a visual way to explore public live broadcasts that are currently happening around the world. Only public broadcasts that have a location tagged will show up here.

In the broadcast screen of Periscope, you can tap the 'location arrow' to allow the app to show your location when you go live.

FIGURES 11.1 See how accurate the Periscope map feature is

Source: Periscope

The advantages of toggling this to 'on' are listed in the Periscope chapter in this book, but what are the security and privacy implications?

▶ Thieves will know almost exactly where *you* are, and that you have an expensive phone that you are literally holding out in front of you ready for the taking. . .

My mobile phone was snatched violently from my hand by a thug on a bicycle. My Periscope broadcast was still live. . . (viewers) heard my frightened scream, and then the screen went black. I have watched the Periscope replay over and over, and it scares me so much.

Rebecca Casserly – @BoopFashionista[6]

▶ A follower on your live-stream account could become a real-life follower (or rather, 'stalker').

▶ Do you really want people to know the area in which you live? If they watch your shows, they know your name, what you look like, what you sound like and your interests and hobbies. You may even have shown the outside of your house or the street. A 'jigsaw effect' means it's not tricky for them to locate you,[7] stalk you or break in when they see you are streaming from elsewhere.

▶ If you stream from a friend's house, will they be happy with that? What if someone presents a live show when *they come to visit you*? What if that person is the babysitter: essentially telling any weirdo that they are, say, a teenage girl, alone in your house or at the park with your kids?

HOW TO SET UP A FALSE LOCATION

You can set up a false location for your Scopes, so you are still featured on the Map page, but your security is not compromised. (This only works on Android phones.)

▶ Settings > General > About

▶ Tap several times on your build number to open Developer options.

▶ General > Menu > Developer > select Mock Locations

▶ Download a fake GPS location app > Open > select and set a location.

▶ WHAT YOU SHOW

Check that you are allowed to stream what will be seen. Complete a thorough recce, so you know when to turn the camera so you don't show certain items:

▶ Where you store valuable items, the location of the plant room housing the IT infrastructure, the possible location of the safe, CCTV controls or the complete layout of the building.

▶ What's on the office desk or wall? Any 'trade secrets' such as strategies on a whiteboard, sales figures on a chart, staff contact numbers?

▶ Any trademarked material such as pictures or logos. Your logo is fine as you will have paid for it, and usually showing another logo is okay as long as you don't give the wrong impression that you are linking yourself with that other company, you criticise them (see below), or make money from showing their material.

▶ Steer clear of car licence plates or people indulging in totally *legal* practices that they may be embarrassed about: people rowing or going into a bathroom, for example.

▶ Showing TV or films/movies is out of the question.

PRIVACY AND SAFETY WHEN USING DRONES

▶ Have you had any training?

▶ Why are you using a drone? What is the need?

▶ Plan what shots you need, rather than just launch. Consider where you will go and what you want to show.

▶ Do you know for a fact that you are allowed to fly a drone in this location?

▶ Think of privacy issues: what you are flying over or alongside (you could potentially have a view through a window).

▶ Consider compassion, say at a natural or man-made disaster.

▶ Also, noise issues, for example, if you fly in the early morning or in a countryside location.

▶ Do a recce for potential hazards, such as trees, pylons, the wind or other drones.

Your viewers may also overhear what is said by other people (see this live-stream from the scene of a triple death, with reporters laughing in the background).[8] Obviously, you have no jurisdiction over what is picked up by your mic in a public place (although if there is offensive swearing, you'd be good to move to another location), but if you are streaming in an office, you may pick up chatter as people pass by while discussing the latest merger or closure.

▶ WHAT OTHER PEOPLE SHOW

Some live-streams have been frankly horrific: rape, torture, death, suicide, threats, bullying and so on. It may be that you stumble across such scenes (or maybe a colleague working as your live-stream producer or community moderator sees them).

The app companies have on occasion been slow to remove such videos. Sometimes they have deleted posts which were innocuous while leaving other more violent streams online. It may be considered that the apps have a moral duty to protect their users, but that needs to be balanced with a 'right to know'.

> One of the most sensitive situations involves people sharing violent or graphic images of events taking place in the real world. In those situations, context and degree are everything. For instance, if a person witnessed a shooting, and used Facebook Live to raise awareness or find the shooter, we would allow it. However, if someone shared the same video to mock the victim or celebrate the shooting, we would remove the video.

Facebook Community Standards[9]

It's understood that Facebook is working on artificial intelligence to automatically detect and flag offensive content in a live-stream. In an article by Reuters,[10] Facebook said it also uses automation to process the tens of millions of reports it gets each week, to recognise duplicate reports and route the flagged content to reviewers who have the appropriate subject-matter expertise.

Questions that remain unanswered: Who are those 'experts' and who has drawn up the guidelines that they work to? Who should make ethical or editorial decisions in such cases? Who decides whether a violent video is 'raising awareness' of an issue or 'celebrating' it? (For example, Facebook's Community Standards ban 'terrorism' without offering a definition.)[11]

▶ COPYRIGHT

Simply put, if you include in your show something that someone else created, and you use that to gain influence or money for yourself, then you could be guilty of 'copyright theft'.

Facebook themselves have a small but significant passage on some of their pages about your responsibilities while using their platform:

> *only broadcasting content for which you own and/or control all rights (or have obtained all necessary licenses/permissions to such rights), globally, including rights in any sound recordings or musical compositions included in the video and any performers appearing in it. Make sure to keep the camera on you, and never broadcast the unfolding event, including what is on a stage, field, or any screens.*

Creators and distributors of a TV show earn money by attracting people to watch the show and selling those 'pairs of eyes' to advertisers. If you stream the show free (or charge people for watching), you are depriving the creators of their lawful income.

The NBA, NFL, and MLB have policies that restrict both reporters and fans from live-streaming game action. The NBA says media are allowed to stream live press conferences and interviews to *their own websites* but not to third-party platforms like Periscope. Aside from press conferences, the NBA also says that 'Non-Game Action Content', which includes video taken at practice, interviews in the locker room, etc. may not be live-streamed. The MLB's media credential policy says, "any video related to Games, captured within the ballpark, and carried online, must be limited to 120 seconds and cannot be carried live."

Other major sporting events have been live-streamed often by the organisers themselves, who state that spectators are barred from doing so. Although some small clubs may welcome the coverage that a live-stream might bring them, for the viewer the scene they see will be distant and poor and without a commentary, and it'll be a drain on battery and data.

If you use someone else's music in your show, you are using their creation to enhance your live-stream. And so, you should pay for the advantages that using their material gives you. This includes sing-alongs and karaoke, despite the prevalence of streams with such content. It also includes any backing track that you may talk over or theme tune that you start a show with. You can buy royalty-free music for a one-off cost at places such as www.pond5.com and http://duenorthaudio.com, but check specific terms and conditions.

If you read from someone else's book or blog, you could be illegally depriving that author of income. If you take someone else's original idea by streaming their presentation at a conference, you may have committed intellectual theft.

Some live-streamers have reported that their streams have been curated on *other people's* YouTube pages, some with pre-roll adverts so that 'thief' gets income rather than the actual presenter. If you believe your copyright-protected work was posted without authorization, you can submit a copyright infringement notification to YouTube: https://support.google.com/youtube/answer/2807622/. (A helpful guide to YouTube and Copyright is at https://support.google.com/youtube/answer/2797449.)

> *Twitter, Inc. respects the intellectual property rights of others and expects users of Periscope Services to do the same. We will respond to notices of alleged copyright infringement that comply with applicable law and are properly provided to us.*

Full Terms of Service and Copyright and Community Guidelines are available on the individual apps' websites, such as:

▶ Facebook Copyright Guidelines: https://live.fb.com/tips/

▶ Periscope Community Guidelines (includes information if you are a victim of copyright infringement): www.periscope.tv/content

Facebook's Rights Manager automatically screens live-video for copyrighted work. If a match is found, the live-stream may be interrupted. This goes for private streams as well as public ones.

▶ WHAT IS 'FAIR USE'?

You may be able to use other people's content through Creative Commons licences (https://creativecommons.org/about/). This is a way that generous people allow others to have access to their work under certain conditions.

You may also have heard of the phrase 'fair use', for when you don't have to seek permission. A full explanation can be found on the YouTube website, here: www.youtube.com/yt/copyright/en-GB/fair-use.html#yt-copyright-four-factors

▶ CAN THE APP USE YOUR CONTENT?

Periscope says in its Terms of Service that you, the broadcaster, retain your rights to any Content you record through Periscope. You grant them:

▶ A worldwide, non-exclusive, royalty-free license (including the right to sublicense to others)

▶ Permission to use, copy, reproduce, process, adapt, modify, publish, transmit, display and distribute the content

▶ YOUR SAFETY

As we saw earlier in this chapter,[12] being distracted when you are broadcasting and watching the screen for comments may mean your personal safety is compromised.

Consider having someone else with you who can 'watch your back' if you intend to broadcast from such a place. At home, consider turning off the location feature on Periscope.

Streaming and driving

We don't reckon it's a very good idea. Here's why:

www.youtube.com/watch?v=JfScUuMAMbA

And yet: www.facebook.com/SocialLiveTVShow/videos/1324182780980370/

Some say live-streaming and driving is no more dangerous than talking to someone in the car, but when you are broadcasting you feel under a bit more pressure to keep talking and you may be tempted to look at the comments.

- ▶ In 2014 in the US, 3,179 people were killed and 431,000 were injured in motor vehicle crashes involving distracted drivers. (www.distraction.gov)

- ▶ Ten percent of all drivers 15 to 19 years old involved in fatal crashes were reported as distracted at the time of the crashes. This age group has the largest proportion of drivers who were distracted at the time of the crashes. (www.distraction.gov)

- ▶ Five seconds is the average time your eyes are off the road while texting. When travelling at 55 mph, that's enough time to cover the length of a football field blindfolded. (www.distraction.gov)

- ▶ Three main types of distractions while driving:

    - ▷ Visual distractions cause you to take your eyes off the road.

    - ▷ Manual distractions cause you to take your hands off the wheel.

    - ▷ Cognitive distractions, such as listening to a talk radio show, cause you to take your mind off what you are doing. (http://thenationshealth.aphapublications.org/)

And an even worse idea is live-streaming while driving *while drunk*:

- ▶ A 23-year-old woman who police said drove drunk and then streamed it live online on Periscope for the world to see. (See YouTube: "Periscope DUI in Lakeland, Fla.")

▶ YOUR PRIVACY

In a previous chapter I mentioned why these apps are free: the developers are using information you give them (what you do, where, with whom) to sell things back to you via adverts on your page.

And because everything you put out there is free for other people to use too, *other* companies use your content to monetise their own businesses.

- ▶ Ditto is scouring hundreds of millions of photos shared on social media to detect brands, objects and context: https://firehose.dittolabs.io/

- ▶ This project scans every Periscope video: http://stream.dextro.co/

Your privacy can also be compromised by what you say or show. Even if it was done piecemeal, over time viewers start to build an accurate picture of you and your family. So be careful what you say and show and consider whether you need to:

- ▶ Say that you are going on holiday/vacation

- ▶ Say your children's names or their school

- ▶ Show the street or house where you live or your car licence plate

- ▶ Tell where you usually stop for a coffee

▶ WHAT YOU SAY

It's not quite a 'free country': you *can't* say exactly what you want. Because if you did that could cause a person to be injured in their "office, trade or profession" in the "minds of right thinking people" (part of the UK definition of defamation). So do you have any legal knowledge? Could you unwittingly make a potentially slanderous remark about rival products or people? Did you know it could be an invasion of privacy if you talk about someone else disparagingly?

Here are some more ways you may find yourself in legal hot water.

Full disclosure

If you are reviewing a product, you have to be honest. So if you are being paid by the company, make that clear in your broadcast. Also mention if you got the product for free or for 'review purposes'.

To use your Facebook page for sponsored content is against Facebook's Terms of Use, and going by the letter, that includes text, photos and live or pre-recorded video. Why? Because Facebook wants to be able to sell advertising space on your page itself, or have *you* pay to advertise. (A workaround for verified pages is to tag the brand within the post.)

A 2015 study by the UK communications regulator Ofcom found that fewer than half of 12- to 15-year-olds who watch YouTube are aware that vloggers are often paid to mention products or services favourably.

Many countries have guidelines about having to make clear that you are being paid (either with money, goods or services) when you write or record certain kinds of content. After all, your audience should be aware that your content may be skewed because of an inducement by the company concerned. In effect, it's an advertisement, so it will likely fall under consumer protection legislation.

There's nothing wrong with having a commercial relationship with a company. What's wrong is misleading people about it. (Again, the following information is based on UK law, but similar regulations will be in place in other countries.)

What's allowed

If you as a well-known live-streamer or personality present a broadcast on the channel (page, stream, account) of a certain company (let's call them 'ABC Conglomerates') talking about their products, it will be obvious that they have paid you to appear. So, you won't need to make that additionally clear, verbally or visually.

Advertorials

If the scenario is the same as above, and you are on ABC Conglomerates' channel talking about their products *but the presentation and production are very similar to your usual shows* (the graphics, location, background), then this is likely to be misleading and so is considered an 'advertorial'. It needs to be labelled as such ('ad', 'ad feature', 'advertorial') so that viewers know before they engage with it (UK's Committee of Advertising Practice Rule 2.4).

Ad breaks

If you run your own content on your own channel but there is an 'advert' within it (a specific section where you will promote a product), *then it needs to be clear to a viewer when that starts.* That could be as basic as holding up a sign or saying that you have been paid to talk about the product at this point.

Product placement

In this scenario, you have your own content on your own channel, but you use a product as a prop that has been supplied by a company, along with a message. For example, you run a programme reviewing tech gear for live-streaming and you show an item given to you.

It should be made clear that the video contains a commercial message, again by way of a sign or verbally: "I'm using these lenses from ABC Conglomerates, who paid me to feature them and explain how they work."

> *The CMA would expect brands and vloggers to tell consumers if an item was given on the condition that it is talked about . . . consumers need to know whether a vlogger has an incentive (financial or otherwise) to talk about a product, and if so what that incentive is.*

▶ THE COMMITTEES OF ADVERTISING PRACTICE (CAP)[13]

If an online review or endorsement is not based on genuine user experience, or displays elements of bias without appropriate disclosure (such as where it has been paid for or solicited without appropriate disclosure), this can have a negative impact on consumers and competition:

- ▶ Consumers can be misled into taking decisions that they would not otherwise have taken.

- ▶ Competitors who do not engage in misleading practices are penalised at the expense of traders who do.

(*Source*: *The International Consumer Protection and Enforcement Network*)

Key Principles for Digital Influencers:[14]

- ▶ Disclose clearly and prominently whether content has been paid for.

- ▶ Be open about other commercial relationships that might be relevant to the content.

- ▶ Give genuine views on markets, businesses, goods or services.

"Paid for" is not limited to financial payment; for example, it could include free clothing or tickets to events. Digital influencers should tell their viewers about any incentive (financial or otherwise) that may have influenced or led them to post particular content.

Again: Check local laws and consult a professional for specific legal advice for your country and content.

Defamation

When comparing product A with product B, explain what your expertise is and what criteria you are using to evaluate the items, and explain why you say what you say.

Let me explain: it would be unfair for the companies to have a review of a scooter by someone who knows nothing about scooters. But to have a review by an expert, or fanatic, means that what they say is more likely to be their 'honestly held opinion' (and that helps protect you, the broadcaster, with what you say).

Why? Because someone with expertise in an area, giving an honestly held opinion, backed up with reasons is better covered by the law when a product is being criticised. Compare that with a non-expert simply unfairly criticising and denigrating a product, person or place.

Here's another legal example: you come across a car crash and decide to start a live-stream showing the aftermath. (Let's leave aside the moral issues of doing this rather than helping.) If you even say something as seemingly innocuous as "the blue car hit the red car", you could be in trouble. Why? Because that presumes guilt on behalf of the driver of the blue car. You could say the blue and red car *collided*, but not who hit whom. You could say "the car ended up on the pavement" as that is fact. But under UK law, it's for accident investigators to decide the actual chain of events and who is to blame. If you blame the driver of the blue car and it's later proven that the fault lay with the driver of the red car, you could be sued (for suggesting that the other motorist had been careless or dangerous).

▶ ABUSE AND HARASSMENT

In 2016 Scottish MEP David Coburn was pranked by viewers who pretended they couldn't hear him.[15]

That was fun, but a more determined troll can ruin your live-stream, your confidence and possibly your life:

- ▶ **By posting offensive remarks** – racist, sexist or sexual remarks (for a while 'open bobs', or 'boobs', was a favourite phrase for trolls, requesting that female presenters undo their blouses).

▶ **By posting disruptive remarks** – such as the same text repeatedly or, in one case, typing each letter of the alphabet sequentially.

▶ **By sending comments which are malicious or mocking** – French President François Hollande got sent comments accusing him of being overweight and worse.[16]

The comments section on live-streaming apps can be disabled, but that stops interaction completely (see more on 'comments' in another chapter). Nothing should be left to chance in this regard. Have a Plan A, B and C ready to be implemented before an important stream begins.

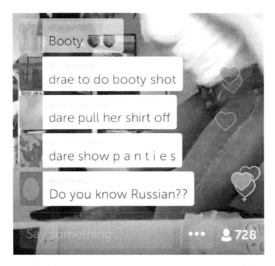

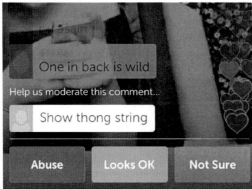

FIGURE 11.2 Abusive comments made to girls who said they were 13-years old, on Periscope

Source: Periscope

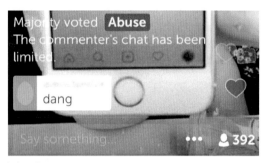

FIGURE 11.2 continued

Amanda Oleander, an artist who used Periscope to showcase her work, agrees that sexist pests are ever-present. Around 20% of comments on her broadcasts are inappropriate statements, questions or requests like 'open boobs' she says.

Kitty Knowles – Thememo.com[17]

Consider what your 'lines in the sand' are regarding comments, so you don't get upset or frustrated on air.

The platform has a 'viewer jury' to help police such harassment. If you want to be called upon to moderate comments made in other people's broadcasts (voting is anonymous), or to have your own broadcasts moderated, then enable those two options in the Periscope settings. You can also report a comment made in replay video, by tapping the avatar of the person who sent it.

Periscope also has a little-known, in-built 'profanity filter', which will pick up potentially offensive words that a user intends to send to the stream. Once identified, a message appears on the screen of that viewer: "Are you sure you want to send this message? Messages like this frequently get blocked. If you get blocked too many times your comments will no longer be seen."

Limiting trolls

▶ **Private broadcasts** – see the settings outlined elsewhere in this book.

  ▷ Do you need to broadcast the content to 'the world'?

  ▷ Could a private stream to your colleagues or a select group of people be more appropriate?

▶ **Comments** – see the settings outlined elsewhere in this book.

▶ In the 'broadcast panel' just before you go live on Twitter Go Live/ Periscope, select the 'speech bubble' icon. This will stop unknown people from posting offensive comments.

What to do on troll patrol

Consider these five i's to help you monitor your live-stream feed:

Ignore them

Simply carry on with your show and hope that they give up their behaviour if you are not rising to the bait. Don't acknowledge them or feed them in any way. If this doesn't work, mention the disruption to all viewers: "It looks as though someone's trying to disrupt our show. You may want to block them so you don't see them again. Just tap their name when it appears."

Interact with them

Ask them who they are, what they mean and why they are doing this. Don't get angry or argue but pose serious questions as you try and engage and understand them. But be ready to block if this enrages them and they step up their campaign of comments.

Identify them

Mention their name and shame them so others know what's happened and they can mass-block them. Ask the troll to post their real name and website. Take a screenshot of their comments and ask other viewers to do the same, so you have evidence of what was said that you could pass on to the authorities.

Interrupt them

If you can, tap the screen and block them while you do so. (It's easier to talk on auto-pilot when you do this, so launch into a well-rehearsed speech welcoming newcomers, how to heart/share/follow, until you are done blocking.)

Inhibit them

Report them to the app authorities, or the actual authorities if necessary. If you have their name or handle, make it difficult for them to follow you or engage with you on other platforms by blocking them there as well. If you see a troll when you're watching someone else's show, block them there so they don't appear in yours.

The live-stream moderator

If you have a 'producer', they could also act as moderator:

▶ By warning a viewer who has made an inappropriate remark

▶   Screenshotting any offensive message

▶   Blocking the sender

▶   Reporting that viewer

How to block a commenter

Facebook Live – You can block viewers during a live broadcast by tapping the profile picture next to a viewer's comment and then tapping Block.

Twitter Go Live/Periscope – As broadcaster, you can:

▶   Limit the comments to only come from your Followers.

▶   Hide all the comments, which rather stops the interactivity of Twitter Go Live/Periscope, but it could be useful if you don't want distraction during a live-stream.

And you can also block people who send you unpleasant comments. Whether you are a presenter or viewer, as soon as you see the comment that you object to (whether when live or a replay video):

▶   Tap on the comment > View Profile > Gear icon > Block User

This will also stop you seeing any of their comments in any other video you see, so they will never be able to:

▶   Follow you.

▶   Watch any of your shows.

▶   Make comments or give hearts in your shows on the app.

And you will not be able to:

▶   Follow them.

▶   Watch any of their shows.

▶   Make comments or give hearts in their shows on the app.

Abuse reporting

Periscope also has an abuse-reporting system[18] that is run during a live-stream itself, by other viewers, or as they are called 'flash juries'.

If one viewer feels that a comment is spam or abuse, a randomly selected group of other viewers will be asked whether they agree. If most of them *do*, then the original commenter receives a 'time-out' and is unable to post another comment for one minute. If they then go on to be found 'guilty' of a second offence, they are banned from the rest of the stream.

The advantages of this are that:

▶ Humans make the decision, not artificial intelligence.

▶ The presenter can continue presenting rather than have the added burden of moderating.

▶ It keeps the *context* of the comment – so a remark that may be considered vulgar in one setting may be appropriate in a serious discussion about FGM, for example.

Both kinds of trolls want an audience.

RECREATIONAL TROLLS

Recreational trolls are usually bored and want attention. Some are nasty individuals using online anonymity to disrupt other people's live-streams. They show up, do their thing and eventually leave.

CRIMINAL TROLLS

Criminal trolls use the same approaches in a much more aggressive fashion. They are cruel and hateful and display an intent to destroy reputations and businesses.

Often times trolls break the law. Their First Amendment Right to Free Speech is, in my opinion, limited. Depending on your state and federal jurisdiction, you may be able to hit a troll with money damages, injunctions and even attorney fees!

▶ **The United Kingdom**. Malicious Communications Act 1988, as well as Section 127 of the Communications Act 2003, 'internet trolls' face up to two years. These laws hold that sending messages which are "grossly offensive or of an indecent, obscene or menacing character" is an offense whether they are actually received by the intended recipient.

▶ **The United States**. Internet trolls can receive 41 months in prison under new state and federal laws regarding cyber-stalking, harassment, bullying and hacking.

Reproduced with kind permission: Mitch Jackson (http://mitchjackson.com/, https://streaming.lawyer/, https://twitter.com/mitchjackson)

Reporting a live-streamer

On Facebook:

> *The rules for live video are the same for all the rest of our content. A reviewer can interrupt a live stream if there is a violation of our Community Standards. Anyone can report content to us if they think it goes against our standards, and it only takes one report for something to be reviewed.*

Facebook Community Standards[19]

You can report a presenter if you believe they are breaking the Periscope Guidelines. In the show:

▶ Swipe right > scroll down > Report

▶ Or you can take a screenshot and send it to safety@Periscope.tv

▶ You can also contact Periscope through the app: People tab > Profile icon (top rhs) > Send Feedback

▶ Or direct at contact@Periscope.tv

FACEBOOK LIVE'S SUICIDE PREVENTION TOOL

According to the World Health Organisation (WHO), there is a suicide attempt every 40 seconds, and among 15–29-year-olds, suicide is the second leading cause of death.[20]

Facebook has a tool specifically for broadcasters and viewers of Facebook Live. They have developed the response by working with the Crisis text line, the National Eating Disorder Association and the National Suicide Prevention Lifeline.

If you watch someone and are concerned about their emotional state because of how they are talking or acting, you can report that live-stream to Facebook. Staff there will send help resources to the broadcaster (such as helpline details and suggestions on working through difficult times), while they are on-air.

Facebook is also using artificial intelligence based on previously reported posts to identify those who are most at risk. If a post or stream is flagged, then a member of staff will review the content and send help.

Account suspension

How might you have your app account disabled? By breaking their Guidelines and also by breaking the *spirit* of those Guidelines.

▶ Because Facebook prioritises live-video over pre-recorded video, some broadcasters show pre-recorded video through the live app to get more viewers. Often these are long loops of content, and often not what they own themselves, such as the three-year-old spacewalk[21] streamed in October 2016. At the time of writing, 19 million people have viewed the 'live' on Unilad's Facebook page[22] and around 26 million people via ViralUSA's page (which is no longer available).

Warning from Facebook:

Live is meant for live content. We want to make sure viewers aren't confused or misled by any uses of pre-recorded content in Facebook Live streams. For example, if a live sports show uses pre-recorded game highlights, they should be clearly distinguishable from the real-time content. Please refer to the Facebook platform policy for the Live API at https://developers.facebook.com/policy/.

▶ One presenter created a short promotional video for themselves, which they played on loop on their laptop overnight, with their phone live-streaming the loop for eight hours. Their account was suspended.

▶ NOTES

1 Adam Sherwin, *BBC Tells Tony Blackburn To Down Periscope*, www.independent.co.uk/ April 17th, 2015
2 Jack Smith IV, *Periscope Livestreaming Gets Reporters Fired*, https://mic.com/ June 26th, 2015
3 Jack Smith IV, *Periscope Livestreaming Gets Reporters Fired*, https://mic.com/ June 26th, 2015
4 *David Davies Jailed for Live-Streaming Cardiff Court Case*, www.bbc.co.uk/news/ February 22nd, 2017
5 James Winsoar, *Let's Discuss Scoping In Public*, www.jameswinsoar.com/ November 13th, 2015
6 Rebecca Casserly, *Getting Mugged Live on Periscope*, http://becboop.com/ September 28th, 2016
7 *Use Periscope? Criminals Could Find You*, www.abc-7.com/ August 4th, 2015

8 www.facebook.com/getsurrey/videos/vb.369041236456978/1521641484530275/?-type=2&theater

9 *Facebook Live Community Standards*, http://newsroom.fb.com July 8th, 2016

10 Kristina Cooke, *Facebook Developing Artificial Intelligence to Flag Offensive Live Videos*, http://uk.reuters.com/ December 1st, 2016

11 Kate Knibbs, *Facebook and Twitter Say They Ban Terrorism. Well, What the Hell Does That Mean?*, http://gizmodo.com/ December 30th, 2015

12 Rebecca Casserly, *Getting Mugged Live on Periscope*, http://becboop.com/ September 28th, 2016. Holding your phone in front of you while presenting a show outside in public is an open invitation to a thief. Consider using a special cord (myBunjee Universal Smartphone Holder, and Highline security leash) to reduce the chances of your device being snatched from your hand by a passer-by on a bike.

13 *CAP Advice and Training*, www.cap.org.uk/

14 The International Consumer Protection and Enforcement Network has downloadable 'Guidelines For Digital Influencers'

15 Ned Simons, *UKIP MEP David Coburn Went On Periscope and Everyone Pretended They Couldn't Hear Him*, www.huffingtonpost.co.uk/

16 Daniela Deane, *French President Gets Ridiculed on Live-Streaming App*, www.washingtonpost.com/ March 3rd, 2016

17 Kitty Knowles, *Periscope Stars Say Sexism Is "Part and Parcel" of Live Broadcast App*, www.thememo.com/ August 11th, 2015; also of interest: *A Live Stream of Sexist Comments?*, www.bbc.co.uk/ August 11th, 2015

18 *Periscope Community Moderation*, https://medium.com/periscope

19 *Facebook Community Standards*, www.facebook.com/communitystandards

20 Source: World Health Organization, *Preventing Suicide, A Global Imperative*, http://apps.who.int/iris/bitstream/10665/131056/1/9789241564779_eng.pdf?ua=1&ua=1 2014

21 www.bbc.co.uk/news/world-us-canada-37778973

22 www.facebook.com/uniladmag/videos/2430165973673114/

12
Tech tips and kit

▶ **INTRODUCTION**

Of course, live-video is all about live, in-the-moment stuff: it's great to point your camera phone at something and go live. After all, it's those qualities that make these apps such soar-away successes. And as long as you speak clearly and have light enough to see, you shouldn't need too much more 'equipment investment'.

But what if you want to take live-streaming a bit more seriously, maybe for work, for a charity, or for a sensitive subject? And you're still *holding* the phone out at arm's length, pointing into the sun, with poor sound and camera-work like something from *The Blair Witch Project*.

Then it's worth thinking a bit more about quality before your reputation, or that of the event, is damaged.

The suggested equipment here is just that: a suggestion. There is no room to list every item, and other makes and models are available, and from different websites at different prices. Satisfy yourself that the items listed on the following pages are compatible with your phone (and its size) and have the features you want before ordering. I have no link with any company or product other than where clearly indicated.

A few pounds/dollars will get you a half-decent external mic and a tripod so people can hear and see you better. A larger outlay will buy you a drone so you can achieve unique overhead views, or a stabiliser which will smooth out shots while you move.

Mobile content needs to look polished nowadays, and even live streams should have a look to them. It's a good idea to bring some production to it.

Al Roker[1]

On the other hand, investing *too much* in tech and set could go against you:

Sets with too many colored lights, effects, or 'professional' furniture tend to create artificial distance, driving viewer engagement down substantially because the hosts are viewed as less accessible. Multi-cam setups, teleprompters, and too many graphical overlays give the sense of an over-produced talk-show, not a piece of organic, relatable content.

Stephanie Patrick[2]

Remember: your topic, treatment and technique is always more important than the tech.

READER OFFER

Some of the equipment listed below is available at www.arkon.com, who have been kind enough to offer a 20% discount for the readers of my book.

Go to www.arkon.com and enter the coupon code 'livestreamhandbook' to activate it and get that 20% discount on your purchase.

I will get a small commission each time the code is used, but you get that massive 20% discount!

▶ AUDIO

It may seem obvious, but it's really important that people can hear you. After all, if they had *no picture* they could probably still get value from what you were saying, but if they had a picture but *no audio*, then they would probably be totally lost. *A stream without pictures is simply a podcast. One without audio is probably a waste of time.*

During your live-stream test-phase of your stream, check the audio quality. You won't be able to do this live (there is usually no audio meter on these apps), so you will either have to rely on a friend to watch and feed back to you, or do a private broadcast and watch it back. (This is easily done on Facebook Live: select the 'only me' option in the broadcast page. In Twitter Go Live/Periscope, go live from an alternative 'dummy' account.)

Doing this will avoid the plaintive "Can you hear me OK?", "What's the sound like?" when you start a live show.

And remember, the viewers themselves will be listening in a variety of situations (e.g. quiet/noisy, through the phone speaker/through headphones), so ensure the audio is as good as it can be when it leaves you.

Other audio tips:

▶ When you change the camera (from front-facing to rear-facing), the microphone flips as well. That means that if you are holding the phone and showing the viewers something in front of you, both the lens and the mic are pointing away from you, and that means that your voice will not be picked up very well.

▶ If you are filming someone in front of you, maybe they are explaining the view or describing how they whittle wood, but when you move the camera across to show the view (or down, to show their hands on the wood), the mic will also move away from the guest.

▶ The way you hear sound and the way your microphone 'hears' it is completely different. The human brain compensates for echoes in a room and filters out extraneous noise so you can concentrate on specific sounds. So if you are streaming from a quiet room, your voice may sound okay to you there in-the-moment, but once it's gone through a mic, it may sound thin, tinny and distant to your viewers. To counteract this, broadcast from a room with lots of items in it to absorb any echo: a carpet, curtains, furnishings. In that respect, offices with bare walls, desktops and big windows are far from ideal.

▶ Know where the in-built microphones are on your model of handset and be careful not to touch them. If you do, the viewers will get an annoying scratchy-rustling on the soundtrack.

▶ Ensure that any external mic you plug into your phone has a TRRS connection. Without getting *too* technical, it's like the one that's on the end of your headphones that you use on your phone. T stands for 'tip' (the pointed end that goes into the socket first), R is for 'ring' (each of the bands of metal on the connection), and S for 'sleeve' (the end of the plug that leads into the cable). Only a connection with *two* rings will work in a phone (hence 'TRRS'; some leads only have *one* ring and so are referred to as 'TRS leads'). Another way to remember: the lead you want has to have three black bands on the tip (these separate the two 'rings' from each other, and the tip and the sleeve!). Plugs which adapt a TRS lead into a TRRS one are available.

▶ Depending on the mic you use and the design of its connection, you may have to remove your phone from its case so the plug can be properly inserted.

▶ If you can be on a Wi-Fi connection, use that rather than a phone data connection. That will avoid the electronic buzz as the phone searches for a signal, appearing on your audio.

Using the mic on your phone is usually fine if you are inside. Some phones come with a set of wired headphone earbuds, which have a microphone built into them which can also be used. You don't need to put them in your ears (after all you're not *listening* to anything), but just tuck the cable into the top of your shirt or blouse (maybe loop it through a button-hole), so the microphone part is about 6 inches under your chin.

Investing in an external microphone is a great idea, especially if you are outside. In that situation, you may have:

▶ Lots more noise for your voice to battle against

▶ The wind against the in-built mic on your actual device

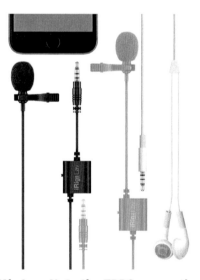

FIGURE 12.1 The iRig Mic Lav. Note the TRRS connection and the adapter to plug two microphones into a single feed to the phone

Source: IK Multimedia Production SRL www.ikmultimedia.com

▶ The phone further away from your mouth (when outside you are more likely to be holding the phone at arm's length and moving it, rather than inside when it is likely to be on a static tripod)

▶ Greater use of the back-facing camera, with the inherent 'off-mic' sound quality

You may want to consider getting a clip-mic/tie-mic (these are also called lavalier or 'lav' mics) that you can attach to your shirt. Consider something like the MXL MM160 (www.mxlmics.com/microphones/mobilemedia/MM-160/) or the Rode Lavalier + (www.rode.com/microphones/lavalier).

A handheld mic like the ones the TV reporters use will make you look more professional whether you are interviewing at a conference or presenting a stream from your office (where you can slip it into a mic stand). Consider mics such as the MXL MM130 (www.mxlmics.com/microphones/mobilemedia/MM-130/) or the iRig (www.ikmulti media.com/products/irigmichd/). Both plug directly into the headphone socket of your phone and come with a splitter jack so you can use the mic and headphones at the same time, so you (or a colleague) can monitor what the mic is picking up.

If you already have a microphone with a larger connection on the end, you can get something such as the iRig XLR to minijack adapter (www.ikmultimedia.com/prod ucts/irigproio/), with a lightning lead that will plug into your phone.

Lots of companies will make a branded mic flag for you (the box that goes around the top of the mic) or a windshield (the foam top).

Extension cables are also available for microphones, to give you a bit more freedom of movement. Of course, it may be easier if you are not attached to your phone at all!

FIGURE 12.2 A range of iRig microphones

Source: IK Multimedia Production SRL www.ikmultimedia.com

FIGURE 12.3 The iRig I/O, so you can use a standard professional microphone into your phone

Source: IK Multimedia Production SRL www.ikmultimedia.com

The Azden ProXD wireless mic (www.azden.com/products/wireless-systems/pro-xd/) comes with a transmitter and receiver with batteries that run up to ten hours. You clip the lav mic to your shirt, and the wire leads to a small pack that you can tuck into your belt. The receiver is plugged into the phone. The Samson Go Mic Mobile (www.samsontech.com/samson/products/wireless-systems/gomicmobile/gomicmobile/) lets you have two wireless mics combine into the same audio channel.

You may also want to get a splitter so that you can put in two *cabled* mics (whether hand-held or lav) through to the same phone. This is great for interviews or double-headed shows. One step further would be getting a mini-mixer. The Saramonic SmartRig+ (www.saramonicusa.com/products/smartrig-2-channel-xlr-3-5mm-microphone-audio-mixer-with-phantom-power-preamp-guitar-interface-for-dslr-cameras-camcorders-smartphones) lets you mix two mics into one output, and the MXL MM-4000 MiniMixer+ (www.mxlmics.com/microphones/mobilemedia/MM-4000/) mixes four inputs. So you can control separate levels for mics, a theme tune or sound effects through a PC and send the mix directly to your phone's audio input.

▶ TRIPODS, MOUNTS AND GIMBALS

Having something to hold your phone means:

- ▶ It's still and steady when you want it to be, so avoiding the seasickness effect for your viewers.

- ▶ There's a smooth and seamless glide when you do move around.

- ▶ Your hands are free to gesticulate, make notes, turn the camera around and turn off the broadcast.

All of which will help your production and performance!

Remember the lens is your audience, so set the phone on a tripod so the lens of the phone is at eye level with your own eyes. That way you will not be literally talking down to your viewers, and they won't be looking up your nose or have a great view of your ceiling. (We like ceilings, there's nothing to top them, apart from the floor of the room above, but they don't make great screen-fillers when you are trying to impart words of wisdom.)

There are a number of mini tripods designed specifically for smartphones, such as the GorillaPod by Joby (https://joby.com/) or the Arkon Universal Smartphone Holder MG2TRIXL   (http://www.arkon.com/product/MG2TRIXL-iphone-tripod-flexible. html) some of which can be twisted around trees or poles for use outdoors.

Or if you already have a large 'photographer's tripod', then get the adapter in which to hold your phone, which will screw onto the baseplate (such as the Glif Tripod Mount & Stand – www.studioneat.com/products/glif).

On-the-road units into which you can place your phone are numerous. Some are handle-and-clamp designs (such as these in the Shoulderpod range – www.shoulder pod.com/), and others (including those by the same company) are more advanced. You can place your phone onto a rig or inside a frame, to which you can also mount an external light, directional microphone and so on, on various brackets.

If you need to stream from two devices at the same time (perhaps from two different accounts, or to a Facebook Live page *and* a Twitter Go Live/Periscope account), then mounts are available that hold two phones. Perhaps be a little creative: one phone/ stream shows 'you', the other shows 'the view'.

FIGURE 12.4 Just a small part of the Shoulderpod range, which will help im- prove the stability of your phone

Source: Shoulderpod, www.shoulderpod.com

FIGURE 12.5 The Arkon TW Broadcaster Pro, Side-by-Side Phone Tripod Mount and TW Broadcaster Live Streaming Kit

Source: Arkon, www.arkon.com

FIGURE 12.6 The iKlip Grip Pro features a large, ergonomic handle that expands into a sturdy tripod, an integrated locking extension pole that extends
up to 62 cm (24″) for getting those 'above the crowd' shots and selfies

Source: IK Multimedia Production SRL www.ikmultimedia.com

A cheap alternative is, of course, a selfie-stick. Although you can't stick it on your
desk or in the ground, it will stop your arm from getting too tired of holding your
phone out in front of you. Additionally, it could help you achieve some slightly different perspectives of a scene.

If you are holding your camera or walking with it, then it's almost inevitable that you
will get shaky shots. Handheld gimbals (also known as stabilisers, steady-cams or gyro-
scopes), support your phone while you are moving about. The three-axis ones are the
best and have motors and counterbalance weights which even out any movement you
make. They are so effective that a walk with your phone looks to the viewer as though
you are gliding, or using a camera on tracks. Going up stairs or running can give the
impression that you are using a drone. Gimbals are expensive, but if you are serious,
then it may be worth investing in one, particularly if you regularly present outdoors or
on location live-streams such as city tours or walks around museums. One thing to be
aware of is that a gimbal's counterbalancing is very sensitive, so depending on the design
of the one you use, if a lead for an external mic touches one of the weights, it can throw it
off-kilter. The same may happen if such a lead is pulled or snagged while you are on-air.

If you are showing a scene, move the camera s-l-o-w-l-y. What may be slow to you in
real life may be like a rollercoaster ride for someone watching on a small phone screen:

▶ They don't see much at any one time.

▶ Neither do they have any peripheral vision, so they can't anticipate what
they will be shown next and could be a little disorientated (e.g. on a tour
around a house).

▶ Some of what they see may be covered in comments.

If you don't have a stabiliser for 'moving' shots or panning, it's best to hold the camera with both hands or, better still, let events unfold in front of you.

▶ LIGHTING

Just as your ears hear sounds differently from what your microphone picks up, so too your brain and eyes interpret light differently from your phone camera. What looks soft and moody to you looks dark and grainy to the phone as it can only average out the light for exposure.

People can take magnificent video or stunning still photos on their phones using focus and exposure settings or pull-focus techniques, but none of these is available through live-streaming apps, although you can adjust the brightness slightly in the Facebook Live menu.

So if you show a sunset, the camera will pick up the sun rather than balance it with the darker land around. (In this situation, lower your phone so the camera picks up more of the land and then adjusts its exposure accordingly.)

It is best to present a live-video from somewhere that is well-lit, whether that is inside or outside. You can get small lights which clip onto some of the mounts described earlier, or if you stream from inside you can use soft-box lights (on stands and with diffuser screens) that give a natural-light look to your presentation. Also available are phone cases (such as those by Lumee – https://lumee.com/) that have in-built, dimmable lights that either shine on you or your guest.

Remember that the lower the light (such as at dusk or under an electric bulb), the harder the phone will have to work. Although you should aim for the light across

FIGURE 12.7 Small battery-powered lights can easily be fitted onto a rig, such as this one by Shoulderpod, along with an external mic, too

Source: Shoulderpod, www.shoulderpod.com

your face to be pretty even, a bit of shadow is good as it gives a bit of depth. So harsh shadows aren't good, and neither is a bright light. If there is some of the latter, draw some curtains or shut a door. Or move outside where the light from that 800,000-mile-wide ball of fire in the sky is pretty much even!

Don't have the camera facing into the sun: it's better for you to have a slight squint and a clear shot than to be silhouetted on the screen, with possible damage to your camera's lens (and annoyance of your viewers) when it picks up the sun's glare.

So if you are the cameraperson for someone else, 'have the sun on your bum'. Remember what the Old Master artists knew hundreds of years ago: the sun is best and more mellow in the morning and afternoon, so avoid the harsh midday brightness if you can.

▶ LENSES

It's inevitable that the lens of your phone will get dirty and dusty. After all, it spends a lot of time in your pocket or bag. Not only will a speck or a fingerprint affect your video, they'll also stop light from getting into the camera sensor. So use a soft lens cloth to give the lens a wipe just before you go live.

Your phone only has a digital zoom, so although you can out-pinch the screen to have more of a close-up of a scene, the picture will become blurry and unfocused. So either be where you want to be to start with or zoom with your feet (i.e. walk closer to what you want to be in full frame).

You can buy additional clip-on lenses or lenses which you can screw to a phone case or frame. The ones made by companies such as Olloclip (www.olloclip.com) can give you a fish-eye or macro view, and also (most useful) a wide-angle view. Using this latter lens will give your stream a greater field of vision so you can have a double-headed presentation team without them being up-close on a couch, and show more of that sunrise or carnival scene.

▶ BATTERY

WARNING! Live-streaming eats power! Viewers will get frustrated if the stream stops at an important point, and having that happen will reflect badly on your brand. So make sure you have enough power before you start your production.

External batteries are pretty cheap and range from small one-time charge options to larger packs which can charge two phones at once, a number of times over. Depending on the model of your device, you may be able to charge and stream simultaneously.

FIGURE 12.8 The different field of view achieved by using a wide-angled rather than a normal lens

HOW TO PRESERVE YOUR PHONE'S BATTERY AND DATA

Your phone is working hard all of the time updating and refreshing apps, checking on your location, finding a signal and sending notifications. Turn off these settings so your battery lasts longer. *(Instructions may not apply to every device or operating system.)*

▶ Reduce the brightness of the screen.

▶ Reduce the time before the phone auto-locks.

▶ Turn on power-saving mode.

▶ Turn off Wi-Fi and Bluetooth.

▶ Turn off auto-updates to apps.

▶ Turn off location services.

▶ Turn off notifications.

▶ Close down apps so they are not running in the background.

▶ Delete and re-install apps, which effectively re-boots them and clears out their cache.

▶ Turn off auto-play for videos.

▶ DATA

WARNING! Live-streaming video is a data-hog! If you are on Wi-Fi using a live-stream app as a broadcaster or viewer, all of this is free. But if you are on 3G or 4G your data allowance is being gobbled, and data-gobbling is the price we pay for immediacy.

You will use more data when the phone is struggling to live-stream your video:

- ▶ In low light
- ▶ When there's a poor signal
- ▶ When you move the phone around a lot

Video is a bandwidth hog. Tests by *The Wall Street Journal*[3] suggested that watching just five minutes of Periscope broadcasts on a smartphone was equivalent to nearly two hours of Web surfing or sending and receiving 300 emails. (Periscope disputes these figures.)

A survey by Krishna De[4] (www.krishna.me) suggested that a two-minute stream on:

- ▶ Facebook Live to a Profile (including downloading the recording to a phone and uploading the recording to the Profile) used 16.285 MB per minute.
- ▶ Facebook Live to a Page (including downloading the recording, but *not* uploading it) used 5.335 MB per minute.
- ▶ Periscope (including saving to the phone, and automatically uploading to the app) was 5.765 MB per minute.

If you are away from home and don't want to lose the connection, check out free Wi-Fi hotspots at shops, restaurants and public buildings or through your contract provider. If not, there are various apps which will map where they are.

If you are in an office or public space, the Wi-Fi connection may be really slow, either because lots of people are on doing general surfing, or because lots of other people are also streaming (often an issue at conferences and major events).

You may have to invest in a bigger data allowance package from your provider. After all, if this is your business or hobby, it may be worth it.

Also worth considering is a mobile Wi-Fi hotspot or dongle. This data is often cheaper than that on your phone (especially if you are using phone data that's extra to your allowance.) It may also be slightly faster and, if so, will save on battery power, too.

Download a data-monitoring app on your phone to check how much of your allowance you are using, to help you decide whether you need to put in a bit more investment.

▶ STORAGE

When you have completed a Facebook Live or a Periscope, you are prompted to save the video to your camera roll. That's often a very good idea, but how much space will you need? After all, the cameras on phones record in pretty good resolution, which will increase the storage required, and that's before the duration of a video is taken into consideration.

To find out how much free space you have (on an iPhone, because Android phones differ so much between makes and models):

   ▶   Settings > General > About > Available

There are also various apps (such as Quickspace) which will interrogate your phone to determine how much space is left and present that in terms of the number of photos or minutes of video that you have room for.

To save space on your phone, you can transfer your videos (or photos) from your Camera Roll to your PC or Mac using flash drives such as the iXpand range by SanDisk (who also make similar models for Android devices) – www.sandisk.co.uk/home/mobile-device-storage/ixpand.

▶ NOTES

1 Troy Dreier, *Al Roker Talks Brand Marketing at Inaugural Stream Con NYC*, www.streamingmedia.com/ October 30th, 2015
2 Stephanie Patrick, *The 5 Secrets to Livestreaming Success From the Game Theorists, YouTube's Largest Regular Livestreamers*, www.tubefilter.com/ February 8th, 2017
3 Yoree Koh and Ryan Knutson, *Watch Out, Live Video Is the New Data Hog*, www.wsj.com/ September 24th, 2015
4 Krishna De, *How Much Data Is Needed to Live Stream Using Periscope or Facebook Live*, www.krishna.me/ August 8th, 2016

PART IV
On air

The pre-show prep is nearly done. Now we can get your show on the air.

In this section of the book is the best advice for what to do and say at the start, middle and end of your live-stream. Plus, explanations are given about features such as the comments and emojis that you'll be sent by viewers.

13

Your vital title

▶ INTRODUCTION

Just before you start your show, Facebook Live says: "Describe your live video" and Periscope asks, "What are you seeing now?"

What you write becomes the 'title' of your show. On Facebook, this appears above your video feed. On Twitter Go Live/Periscope, it's on the screen when someone joins the show and is also what you can choose to be auto-tweeted as a Notification to your followers.

A compelling description will help attract more people to watch your video when it is live, or once it has ended. It is the advert for your show and entices people to watch. Unlike, perhaps, these actual titles:

Pausaaaaaaaaa

Asian food

we cos

Garden

TRIPLE FOAM

Hanging

Love you too

Blahblahblah

FIGURE 13.1 The title page on your Periscope, which you can have tweeted to your followers (If you broadcast via Twitter Go Live, your standard tweet text becomes your 'title'.)

Source: Periscope

You need to spend some time coming up with an awesome title. Tell people why they need to spend minutes and megs watching you. So:

▶ Make the title honest.

▶ Make it catchy.

▶ Sell the content.

▶ Ask yourself: Why should they watch?

▶ WHO WILL SEE THE TITLE?

▶ Your followers *now* on Facebook and Twitter Go Live /Periscope

▶ Anyone else your followers have retweeted that tweet to or shared the show with

▶ Anyone on Twitter who searches for the # that you have used

▶ Anyone whose @name you use, or people searching for that @name

▶ Everyone scanning the list or map of every show that is live now, or recently live: www.facebook.com/livemap and www.periscope.tv

▶ People who later scan your Facebook page (or the messages they have received from it), your Twitter feed (or the messages they have received from it), or your list of videos on your Facebook or Periscope bio (if you have chosen to save them)

▶ Your followers' followers, who had the show recommended or shared to them

▶ YOUR TITLE FORMAT

Of course, you can be unplanned and off-the-cuff in titling your show in the same way as you can be about presenting it, but it stands to reason that you will get more viewers if you give them some clue about why they should watch.

'Hanging' may not get many of your friends to watch.

'Hanging at the beach' may get more.

'Hanging at the beach with the kids and a drone at sunset' is likely to persuade an even greater number to jump in and take a look.

You may want to consider creating a simple and compelling title style and use it consistently. That may be a format like this:

#Paris On Foot: Ep 1 "The Left Bank to the Sacre-Couer"

In this example, the show has a name (*'Paris on Foot'*), and each 'episode' has a number (*'Ep 1'*), and then follows details of that particular episode (*'The Left Bank to the Sacre-Couer'*), and it's the same format each time. This consistency helps with brand awareness and also post-live viewing: someone whose first experience of the show is, say, episode 10, will realise that there are other previous episodes to watch, too.

In the example above there was also a hashtag. If you use one of these (e.g. #travel, #music, #food), your Periscope will be curated into that topic when you end the show. This will make it more discoverable. See suggested topics in the Periscope Global List in the app.

▶ YOUR TITLE CONTENT

Create a catchy title that humans will like and algorithms will love. You need to give context to the pictures and persuade a viewer who is scanning their feed to click through and watch (and hear) the actual show.

Make the title short so it doesn't overflow the character quota on any of the platforms, meaning that your title runs out mid-way through. Your title for a Facebook Live broadcast can be longer than the 120 characters for Periscope, as it appears as a traditional Facebook post.

Sometimes, the most effective title is the simplest and most straightforward:

▶ Elijah Wood posted a show with the title *"Jellyfish"* while visiting an aquarium, which is exactly what the video showed.

▶ *"Watch our live unboxing of @Microsoft's @Surface 3 now!"* literally does what it says on the box.

▶ Or use a title that explains *"This is what we'll do . . ."* or *"This is what you'll learn . . ."*.

Or maybe use a headline and content based around a list:

▶ *"10 Ways To Win At Life"*

▶ *"6 Ways To Use Fresh Lemon In Cleaning"*

Or spell out a word as an acronym:

▶ *"Why fruit is B.A.D. for you"* where the letters b, a, and d stand for the initial letters of your bullet points.

You can also add other terms that will be eyeball-grabbing:

▶ *"Followers Only"* or *"Members Only"* will get people who think they will get exclusive information.

▶ *"Exclusive"*, *"News"*, and *"Breaking News"* will also get attention.

Emojis and CAPITAL LETTERS, used *sparingly*, will also stand out in someone's stream, especially if you use the same series of them each time, as part of your brand. (Beware: an icon you use on your phone may not appear the same way on someone else's.)

But again, don't mislead. The Periscope entitled *"How to invite ur followers to ur own broadcast . . . a 60-second tip"* was actually over 40 minutes long.

Sure, you'll get more viewers if you write *"Porno"* or *"18+"* in the title. But unless that's what you provide (and I suggest you don't), then you'll most likely get more viewers, but they won't stick around and they won't come back.

Trust: work to earn it and keep it.

Once you have composed your title, and checked it for typos (your brand reputation is at risk), copy it into your phone's memory. Then, if you have a glitch once you are live and you need to start the show again, the title is ready to paste back in.

POWER WORDS

Use upbeat, positive and dynamic words in your titles as a way to encourage people to stop and watch.

So instead of "*Here's a* good *view of the cathedral*", consider using:

▶ *Amazing*

▶ *Spectacular*

▶ *Wonderful*

Instead of "*5 Ways to Save Money*", maybe talk about:

▶ *Hidden secrets to save a fortune.*

▶ *Confidential tips to make massive savings.*

▶ *Insider tips to hit the jackpot.*

It's the same content but with a much more alluring title.

You can find more words and phrases that will help you sell your show in the book *Find-a-Line* on www.lulu.com/shop/peter-stewart/find-a-line/ebook/product-20728719.html

▶ TITLE TRACTION TRICKS

You could base your show, and therefore its title, around what people who are interested in your *overall topic* are talking about specifically *right now*.

So if you present a show on football/soccer, see what's trending on Twitter to give you a suggestion on what you could be talking about, and include that reference as a hashtag in your title.

Buffer says that:

▶ Tweets with hashtags get 2x more engagement than those without.

▶ Tweets with one or two hashtags have 21% higher engagement than those with three or more.

▶ Tweets that use more than two hashtags actually show a 17% drop in engagement.[1]

If you use a hashtag, when people search on Twitter for the hashtag to do with their favourite topic or TV show, the link to your show also comes up in their results. *So to be clear, hashtags in a Periscope title don't work independently in Periscope itself. But you want to have them in a Periscope title, so your show is more easily found by people on Twitter, when your title is auto-tweeted at the start of your broadcast.*

USING UNIQUE HASHTAGS

People don't necessarily tag you in tweets, and if they are tweeting the link to your live show or the replay, then your Twitter name may not be mentioned then either.

But if you create a *unique hashtag* that you always use in your Periscope titles (or in links you tweet to your live or once-live Facebook videos), then you will be able to track your supporters by simply searching for references to that hashtag on Twitter.

So in the example above, as well as writing *#Paris* (which would have attracted those searching for the city's name), you could also regularly use *#ParisOnFoot*. Then, either by doing a basic search on Twitter or using lists on Hootsuite or TweetDeck, you'll quickly see who has re-tweeted or liked your original post. Those people are your supporters, and so it'd be good to tweet and thank them.

These tools will help you decide on the best hashtag to use:

▶ www.twitter.com – just go to Twitter itself to see the trending hashtags (online it's on the LHS). They're already tailor-made for you so they're not 'universal'.

▶ www.trendsmap.com – shows popular hashtags by location.

▶ www.hashtags.org – includes the trends of the hashtags, that is when they are popular during the day or year.

▶ www.keyhole.co/ – shows a cloud of popular hashtags.

You could also use the auto-complete suggestion drop-down menu on YouTube or YouTube's Trends Dashboard (www.youtube.com/trendsdashboard) that lets you quickly explore what's popular in different places around the world, as well as within specific demographic groups. Or use Google Trends (www.google.com/trends). So, tie your show in with what people are talking about right now, if it fits, but don't lie or mislead them.

All these tips should help you get more traffic to your show and more traction on what you are saying or selling. But remember: *Titles will help you get the viewers, but good content will keep them.*

THE HEADLINE ANALYZER

This great website will help you:

▶ Use headline types that get the most traction for social shares, traffic and search engine ranking.

▶ Make sure you have the right word balance to write readable headlines that command attention.

▶ See the best word and character length, while also seeing how your readers will scan your headlines.

http://coschedule.com/headline-analyzer

▶ NOTE

1 Source: Kevan Lee, *How to Use Hashtags: How Many, Best Ones, and Where to Use Them*, https://blog.bufferapp.com January 27th, 2016

14

Comments and reactions

▶ INTRODUCTION

One of the reasons live-streaming is so much more powerful than other social media, is the real-time interaction between who is presenting and who is watching.

The feedback that viewers give is shown on the screen for the host and other viewers to see, and are either written comments or pictorial reactions. On Facebook Live viewers can choose from a series of 'emotion' emojis, and on Periscope, they tap the screen to give hearts.

▶ COMMENTS

(There's much more on 'abusive comments' and 'trolls' in the chapter on 'live-stream privacy, security and safety'.) According to Facebook, people comment ten times more on Facebook Live videos than on regular videos. Comments, such as suggestions and questions, are important because:

- ▶ **Introductions** – They give the opportunity for people to say who they are, where they are watching and what they do.

- ▶ **Interaction** – They provide live and instant feedback: the chance for viewers to ask questions, ask the broadcaster to move the camera, ask the guest something specific and to dis/agree with what is being talked about.

- ▶ **Relationship-building** – The broadcaster and the viewers get to know who's in the audience and begin to recognise names and people. The broadcaster can greet people personally and start building a personality. In some apps, the viewers can respond directly to other people in the audience, and in Periscope anyone watching can tap on a comment to discover more about that viewer and follow them, thereby increasing their own community.

▶ **Data-capture** – After the live-stream, the broadcaster can approach the viewers individually to thank them for watching, offer extra help or advice, and strengthen the relationship.

▶ **Audience building** – On Facebook Live, the more people interact with your live-stream with suggestions and questions, the more your video will automatically be shared to other newsfeeds. That's because the show will be spotted by the algorithms as having active viewers and, so, great content.

▶ **Stickiness** – The more people are commenting, it's inevitable that they are staying on the stream longer, which helps your overall analytics.

You want an active audience, and acknowledging and responding to messages encourages engagement and fosters a two-way conversation. So urge people to message you on the screen and then try and spot and answer questions, thank those who sent them for their contributions, and comment on the comments! Don't just stare at the chat-feed in silence! Indeed, you'll get *more* comments if you reply to the ones you already have!

It is most effective to ask a question and then say something along the lines of "I'd love to know what you think, put your thoughts in the comment box". In other words, specifically explain what it is you'd like viewers to do and how. Obviously, you don't want to be patronising, but psychologically they are more likely to send you a message if you subtly remind them how to do it.

> *You may have a well-planned live broadcast . . . but . . . you should be ready to change. Addressing your viewers' feedback live is . . . an opportunity for your brand to engage with your audience. . . . Learning about what your audience actually cares about can help guide what content you choose to share.*

Jacob Warwick[1]

ENGAGE WITH YOUR VIEWERS

If you build a personal connection with people and give them valuable content, you will strengthen the 'know, like and trust' factor. You can do this by:

▶ Welcoming people to the show

▶ Using their names

▶ Thanking them for watching

▶ Asking for their comments, questions, thoughts and feedback

▶ Responding to their comments, questions, thoughts and feedback

▶ Humanising your brand by showing your genuine personality

▶ Tailoring your content to the needs of the viewers and restructuring it in the light of their reactions

▶ Being honest and open in your role as a producer/presenter:

▷ Having a show title that doesn't mislead

▷ Being open about any sponsorship or products reviewed

▷ On Twitter Go Live/Periscope particularly, not buying hearts or followers

Questions that get comments

Ask questions that engage and involve your audience:

▶ "Thanks for watching; where are you from?"

▶ "What did you want to get from this show?"

▶ "Are you ready for the next idea/suggestion?"

▶ "Shall I go left, or right?"/"Shall I go inside?"

▶ "What do you think?"

▶ "Has the same thing happened to you?"

▶ "What would you have done?"

▶ "What kind of content would be of benefit in the future?"

When viewers can't comment

In Periscope this may be because:

▶ The broadcaster has decided to limit comments to only those that they themselves follow. This limits the viewable chat to more of the people they trust and helps the broadcaster control the conversation to a larger extent than having it public. You do this by tapping the 'speech bubble' in your broadcast screen just before you go live.

▶ The viewer has been blocked by the broadcaster or by other viewers.

▶ Commenting abilities have been limited, perhaps because the viewer has been considered responsible for excessive spamming, trolling and harassment.

Hiding comments

The Facebook Live or Periscope viewer or broadcaster can hide the comments (and hearts) during a show. You may want to do this if the reactions cover too much of what you want to see (e.g. a view or whiteboard notes). On Facebook, swipe right on your mobile device. On Periscope, tap on the '. . .' at the bottom of the screen for the option.

Seeing comments better

Broadcast via one phone and have another device with a larger screen, such as an iPad, alongside you on which you will be better able to see the comments.

On Facebook Live, a broadcaster can scroll up and down the screen to see comments and answer or address them their leisure. On Periscope they float up the screen and then disappear. On both apps, when a video is replayed, the comments will appear at the same point that they did when the show was live.

Incidentally, help for blind users of Twitter Go Live/Periscope can be found in the article *Live Video Streaming Around the World* at www.applevis.com.

CHATTERBOX

For popular users of Periscope, the comments can fly up the screen so fast they are missed. 'Chatterbox for Periscope' (search for it in the Chrome web store or at https://chrome.google.com/webstore/detail/chatterbox-for-periscope/bdg-kofekoejgkpjbjmdhmmdfckgfgigg) is a Chrome-only extension that helps you by archiving your comments so you never miss a comment or question during your broadcast. Install the extension and then open up your browser window on your computer while streaming on your phone, and comments will then start appearing in the browser window.

Click on a comment and you will see who sent it and then can reply to it directly. You can also use Chatterbox to monitor other people's Scopes, so you can scroll through and see the questions sent to, say, a show that was broadcast by a competitor! Why? Because:

▶ If that Scoper didn't answer questions sent to them, then you can instead . . . and position yourself as more of an authority than they are!

"Hey, I spotted your question in a recent Scope about XYZ. The answer is because ABC. I hope that helps!"

▶ The questions they are asked most often will give you a tip-off about what people want to know, and hence ideas for future content for your show.

You can also create a simple poll in which you can ask a question with an 'A' or 'B' alternative answer. Each time one of the words linked to the A or B response is included in a comment from a viewer, a bar-chart alters to give a running percentage.

Answering comments

While you are presenting the show:

▶ Glance at the comments and take in what people have written.

▶ Try not to stop dead while you read them to yourself. . .

▶ or to read all of them out loud (after all, everyone else can see them too, they don't need them read to them!).

▶ During your presentation, at a convenient moment, pause your show to answer and engage comments.

When you answer a question, start by summarising it in case others may not have seen it (or in case you repurpose the stream as an audio-only podcast):

▶ "Gerald has just asked whether we have these in blue. Yes, that's one of the updates we'll have in stores this spring."

▶ "So Susan, you want me to go show more of the production line?"

▶ "To answer Simon's query, yes, we are part of the Fairtrade Alliance."

▶ "A good point from Jen there, and she's right, there are four ways that you can . . ."

Over time you will develop a knack for saying one thing out loud while reading something quite different to yourself, judging its significance and either answering it immediately (perhaps by incorporating it directly into your verbal flow, as above) or remembering it to respond to later.

Thanking those who comment, and addressing them by name, validates that person. It is personable and relatable and another thing that TV presenters can't do. (Did you ever call a radio station to get a song request played, and got a thrill when they said your name on air? That's how it is when a viewer gets a name-check in your show.)

THE READER-REPLIER BROADCASTER

When you are presenting, it is quite tricky to read comments internally and stay fluent verbally at the same time. Stopping to read the texts (either to yourself or out loud) can interrupt the flow of your show as you get side-tracked. If that happens, then both parts of your role suffer:

▶ Your presentation of the show

▶ Your response to the comments made by your viewers

Perhaps you have seen a number of people, some 'professional live-streamers', who struggle to cope with the comments and 'self-interrupt': they get halfway through a sentence and then stop to say hi to someone who's just joined or to answer a question that just popped up. They are satisfying that single person but ignoring their main audience.

So decide in advance how and when you will respond to comments:

▶ If you have several points to make in your show, you may want to invite questions in between each of them,

▶ After two or three points,

▶ Or ask viewers to send them just at the end.

Also politely suggest that viewers only ask another question as you finish the answer to the previous one, not *while* you are answering it!

If you ask a question and suggest viewers write a response, wait while they do so. Don't charge straight on with your next point.

When you can't respond to comments

If you are in a place where you can't speak out loud to your viewers (maybe you are streaming a church service, or conference, or during a one-minute silence), then:

▶ **Set expectations** – and say at the start of the broadcast that you won't be able to respond verbally, and why that is.

▶ **Consider having a sign** – and show this periodically to explain the situation.

▶ **Have a colleague** – who can write in the chat to explain the situation.

▶ **In Facebook Live** – (which allows more characters), explain the situation in the description of the show, or post a pinned comment in the chat.

There are different kinds of commenters that you will soon become used to, some of whom will disrupt your stream deliberately:

▶ The person who SHOUTS MESSAGES IN CAPITALS TO GET NOTICED or includes dozens of emojis

▶ Those who constantly react to everything you say and send a comment every few seconds

▶ Thunder-stealers who anticipate what you are about to say and write it on the screen first

▶ Viewers who carry on a conversation between themselves on your screen

▶ People who ask dumb questions such as "What's this all about?" or "Nice top. Where did you get it?" or "I've just joined, can you repeat everything so far for me?"

▶ Commenters who jump in to show off that they are there, but only stay for a minute or two, perhaps just waiting for you to say their name. Such people often make a comment such as "Hi everyone!" to get personal validation from other viewers.

▶ And of course, the troll (See elsewhere in this book.)

Also see:

▶ How to deal with abusive comments, in the chapter "Live-Stream Privacy, Security and Safety".

▶ More about having a colleague to help monitor comments and write comments themselves during a stream, in the chapter "The Live-Stream Producer".

▶ REACTIONS

During your broadcast, your viewers can send emoticons (smileys, emojis) onto the screen. This is instant feedback like Instagram's hearts or Facebook's 'Likes', given by viewers when they appreciate something that you have said or shown. They can be considered your 'applause', a 'popularity rating', or 'momentum meter', and it's often heartening to get them. Indeed, on Periscope they are actually cartoon hearts.

The developers of Periscope say another reason they developed the hearts was to make the process of going live more friendly than having a big red blinking 'live now' light that you see on the front of video cameras, and to indicate to the presenter of a show that their stream is 'live'. Non-verbal feedback from this type of interaction gives you as a broadcaster confidence and helps you grow your presentation skills.

Facebook Live – viewers can choose from symbols that represent 'like', 'love', 'haha', 'wow', 'sad' and 'angry'. Comments and emojis can also be given to the broadcast when the viewer is watching the archived show. At Hallowe'en, these have been added to with a limited-edition range, including a 'cackling witch' and 'Frankenstein'.

Periscope – viewers on this app simply tap the screen to send a flurry of 'hearts' up the screen. There are no other regular symbols to indicate other emotions, although the developers sometimes introduce designs on a short-term basis during events such as Hallowe'en (bats) or Thanksgiving (turkeys). The colour of each heart corresponds to the tint of the bio-pic of the viewer who has sent it, and the colour changes each time that viewer logs on to a different stream. Colours are allocated randomly and you can't change them, although it has been suggested that purple is always the first colour to be allocated. Each Periscoper's tally of hearts-received appears on their bio page. Hearts can also be given to the broadcast when the viewer is watching the archived show.

Some Periscopers buy hearts (and Followers) via sites such as http://scopefuel.com/ to appear more popular. After all, it's the classic domino effect: appearing to be popular encourages more people to watch and follow. But as Periscoper Mike Hand once

FIGURE 14.1 Facebook Live reaction symbols

Source: Facebook

wrote in a tweet: "buying social proof like fans, followers and hearts is like a bloke taking Viagra and not telling his girlfriend".

With analytics, it's easy to see whether someone's heart-rate has jumped considerably overnight, and if you are caught by Periscope, then you may well have your account suspended. As they point out in their Guidelines, "Purchasing 'hearts' or paying to have a broadcast 'shared' to increase the popularity of the content.... Using or promoting third-party sites or services that claim to get you more followers" are explicitly banned.

Asking for emojis

One big takeaway from this section: your 'engagement' score on your live-stream is in part calculated by the reactions that you are given – as well as the shares and the comments. But of these, a reaction is the easiest for a viewer to give. Therefore, encourage generous use of these icons ("Send me hearts if you love what I'm talking about", "Send me angry faces if that makes you cross, too . . .") to increase your engagement score in the easiest possible way. (Note the use of the plural in those two examples: "*send me hearts*" not "*send me a heart*", to increase your score even further.)

But remember, it's not the number of smileys or hearts that are important (or even the number of followers you have), *it's the number of people who watch your stream* (or better still, how long they stay watching!). So give viewers great content during the show, and support and advice after the show, and brilliant value all around.

Shows which consist of little more than "*send us hearts*" add noise, not value. Beg for them, and you become a 'heart whore'.

> *Asking for hearts is like asking for a client to like you. . . . Love the hearts, be grateful for them, thank people for them . . . but get more excited when someone watches your broadcast, comments, shares it with their friends and clicks through to your website.*
>
> Donna Moritz[2]

If asking for hearts is *all* you're doing, it makes the show more about *you* and less about the *audience*.

Reacting to reactions

Watch the screen and monitor the type of emojis (or the amount of hearts) that you are getting. If lots of 'thumbs up' turn to mostly 'thumbs down', then consider why this might be.

It was intriguing watching the live reactions changing from amused to angry as soon as viewers weren't seeing what they wanted. This opens up a whole new dimension to how we engage with news, brands, and organisations.

Alice Reeves[3]

If your viewers are showing you that they are bored or frustrated, then that could be a good thing. At least they haven't left, and you have a chance to engage them better:

▶ Refocus your content or change direction entirely.

▶ Show another more interesting view.

▶ Engage more by responding directly to the text comments that are being made.

▶ End the show.

▶ NOTES

1 Jacob Warwick, *How to Create Compelling Live Broadcasts*, www.adweek.com/ July 22nd, 2015
2 Donna Moritz, *21 Periscope Tips for Winning Broadcasts*, http://sociallysorted.com.au/
3 Quoted in Nikki Gilliland's article *v Biggest Social Media Trends of 2016?*, https://econsultancy.com/ December 12th, 2016

15

Shares, follows and notifications

▶ INTRODUCTION

Live-streaming is all about engagement and interactivity, sharing and recommending (this is *social* media after all), and the more your viewers do this with your content, the more valuable your video becomes. Their interaction has a snowball effect:

▶ Their individual sharing will bring more viewers to your show.

▶ Facebook Live algorithms will notice the activity, and so will share it to more of your follower's timelines, automatically.

It's good practice to suggest to viewers during your broadcasts "Follow me so you don't miss out on future shows . . . and Share this show with your friends so they don't miss out on this one".

After they *follow* you, they will then get a Notification to alert them each time you go live with a new broadcast.

When they *share* the show, it spreads the message that you are delivering and increases your profile and the number of followers and emojis/hearts that you may get. And that does wonders for your presentation confidence!

In this chapter, we will look at each of these features in turn. Again, we look mainly at Facebook Live and Twitter Go Live/Periscope, although other apps are similar.

But remember with Periscope specifically, some features and accessing them may be different on iOS and Android devices.

▶ SHARES

Boost and build your broadcast audience by requesting that viewers share your show with the people who *follow them*, to compound your viewing figures.

Having people share your show is the single most effective way to extend your network.

> When people like a video, they're more inclined to share it with their friends, which helps get that video in front of new people. Recommendations from friends are powerful: in fact, 48% of video watch time on Facebook comes from shares.
>
> Facebook.com[1]

As there is no listings or comprehensive search facility for any live-stream platform, the main way for you to build an audience is by:

- ▶ Pre- and post-promoting it to your existing friends, followers and fans
- ▶ Relying on organic sharing and notifications

Mention how they can share at the start and end of the show, and throughout it.

Again, things are different between the two main apps and the device on which you may be watching.

Facebook Live

On Facebook Live, the number of people your link is shown to (remember, no one sees every post from every page they 'like'), will be increased as more people share your live-stream.

> If a stream gets lots of viewers and feedback, Facebook can automatically push it higher in the feed so it's more visible. Basically, Twitter relies on explicit amplification by viewers while Facebook's algorithm chooses who sees what stream.
>
> Josh Constine[2]

And to share a show manually, ask your viewers to tap the 'Share' box on the screen while you are on air.

FIGURE 15.1 The 'share' button and 'notification' prompt in a Facebook Live feed

Source: BBC News, Facebook

Twitter Go Live

To share a live-video, viewers simply retweet the post it appears in.

Periscope

Viewers don't need to be following you to be able to share your show; after all, they may have stumbled across a Scope in the Global List and want to invite others to come and watch too, without committing themselves to following you until the end of time.

They can share by:

▶ Tapping on the prompt message that comes up on the screen as they watch

▶ Tapping '. . .' and following the prompts

▶ Swiping up from the bottom to go to a page on Android or left to right on iOS devices

▶ Tapping the watching number at the bottom of the screen to see your mini-bio and following the prompts. There they will also see your show title, a map of where you are (if you have enabled this feature) and a list of some of the other live viewers (someone can tap on each person's name to see their profile page from where you can follow them if they wish).

People watching you on Periscope have the option to Share the show on Twitter:

▶ To all of their followers

▶ To *specific* followers

▶ On their Facebook page (if they are logged in to your Facebook account on their phone)

▶ To copy the link (say, to put into an email)

Some of these options aren't available if they are watching a replay of a show. *As some of your viewers may be a bit reticent to invite all of their contacts to watch your show, remind them that they can select specific people to watch if they wish, not necessarily all of them.* While broadcasting, you can easily send an on-screen message to your viewers to request that they either follow you or share your broadcast. Tap the button '. . .' to bring up these options.

When to ask to share a show

Sharing means that even more people can get to see your show:

▶ Encourage people to share at the *start* of your show (they will do this if they know you and trust your content).

▶ Encourage people to share at the *end* of your show, once they have seen and evaluated the content and know that it was good enough to recommend to their followers.

Reciprocal sharing

Of course, such sharing of broadcasts should also work the other way: you ask people to share your show, and you should share those of *other* people that *you* watch. So if you dip in and see a stream that you think your followers would be interested in (and it fits with your brand values), then tip-off either *all* of your followers or a selected group of them.

Beware the share

If your viewers invite their followers to watch, you have a second chance to be discovered by people who don't follow you, but have had your show recommended to them by people that they *do* follow and who *also follow you*!

And having a show shared is of greater value than having people give you thumbs-up or heart icons. That's because giving hearts is telling someone *'I like you'*, but *sharing* is having someone tell their friends *'I like this other person'*: it's more public and therefore has more resonance.

But when you are *a viewer*, consider this: when *you* share *someone else's* show, you are putting your own brand on the line. In other words, if you recommend to the people that follow you that they watch a stream that they subsequently consider to be of no interest to them, they will blame *you* for the recommendation, not the presenter of that programme.

Additionally, if you invite *all* of your fans to watch lots of other people's Periscope shows:

▶ They will be bombarded with notifications from you, which again will become annoying (and they may 'unfollow' *you* as a result).

▶ Their Periscope 'Watch' list will become cluttered with shows they don't want to see, and they'll notice your name under the title as the person who recommended it to them.

So, don't spam-share, or over-share as people will unfollow you, not the presenters you are promoting. Only invite people to high value and relevant shows.

So, as a viewer, before you tap the 'share' button consider:

▶ Are *all* my followers actually going to be interested in this? Remember: your audience isn't made up of one homogenous group, but of different sub-sets: local people, people you know through work, friends/family, your children's friends' mums, or the guys at the gym.

▶ If the answer is 'no', consider (on the Periscope app) sharing the show with just a *select* group of them.

Your takeaway from this section: a lot of the success of a live-stream will be down to getting people to watch the show while it's on, so do all you can to get people to share the link while it's live.

▶ FOLLOWS

If your viewers enjoy the show you are presenting, encourage them to follow you. Then they will get a notification sent to their phone when they start a new show (if they have turned that feature on).

Facebook Live

Of course, your viewers are likely to be following you on Facebook already (that's how they got to see your video in their feed), but it may be that they came across it by another means (they saw a tweet linking to it, or it was shared by a friend). So remind viewers that they can tap on the Follow button on live-videos, and videos that *were*

Follow BBC News   Follow

FIGURE 15.2 The 'follow' button in a Facebook Live feed

Source: BBC News, Facebook

live, and then opt-in. Then they will get a notification the next time you go live, and be more likely to have your videos shared to their newsfeed (as you know, you don't get sent everything from everyone you follow, although you are more likely to have live-video shared than any other content). The button is at the bottom of the Live screen.

The first time someone joins a Facebook Live of yours, they will get an on-screen prompt to subscribe to see more in the future.

Periscope

If someone follows you on Periscope (different from following you on Twitter), they will get a notification when you go live, and your shows are put into their personal Watch channel list (for 24 hours), which they can see the next time they log on to Periscope.

There are several ways that they can follow you:

▶ While watching a Scope:

  ▷ They can tap the automated in-stream prompt to follow you.

  ▷ Tap '. . .' and then the follow button.

  ▷ Tap on the 'number of viewers' tally while watching a Live Show to see the short profile of you, the presenter, and then tap the button to add you to a list.

FIGURE 15.3 The 'follow' and 'share' menu in a Periscope feed

Source: Periscope

▷   While watching a replay, swipe right (in iOS) and swipe up (on Android, to see the follow option.

▶   Tap your small bio-picture to be taken to your main bio page where they can Follow you.

Follow-backs

Make a point to consider following people back, especially if they are regular viewers and 'power users': it's etiquette and encourages engagement. And to be strategic, that follow-back could lead to an influencer marketing opportunity when that other user promotes your stream on *theirs*. Think how that could boost your profile to a whole new audience segment and bring you new viewers.

Personally engage with your followers: contact them off-screen and reinforce a connection. Watch their shows and make comments, click on their profile and send them a tweet of thanks, or subscribe to one of their newsletters.

HOW TO SET UP THE FACEBOOK FOLLOWER OPTION

Enable this up on your personal profile so anyone can follow your updates and see when you go live, and so you get a wider reach:

▶   Go to Settings > Followers > Who Can Follow Me > Everybody

So now you have started a new relationship, don't just keep meeting up in the same old place! Follow your fans on *other* social media channels as well. Remember, live-streaming doesn't exist in a vacuum, it's just part of the social media mix. For example, as social media consultant Katie Lance suggests, have a Twitter list of people you have met on Periscope.

You want to follow people or businesses because they have a benefit to you, not just 'following for following's sake' or because you want them to follow you back. Such actions are a 'follow-train'. Instead:

▶   **Collaborate and reciprocate** – Refer each other's shows and help each other's networks.

▶   **Show up on other people's shows** – You have to watch them, get to know them, build a relationship and interact with them in the stream and elsewhere. When you get on their show and they say 'hi', people will tap and follow you, as you will have been referred to them by someone they already respect.

▶ NOTIFICATIONS

We all like to have control over when our phones decide to tell us about things. Some of us like a notification for every interaction across social networks, and then there are those who only want to hear their phones go off for something of monumental importance.

Jen Karner[3]

As soon as you go live, those who have chosen to do so will get a notification and will be able to join and engage in the conversation. This is a greater advantage to the broadcaster and the viewer than watching a replay of the show.

Sometimes they may not want to be told every single time some people start: the deluge can be simply overwhelming. (Notifications are usually 'on' by default.)

Remember: turning off a notification is not the same as Unfollowing them. You will still be able to see their content in your feed, but you won't be told each time they go live.

Facebook Live – Go to Settings and Notifications to toggle the live-video Notifications that you will get to 'all live posts'.

Periscope – on Android it's People > Profile > Settings > Notifications. On iOS, you will have to go through the profiles/accounts of everyone you Follow to turn them Off, by toggling the bell icon. To get a Twitter notification every time someone goes live with a video (but not get every Tweet they send), go to follow them in the usual way on Twitter, then select the notification icon, and then 'only tweets with live video'.

▶ NOTES

1 *New Video Metrics: Understand the Audience and Engagement of Your Facebook Videos*, https://media.fb.com/
2 Quoted in *Facebook Takes On Periscope by Giving Live Streaming to All U.S. iPhoners*, https://techcrunch.com/ January 28th, 2016
3 Jen Karner, *Using Periscope's Notification Settings*, www.androidcentral.com/ June 9th, 2015

16

The presenter

▶ **INTRODUCTION**

Let me take you back millions of years to the plains and the caves of early man. After a hard day's hunting on the savannah, our tiger-skin-wearing hero (let's call him, Fred, because he works with flint-stones) returns to his community. Sitting around the campfire, Fred communicates to his friends about what he got up to that day. Enthused by their cheers, and without speech or the written word, he jumps around in the shadow of the flickering flames and with nothing more than grunts and gestures, shows them how he out-ran a lion, killed a woolly mammoth and the direction and distance of the hoard of honey that he discovered.

Fred is given confidence in explaining his exploits by the feedback of his audience: his brain is processing all the visual and audible cues from those around him – the wide eyes, the gasps of amazement. He's building rapport with his audience as his tale becomes taller.

This is how humans are still 'programmed', but live-stream technology confuses us: it's not easy for us to have that rapport when we can't see or hear those we are talking to and don't have natural feedback from them.

Just as Fred may have 'frozen' at the sight of his first sabre-toothed tiger, we may freeze at the sight of a cold camera lens, with a moving picture of ourselves underneath it. It feels unnatural because it is: cameras aren't alive.

There are two types of speakers in the world: the nervous and the liars.

Mark Twain

So when we present on video, we have to remember to *build in* inflection, tone and body language to be more human and more authentic. This is good: it restores a lot of *human* elements back into the cold, mainly written world of social media. People engage with presenters when they look natural, not 'corporate', when they have 'formal informality', or a balance between 'casual and professional'.

In my several years as a voice and presentation coach for the BBC, I developed a series of techniques to help people perform better, and I have previously outlined these in my other books. In this chapter, there's lots of help to overcome the nerves and the self-consciousness, repackaged just for you so you too can perform like a pro.

▶ ON-CAMERA CONFIDENCE

You should be prepared and comfortable with:

- ▶ Where you are
- ▶ And what you are going to say

The audience will spot someone who is unprepared or nervous a mile off, and you could lose them.

> *Choose talent who are not only prepared to handle any issues when live-streaming, but also have the ability to interact with the viewers. Our hosts work closely with us on creating a detailed run of show, enjoy interacting with viewers and are comfortable handling any issues that may come up.*

Melanie Cohn[1]

Your personal pep-talk

Guess what? Most people feel awkward on camera, and even more of us hate to watch ourselves back. We don't think we look right. We don't like our hair. The skin isn't perfect. Our nose is too big. But your looks are what make you, you. And here are some other things that make you, you. Your authenticity. Your passion. Your style. Your knowledge, experience and expertise.

Everyone's voice, career experience and personality are different, so don't force a show out of something you don't understand or believe in, as then you really will feel awkward and look like a robot.

Be authentic by talking about something you love. When you do that, you will only have to glance at your notes occasionally as you'll be speaking from the heart, giving unscripted answers to questions and having a real conversation with your viewers.

Tell your story and be yourself. There's nobody better to share your passion than you! Show your insight and passion and your personality. Be informed, useful and relevant. Don't think about it as *broadcasting*, think of it as *engaging*.

Your physical warm-up

If you are nervous, then you *may* experience *some* of these characteristics:

▶ Your voice will rise in pitch.

▶ Your tone will become flatter, more monotonous with less variety.

▶ You talk faster.

▶ You have a shaky voice.

▶ You lose your train of thought.

▶ You stumble over words or develop a verbal tic.

▶ You blush.

Woah! Take a deep breath and stay calm, and carry out these Tension Busters:

▶ *Relax your body* – have a good stretch, shrug and (carefully) move your head from side-to-side and back-to-front.

▶ *Relax your mouth and throat* – yawn, do an exaggerated smile, hum, stick out your tongue, curl it up, repeat tongue-twisters.

Your mental warm-up

You will be less nervous if you have *prepared your content*. You don't need to memorise your entire show but have some notes to hand: your opening, key points and conclusion (after all, the only rambling you want to be doing is if you are presenting a live walking tour).

If you are doing an indoor programme, consider putting your notes alongside your phone, or taped to the wall just above the phone, so you don't have to keep looking away.

If you are presenting an outdoor show (coping with walking, the wind and possibly holding the phone as well), consider having your notes easily accessible in a transparent map holder around your neck that you can glance at and so have your hands free most of the time.

Some presenters talk until they've got something to say. Don't be one of them.

Know why you are making the journey, the route you will take and what you will do when you get there.

Otherwise, it's like a Sunday afternoon drive in the car: going nowhere in particular, taking the 'scenic route' and where the whims and the wheels take you. And if I'm a passenger, I probably won't be that interested.

Have a structure of the show, know where you will go, and what you will say at each point. All this will help give you and your viewers confidence in what you are saying.

It will make the difference between a pretty good performance and a p*ss-poor one: full of mistakes, trips, fluffed lines and giggles, cul-de-sac comments (which lead to a dead end, and leave you dying on air), ramblings, out-of-sequence steps and awkward silences.

Rehearse your opening every time

You wouldn't expect someone on *Dancing With the Stars* or *Strictly Come Dancing* to go straight onto the dancefloor without going through the moves one last time and feeling the music. So, follow their lead: rehearse your opening link. Get that right and the rest may flow. Get it wrong, you'll feel awkward and it's going to be tricky to recover.

Practice what you are going to say, but don't read it. You have to engage by looking into the camera and imagine you are simply talking to a friend or colleague. How would you talk to them? Talk like that on camera. Be well-researched and well-rehearsed.

▶ MAKE FRIENDS WITH THE LENS

It's certainly odd: talking into a phone and seeing yourself right there on the screen. And then spotting that number in the corner of how many people are watching you right now, even though you can't actually see any of them. As I said in the introduction, it's unnatural.

New radio presenters are often advised to put a picture of a friend just on the other side of the microphone, so when they are talking to their unseen audience they can focus on that one single person. They are advised to imagine their friend giving support, smiling and encouraging them. That helps them talk one-to-one 'to everyone' and come over as conversational. You may want to try the same trick.

Your voice

There's no need to raise your voice, which is the natural thing to do when you can't see who you are talking to. Remember, this is more intimate than TV, and they may be listening to you via earphones.

It is natural to have a voice, pitch and speed that reflects the content and your enthusiasm for it, so use a slower, quieter, more deliberate tone for:

▶ Straightforward background detail

▶ Complex ideas

▶ A way to reassure your viewers with the information you are giving them

And conversely, use a more upbeat style and speed, with more variation in the tone to show your:

▶ Excitement and enthusiasm for a product or idea

▶ A 'call to action'

Your tone

Talk to everyone all at once, but individually. That's because people are probably watching by themselves with their phone only a short distance from their eyes. It's an intimate experience.

Your language

People want to be treated as individuals, so be personal by welcoming viewers by name, or reacting to individual comments. Try and avoid using words and phrases like "everyone", "all of you", and "everyone out there" or "all of you watching".

Simply say "how are you?" (rather than "how are you all?"), and "thanks for joining me" (not "I must thank every one of you for joining me") and "today I'm going to show you . . ." (not "all of you are about to learn . . ."). It's a subtle but important differ-ence that radio presenters have used for decades to build a better relationship.

Corporate buzzwords have no place in communication of this type: talk normally and informally. One of the quickest ways to get people to stop watching is if you fill your show with jargon.

Your eyeline

Remember the camera is your audience. The lens is like the human eye. Treat it like a person. Smile and be natural and look into the lens, not continually away.

Don't look at the screen unless you are reading comments. Instead, look at people who are watching you, by looking *down the lens* at them. Make sure you know where the lens is on both the front-facing camera (the one you will use when you see your-self as you broadcast) and the back-facing camera (the one you use when someone else is your cameraperson).

If you don't look at the lens, you will not be looking at your viewers in the eye and therefore appear shifty! If you keep forgetting where to look, put a sticky arrow or smiley face label near the lens (but not covering it!) to remind you.

When you are broadcasting in landscape orientation, you still need to look at the lens, not the screen! That's a little awkward as it's more natural to look at the lens in portrait as it's at the top of the device. In landscape, the lens is way over to the left. However, if you *don't* look at the lens, you won't be looking your viewers in the eyes but off to the side, and will unintentionally appear rude, certainly awkward: https:// twitter.com/Lord_Sugar/status/845048870753243145/video/1

You can glance down at your notes, or look away briefly, that's natural. Looking dis-tracted and uncomfortable isn't. Viewers will be able to tell when you are reading a script that you have just off-camera or looking at yourself on the screen rather than *them*! But don't stare at the screen. It's rude and intimidating. Oh, and don't forget to blink!

And a reminder to have the lens of the phone at the same level as your own eyes. If the camera is lower than your eyes, you will be looking down at your audience literally and maybe metaphorically, and they'll have a great view of your ceiling and up your nose.

Your gestures

People connect with people, so if possible, show your face, smile and gesture. That's because your presentation is not just in the words. Using gestures are natural and will give you a more relaxed and conversational style. Use your hands to gesticulate and animate. It's natural and engaging body language.

Some of how you hold yourself and 'come over' to your audience may be subconscious and linked to the way you feel about your performance or content or a thousand other things about your life, work, family or health. So if you are excited and energised, you will appear bigger and brighter, and your voice will be louder and have more variation. And if you are worried, embarrassed or depressed, then you may appear on screen as small, with a voice to match.

You can trick your audience to a certain extent: if you want to suggest confidence, then 'stand tall' and be expressive with your face and hands. Match your emotion to the message.

If you are talking about the various steps to success in a seminar, then use your hands as building blocks on top of each other; if asking your viewers what they think of what you have mentioned, point at the screen ("what do you think?"); if you direct them to tap a button on the screen to share the show, gesture to where it will be. All this helps tell the story, aids communication and is far more natural than either the written or spoken word.

And if you are enjoying your own show, don't forget to tell your face, and smile!

Don't *overuse* gestures. Remember that you are quite big in your viewer's screen and whatever you do is 'magnified' (a movie actor can have much more subtle expressions than a theatre actor). Instead, look on these tips as a reminder to tap in to what we already do naturally, have them as part of your arsenal of 'tactics of persuasion', and rehearse them in the same way as you would the rest of your content.

Stand straight, keep eye contact, smile, take your time, show your hands and relax. And try and eliminate any strange tics such as earlobe pulling, brow wiping, or lip pursing.

Your pose

Sit like the TV anchors sit: on the front of the seat, with your body slightly forward but keeping your body level.

If you are writing on a whiteboard, have your body half-turned towards the camera to keep a connection with the viewer. Try never to turn your back on them.

If you are interviewing someone on location, don't stand face-to-face to them, as the camera will only see the profile of each of you. Instead you should both half-turn towards the camera.

Be you +

Think about how you talk and present yourself in these different circumstances:

- ▶ To your partner on the sofa on a Saturday night, with dimmed lights, a glass of wine and a movie on the TV

- ▶ With your partner on a Saturday morning when you are doing chores and leaving the house to go shopping

- ▶ At the office talking to a group of four other people around a desk in a meeting room

- ▶ At the office doing a presentation in front of 20 people

- ▶ In a theatre in front of 200 people accepting an award for great live-streaming shows

In each of those scenarios, you will use a different voice (it'll be softer or louder), you will have a different energy in your personality and you will have a different 'attitude'. In short, when you are physically or emotionally closer to a person, everything about your 'presentation' is smaller, including your vocal range and gestures. When you are *physically and emotionally distant* to a *lot* of people, you will be bigger in your voice and energy.

Now bear in mind that some of your charisma will be 'sucked up' by the screen. Still be you, but 'you+'. So, channel the feeling and attitude you have when you talk to a small group of people, not one or two, but about four or five, and then when people see you on their phone, it should look natural.

(Oh, and never go to air if you are tired, cross, tipsy, rushed, high or low. People will see the 'real you' from a mile off and you will let down yourself and your brand.)

▶ YOUR PERSONAL APPEARANCE

How you dress is also part of your presentation. It may be that you consider wearing the same things each time you appear on camera. That may help with:

- ▶ **Your branding** – you always wear a hat, or always something yellow.

- ▶ **Your own comfort** – the same outfit helps you get 'into the zone': you feel dressed to perform when you have that particular item on.

Bear in mind that being on camera can throw up a few issues that you may not have considered before:

- ▶ The camera lens will see things in a different way from your eyes, so patterns and colours may appear different from how you expected.

▶ Any extra lights may show a colour slightly differently than it is in real life and may cause something to shimmer or glint.

▶ An extra mic will pick up noises that you may not have noticed before.

Grooming

Comb your hair, have a shave, straighten your collar, sit up straight (is that spinach between your teeth?). A touch of blusher or lipstick may save you from looking washed out, a wet flannel over your face may save you from looking too shiny. Powder may take the shimmer off a bald spot.

Keep hair away from your eyes, and don't continually flick it on camera. And if you are going to point to something, make sure your nails look presentable.

Clothes

Wear something appropriate. Is it a business suit or shirt and skirt? Think twice about anything that is tight, short or low-cut.

If you are, say, a chef, wear something that says to people who see you for the first three seconds in their feed with no sound: "this guy's a chef!"

Patterns

Remember what they say: the camera adds ten pounds! Do yourself a favour: stripes can make you look fatter, solid colours more slimline and a 'loud' Hawaiian shirt can be distracting.

Fine checks and some textures (such as glossy or man-made) can play havoc with a camera and seem to shimmer to a viewer.

Colours

Depending on your skin tones, big blocks of colour may not look good on screen. All white or all black, or clothes with big contrasts, will cause the camera to have to work hard to balance with your face, hands and background. Consider wearing colours that fit with your company brand.

Accessories

Rings, bracelets, necklaces, earrings and a nice watch, they can all look good on screen but ensure they're not too reflective, or make a distracting noise each time you move. A heavy watch may knock on the table as you go to show something. Expensive jewellery when worn on an outside live-stream may attract a mugger.

▶ THE TWO CAMERAS

Show me, or what I can see?

You can use the front (the 'selfie' camera) and the back-facing camera on your phone. Tap the screen to toggle between which camera is being used, and so what the audience can see: either you or your surroundings.

If you are self-shooting, a combination of the two views might be best for variety. If you are the cameraperson for someone else, you will want to keep the camera on them, with you watching the screen to ensure they are well framed.

Remember that each time you swap cameras:

- ▶ The camera lens and microphone are linked as the phone will 'presume' that you will want to use the audio from the view that you are showing. That's fine if you are filming a colleague as what you want the audience *to see* and what you want them *to hear* are both coming from the same direction. If you are alone and talking to the front-facing camera, the situation is the same: front camera + the front mic. But if you then swap cameras to show *what you can see*, what you *say* will then be 'off mic'. So, if you are filming away from yourself, speak up . . . or use an external microphone.

- ▶ The microphone will swap at the same time as the lenses, and as this happens your audio will be cut off for a split second, so stop talking when you change perspective.

- ▶ When you turn the camera from the 'view' to 'you', you won't immediately be well-positioned, so try to avoid sudden re-alignment as your face comes into frame.

- ▶ The 'view' is usually best shown in landscape orientation. 'You' are usually best shown in portrait. But don't alter the camera lens and the perspective at the same time, or the viewer will feel as though they are navigating Cape Horn in a dinghy full of stray cats.

Off-camera streaming

You *don't have to* appear on screen (after all, the on-screen message says "what are you seeing?"):

- ▶ You may be worried about your personal security.

▶ You may be worried about how your looks may be perceived by others.

▶ It may be against your contract of employment in your 9-to-5 job.

▶ You maybe feel as though you don't have an appropriate home location to show.

▶ You may be shy.

Well, that's a shame because humans relate best to other humans[2] (which kind of makes sense!). It's all part of the 'know, like and trust' philosophy of social media. So if you can, instead of always live-streaming *what you are looking at*, flip the camera around and talk to viewers so they can see you.

If you simply can't bear to show your face, you have to up your game in other aspects of your broadcast:

▶ What you *do* show has to be even more fantastic.

▶ And your description of it has to be ten times as compelling.

Double-headed shows

If you feel awkward presenting alone, you could buddy up with someone else, so it's not just you carrying the event. If you do have a co-host, there's a chance that you will both try and get in shot at the same time and juggle position as you each lean forward to take a closer look at the comments on screen. That will look awkward and it will probably feel awkward, too.

There are solutions to this problem:

▶ Sit further back, and broadcast in landscape mode or buy a wide-angled lens for your phone so more of the scene is seen.

▶ Get an external mic or two so neither of you have to lean into the phone to be heard.

▶ Log onto your own stream on another device that you can have in your hand and on which you will be able to see comments more clearly.

▶ YOUR DRY RUN

Now you have worked out what you will show and talk about in your show, how to dress and present, the time will come to go live. It may be a bit nerve-wracking, but don't wait for the 'perfect' opportunity or you'll *never* do it!

It's probably a good idea to have a dry run first. Save 'spontaneous' for a once-in-a-lifetime moment or when you are comfortable and experienced.

A rehearsal is good so you can:

▶ **Get used to being on camera** – and more importantly *seeing yourself* on camera.

▶ **Check the lighting and the sound** – see what other people will see, before they do.

▶ **See whether you can be fluent** – and can refer to your notes without losing your train of thought. So, do a dry run so you don't dry up!

▶ **Know where to go and what to show** – if you will walk around during your broadcast you will want to check the route, think of what you will do at each location (and what you will say as you travel between each), and confirm that the Wi-Fi or phone connection will be strong enough.

Don't be afraid. FEAR can be defined as: *F*alse *E*vidence *A*ppearing *R*eal!

It's okay to be a bit nervous, thinking "who will watch me?" and "will they like me?", but if you want to do this, let's do it! After all, with all the previous pages of help, advice and inspiration, you are better placed than most people to make your livestream sensational!

There are two ways you can give yourself a dry run so you don't break into a cold sweat:

▶ **Do a video** – remember them?! The facility is right there on your phone already, and there's no danger of going live! You can still check everything out and, crucially, you can play it back straight after and see what you thought. And then if necessary, do it again before you live-stream.

▶ **Do a private broadcast** – perhaps to a family member or to a 'dummy' alternative account of your own (that you invite 'yourself' to watch). On Facebook Live you can broadcast from that account so only you can see it.

On Facebook Live

In the broadcast screen, tap on the button under your name, and choose to share your broadcast with:

▶ **Public** – so anyone can see the show

▶ **Friends** – your friends on Facebook

▶ **Friends except** – tap-through to select those who you don't want to see your show

▶ **Your smart list** – those people in a particular group

▶ **Specific friends** – again, tap though to select those

▶ **Only Me** (on your Profile page only) – with a padlock alongside it. This is the option you want so you will see the video exactly as it would appear to anyone else . . . they but won't!

If you can't change your preferences in the Facebook app, do it via Facebook.com on your desktop. Any changes will be integrated into the app directly.

On Twitter Go Live

Do a rehearsal through a dummy account.

On Periscope

▶ In the broadcast screen, tap on the 'public' button and invite selected trusted people (or another account that you own) to watch. (You can only invite people to a private broadcast if they are already following you.)

▶ Or select a 'group' that you have set up or belong to.

Remember: the option you have chosen may become your default for the next time you go to do a live-stream. So make sure that you change it back if necessary or you may be streaming and wondering why you have no viewers!

One last thing: when you start your dry run, don't worry too much about how *you* are coming across. Focus more on how *your message* is coming across.

Portrait and landscape views

Facebook Live, Twitter Go Live and Periscope allow you to stream your video holding the phone either way around:

▶ Portrait (aka vertical or 'up-and-down')

▶ Landscape (aka horizontal, lengthways, or 'across')

The benefits of vertical video

▶ It's how you naturally use and hold a phone to call, read messages, scroll through Facebook and so on, so it's easier to shoot this way and also for people to watch this way.

FIGURE 16.1 The different perspectives achieved using portrait and vertical orientation

Source: Periscope

▶ It's the way you use your phone for other similar video apps such as Snapchat (there are even 'vertical video film festivals').[3]

▶ If you are doing a 'piece-to-camera', such as a tutorial, the human frame fits better into the portrait orientation (hence its name!).

▶ Vertical video is also often best for shorter live-streams.

The benefits of horizontal video[4]

▶ We live in a landscape world where so many things are wider than they are tall.

> ▶ Horizontal is the ratio that our eyes are.

> ▶ It's how TVs, movie screens and computer monitors are made.

> ▶ Horizontal video is often better for longer streams, where a viewer will turn their phone for a more immersive experience, and for landscapes (hence the name!), two-person shows and so on.

Again there's a slight difference between the two main apps, Facebook and Periscope.

On Facebook Live – the orientation you start your show is the way it will remain throughout. So if you start in landscape, you can't change to portrait later. Also, ensure that the 'zoom' setting is off on your iPhone as this may also interfere with the orientation of your picture.

Twitter Go Live/Periscope – if you shoot in landscape, the viewer can decide which way they watch: either in landscape (in which case the view fills the screen) or in portrait (in which case the view only partially fills the screen).

That means that a viewer can continue holding their device in portrait to watch, or match the broadcaster's orientation to maintain full-screen video (regardless of how they are shot: the app will auto-rotate the video to compensate how the phone is held), and the comments will adjust themselves to flow the best way.

On Periscope, you can change the orientation of the phone as you broadcast and the image will automatically re-align itself.

Other portrait/landscape tips

> ▶ If the image doesn't rotate when you stream, make sure that the 'orientation' setting on your device is not locked! *(Some older phones may not correctly manage landscape views.)*

> ▶ If you know you want to upload your broadcast to another platform (like YouTube or Instagram), make sure you start your broadcast in the mode you want it to be and keep it that way. Note that if you do a live-stream in portrait, when you upload it to a landscape-playing platform such as YouTube, black bars will appear on each side of the playback screen, and that will detract from the viewer's experience.

Framing yourself

'Headroom' is the space viewers see between the top of your head and the top of the screen, usually when you are close to the camera.

Watch TV and you will see that often the very top of someone's head may be sliced off but no more. Rarely is there lots of headroom: that is a waste of space and gives the impression that you are a 'minnow in a small pond'.

If you are talking to the camera, use the top third of the screen for your face: if you are *too low* in the frame, then you will be blocked by the flow of comments.

If you are too close, the camera may have trouble focusing on you and you will appear to be h-u-g-e to the viewer. Additionally, although viewers can hide the comments, allow plenty of room for people to see you once they start to appear.

Have your face so viewers feel connected but without filling too much of the screen. So if you are 'self-shooting', have the phone a selfie-length (an arm's length!) away from your head. This distance will still create a personal connection with your audience.

The face is the most interesting part of the body: it's what other humans connect with. So another waste of space might be showing too much of the rest of someone's body, say their legs. Get closer to the person so you can see and hear them better, rather than show things that don't add to, and may distract from, the message. When you do this, be careful what part of the body now appears cropped at the bottom of the screen: across their stomach is fine, but it doesn't look right to cut someone off at their knees.

Zoom with your feet. In other words, even though you can pinch on the camera screen to show a scene closer than it actually is, because the camera has a fixed lens, the picture will become fuzzier. If you want to show something that is in the distance, it's often better to move closer to it.

You want to get your message *across* to your viewers, and you don't want to *look down* to them. If you position the lens of your camera at your eye level, you will

FIGURE 16.2 Good framing for a live-video

avoid coming over as 'threatening' or distant to your audience. (After all, when we speak with someone in real life, eye contact aids communication and relationship building.)

If you are out of doors for your show, avoid the classic tree-out-of-your-head shot or the almost-inevitable 'photo bombers'.

When you take a *photo* on your camera, you have the opportunity to have gridlines superimposed on the screen, so any lines in the view are straight. You can't do this with Facebook Live or Twitter Go Live/Periscope, so make sure you keep an eye on the screen so the bookcase behind you, for example, doesn't look as though it's about to topple onto your head, or the yacht on the horizon doesn't look as though it's going to slide off the edge of the world.

Also, make sure these fit the frame:

▶ Any props you hold up, including signs, web addresses, logos

▶ Your hands when you gesticulate. Moving arms with nothing on the end of them will look odd.

Review your rehearsal

Like the first time you do *other things*, your first live-stream may have been a bit awkward, but (to continue the analogy) it was probably over pretty quickly, you'll get better at it in time, and anyway you may have done it alone and in private.

With live-streaming you can't re-shoot and start again, but you can in a dry run. You had a rehearsal so you can work out all the kinks that you might come across when it's for real.

So, review your rehearsal (indeed, you should regularly watch back most of your shows):

▶ **The Technicals** – were you in frame, what were the sound and lighting like?

▶ **The Presentation** – were you fluent, did you fall back on verbal crutches ("like", "y'know"), which may be annoying; did you say what you needed to?

When you watch yourself back, it may be really awkward, but try and determine what worked and what didn't. Identify strengths and weaknesses, what you can change and how. And watch other people's live-streams, too. See what they do and what works for them: a style, a production, a format . . . how do they use their voice or visual aids?

You are bound to make a few mistakes. Correct the problem and move on. And you know what? You've started! You're under way!

This whole thing needn't be daunting. It's fun, but most people have to prepare. Rehearsing will free you from the worry of the technical aspects and let you concentrate on *communicating*.

▶ YOUR FIRST LIVE SHOW

Some people, quite understandably, suffer from 'analysis paralysis': they think so long and hard about getting onto Facebook Live or Twitter Go Live/Periscope that they never actually do it.

They always have more reasons *not* to jump in than they do *to* jump in. They watch other people's streams, make notes, plan the best time to do a show (should they ever do one), and then get distracted because "we're just about to go away for a week", or "I'm not feeling well" or "it's a bad hair day". But deep down they know they really do want to dive in.

My advice? Get on with it. If you don't know how to start, start! Then you will learn from experience. And you'll never get experience of doing something if you don't do it.

And for that very reason, when you do your first show and you feel as though it might help, tell your viewers that it's your first time live. Some people do their first broadcast about the fact that it's their first broadcast and get lots of on-screen support because of it. Don't get stressed about your first stream. It may be daunting, but after it's done you'll be on a roll.

As well as publicising your show to your contacts and clients, make sure that your friends and family know, too. You can ask them to send lots of hearts, make helpful comments and ask easy questions to get the conversation going.

So are you now ready to be a Facebook Live virgin? Are you ready to 'pop your Peri cherry'?

▶ YOUR FIRST 100 SHOWS

You may not actually want many people to watch your first few shows as you will be on a learning curve. So don't get hung up about the viewer tally at the bottom of the screen!

Indeed, your first several dozen live-streams are likely to suck because:

▶ You are new to the platform.

▶ You need to get experience.

▶ You need to get comfortable.

▶ You need to learn to multi-skill.

▶ You need to find 'your voice'.

▶ You need to develop your niche and format.

You will not be an 'instant celebrity': go with the flow and realise how you grow. Your tenth live-stream will be a bit better than the first; the twentieth will be better than the tenth and so on. Stick with it and time will show you how to make a good show.

You will get better by practising. It will take time, training and a bit of effort, but to start off everyone is a bit nervous. Even the most experienced presenters have butterflies.

Of course, if you are excited by your material, your audience will feel the vibe and will help carry you along. So identify what makes you passionate about your topic and zone in on that.

▶ NOTES

1 Tanya Dua, *Dunkin' Donuts, Wendy's And Other Brands Sound Off on What Works in Live Streaming*, http://digiday.com/ November 30th, 2016
2 Paras Chopra, *Do Human Photos on a Landing Page Increase Sales and Conversions?* https://vwo.com/blog/
3 See: Benjamin Starr, *4 Reasons Vertical Video Is Suddenly OK*, www.visualnews.com/ July 27th, 2015
4 More benefits of horizontal video are in the YouTube video: *Vertical Video Syndrome – A PSA*, June 5th, 2012

17

The producer

► **INTRODUCTION**

Your shows may become so popular that you have lots of viewers making lots of comments, perhaps at the same time. Responding to those as they fly up the screen can be a challenge for a single-person production. Blocking people who are deliberately disrupting or dominating the stream just adds to your headache. (One of the first live-streams by an international cruise liner company was hijacked by one person clogging the screen by posting the entire alphabet . . . one letter at a time.)

So, you need a plan for:

► Promotion

► Moderation

► Discussion and conversations with your viewers

And that's where a producer can help.

Your producer

If you have a cameraperson (someone who is holding the phone for you), they see the screen (so they know you are in shot), but *only they* see the messages (obviously!). So they could block any awkward viewers.

FIGURE 17.1 A presenter being filmed with the iKlip AV phone mount with integrated wireless mic facility

Source: IK Multimedia Production SRL www.ikmultimedia.com

FIGURE 17.2 A producer using a Shoulderpod pocket rig with Rode directional mic and windshield

Source: Shoulderpod, www.shoulderpod.com, www.rode.com/microphones/videomicme

Or you could have another person (a 'producer' or someone from your marketing or social media team) who is watching your show and makes notes of most relevant messages and passes them to you on paper or via another app (say WhatsApp). Or maybe have them capture the comments that you can answer in another show.

Better still is having that producer log in to the *same account* as the one you are broadcasting from. Then, as you broadcast they can:

▶ Reply to comments in text as you answer some verbally.

▶ Reset the show, explaining to late joiners who you are, where you are and about the content.

- ▶ Forward and back-promote the show:

    - ▷ "If you missed the view of the turret be sure to watch the replay."

    - ▷ "Stay for a few minutes when we tour the room where Queen Elizabeth slept."

- ▶ Put in links to sites or products that are mentioned in the show or may be of added value to the viewer.

- ▶ Block people.

- ▶ Take screenshots.

- ▶ Invite people to join the live-stream.

- ▶ Pin a comment to the Facebook Live feed.

- ▶ Remind viewers to like, follow and share.

Doing this is a great advantage for brands who want to take their engagement one step further.

Brand guidelines that you set up may dictate how your producer responds to comments in the stream:

- ▶ The tone, especially when responding to complaints or comments from trolls on the live screen[1]

- ▶ Whether they use the name of the person they are responding to

- ▶ What sites they link to and how often

- ▶ And so on

During and immediately after your live-stream, have a colleague engage by:

- ▶ Welcoming and thanking viewers

- ▶ Asking questions and answering questions

- ▶ Making and replying to comments

- ▶ Saying what's coming up in the show

- ▶ Putting in URLs

- ▶ Promoting the next show, when it's on and the content

Doing this helps engage the audience and makes them feel more involved as participants rather than just spectators, gives valuable information, and helps reinforce your brand identity and audience community.

Additionally, they can see how people are reacting to the stream and work out where and when this happens, to determine what works best and the possible content of future shows.

▶ NOTE

1   There is a useful flowchart regarding this, here: Jonathan Michael, *Social Media Response Flow Chart for Small Businesses*, http://articles.bplans.com/social-media-response-flow-chart/

18

The viewers

▶ INTRODUCTION

During your show, individuals will inevitably drop in and drop out. In broadcasting, we call that 'the churn':

- ▶ Some will join you at the start and stay all the way through. We love these people! Let's call them **The Superfans**.

- ▶ Some will join you late but stay: **The Johnny-Come-Latelys**.

- ▶ Some people will join you on time and then leave: **The Toe-in-the-Water Viewers**.

- ▶ Some will join late and leave early: **The Uncommitted**.

You need to consider all of these groups, so:

- ▶ You get more viewers.

- ▶ You get more comments.

- ▶ Your stat-numbers improve.

- ▶ You will feel supported and that your content is valued, and so do a better show.

- ▶ You are more likely to be recommended to others.

▶ TARGETING YOUR VIEWERS

The Superfans

You need to love and reward the people in this first group. They are your apostles who will go out and spread the word about you:

- ▶ Make sure you are following them on social media.

- ▶ Watch their shows and comment in them (think how supported they will feel when they see that you have taken the time and trouble).

- ▶ Make sure you are following them on Twitter and other platforms, re-tweet their material and comment on it.

- ▶ Thank them and mention them by name on air (but not so much that the show becomes a 'club' and other people feel excluded).

- ▶ Ask them to share the show, so you get 'double exposure'.

- ▶ Give them added value – for example, a private show with extra material or a guest interview, or a way they can get their questions answered. (With fewer viewers in a closed show, they get more time with you and more personalised advice.) Or maybe a VIP club that they can join via email for extra content and engagement. Perhaps people should aspire to join this, or they have to be asked by you or recommended by another of your followers.

The Johnny-Come-Latelys

You need to promote the show better to the people who join you late:

- ▶ Pre-promote the show on all your social media, so they know what the topic is and are more likely to arrive on time for fear of missing out (FOMO). Such a message could be posted several hours before the stream starts, so potential viewers can schedule their work and join you live, and on time.

- ▶ Create must-watch content at the start of the show that people won't want to miss, and refer to this later in the show.

- ▶ Consider a contest that rewards early joiners – perhaps "the person who has the red heart [on Periscope] in the next show, will get a shout-out and follow".

- ▶ Welcome viewers by name when they do join, to make them feel more appreciated.

▶ Maybe set a question at the start that will be answered by you at the end. (Perhaps just do the *answer* at the end without repeating the question, to encourage people to watch from the start in future!)

▶ Remind them that if they missed the start of the show, they could watch the replay later. That way, at least they'll get the content and you will get the views.

The Toe-in-the-Water Viewers

These people join you on time but then leave:

▶ Do fantastic teasing during the show to convince these viewers to stick around for longer. We need to let these people know what fantastic content they'll be missing out on if they 'leave the party' early.

▶ Leave some best bits of information until last, or maybe set a question at the start that will be answered by you at the end.

The Uncommitted

And as for the fourth group, who join late and leave early:

▶ Welcome them to the show when they do join you (you get a message on the screen).

▶ Consider an end-of-week/month summary episode. They will get the highlights in one place, although they won't get it as early as everyone else.

▶ Or maybe a show that says "this is what we spoke about" without giving *all* of the tips and tricks: "for details on how we did that, watch again on YouTube and so you don't miss out in future, catch each new episode live."

▶ PROMOTING YOUR SHOW

Market yourself

People have to know they *could* watch you before they decide whether they *will*! So go to all those places where you have your email address, Facebook page and Twitter @name (like on your email auto-sig, your website and your newsletter) and say that you present shows on Facebook Live and Twitter Go Live/Periscope and what the content is.

We also have regular live video shows on our Facebook page, showing how you can use all the local ingredients we sell in our farm shop.

Watch our Periscope show every weekday at 12.30 CDT for our top DIY tips.

Produce a short pre-recorded video to promote the longer live one, explaining what you do a show about and when, and put it on Facebook and pin it to the top of your Twitter page.

Produce some enticing graphics-and-text for other social media such as Instagram and Pinterest.

Pre-promote your show

Maximise the effort that you are putting into the production and presentation of your performance by pre-promoting it. So when you know that your show will be on at a certain time, tell people.

If people across all of your platforms (there is a world outside of Facebook!) know you will be on at a certain time, and they want to see you, they can plan their life around the event and try and ensure that they are available to watch. If they're *only* told as the show starts, chances are they won't be free or maybe won't even see the message.

Yes, a notification may go out (both Facebook Live and Periscope send Notifications to those who have opted in to get them), but that will just be sent once and only when the show actually starts. You will miss lots of people if they only know it's starting in "three minutes" or is "just starting". But if you tell people that you have a show at six tonight (give a time-zone reference), and this is what is in it, and then send another message to your Twitter friends a couple of hours later and so on, you stand to get a larger audience.

FIGURE 18.1 Pre-promote specific shows so people can plan their day around watching you live

Source: @KrishnaDe

YOUR WEBSITE LIVE-STREAM EXPLAINER SHEET

Have a page on your website on which you explain about your live-streaming show, its content and broadcast times that you can refer people to.

***

(Your Show/Episode title)

On [*date*] at [*time*] we'll be hosting a show entitled [*Your Show/Episode title*], live on Facebook.

In it, we'll discuss [*list two or three key points, or explain what they will see or learn during the show*]. You will be able to watch and listen and submit your questions to us via the on-screen messaging service. All for free!

To watch the broadcast:

Follow us on Facebook [*your name*] and look out for our show starting at the above time.

If you miss the show, you can see it later at [*your Facebook, website and/or You-Tube page*], although obviously you will not be able to ask questions.

If you have any questions or comments before or after the show, you can contact us at [*Twitter, email etc.*].

Our show will last about [*minutes*].

We look forward to you joining us!

***

Then you can direct your fans on various social media to that page so they can see details of how to watch your upcoming shows:

"We have a live video show about _____ on Facebook today with @____. How to watch details: www . . ."

In 'pre-show promo tweets' advertise your show's content with #hashtags and @names to encourage people to turn up. Offer to send an email reminder to your fans. If you have a 'sign-up' box on your website, as well as potentially getting more viewers, you'll also capture their addresses for future marketing events. Include in the pre-promotion, the time (in various time zones) that the show will be on (e.g. GMT, EST, CST). How do you work the zones? www.timeanddate.com/worldclock/

Harness the power of other platforms, too. So advertise your broadcast in the *real-world area* about which your show will cover. So if it's a cooking show, tell people at farmers' markets. If your show is about the local town, then get a mention in the local paper or council guide.

Or if you are 'on location' and you will go live shortly:

▶ Twitter allows you to post a short video up to 140 seconds' duration, which will play right in your follower's feed. So, record a short promo video of where you are, explaining what you will show live in **XX** minutes.

▶ Take a still picture of the scene and send that as part of your pre-promotion Tweet.

▶ Take the picture and then add words to the image to make the Tweet even more eye-catching:

▷ https://buffer.com/pablo

▷ https://behappy.me/generator

▷ www.facegarage.com/photoEditors/instagramQuotes

▷ www.pixteller.com/

Or use free website apps like Canva to design something even more eye-catching and as memorable as possible. Many of these sites have app-equivalents so you can design and post directly from your phone.

And there's more to think about doing:

▶ Put together a photo-montage about your show topic, in a Facebook or Twitter post.

▶ Tag your picture with @names to get the attention of people on Twitter you want to watch your show.

- ▶ Use Google Form (www.google.co.uk/forms/about/) or Survey Monkey (www.surveymonkey.com/) for other ways to promote your show and have your followers contribute towards it:

  - ▷ If you will have a lot of viewers, then this allows people to post a question before you go live, in case they are unable to comment during the stream. Or ask for questions and topic ideas in advance through other social media channels. Doing this increases participation and helps break the ice on air.

  - ▷ It gives you potential content for this or any other show.

Use all these tools as building blocks towards your final goal.

Promote your show live

Once you go live, get a friend or colleague to grab the link and put it out on other social media channels. And yes, you could promote your Facebook Live on Twitter, or your Periscope on Facebook!

On Facebook Live

- ▶ Share the page to your other Facebook pages.

- ▶ Get the link to the stream and repost it to Twitter.

On Twitter

- ▶ Get a colleague to re-tweet the auto-tweet that was sent from the account when the live show started on Periscope or re-tweet the live-stream on Twitter.

- ▶ Have them send out other tweets while you are broadcasting, or schedule Tweets to go out while your show is live. As your auto-tweet to your live-video will drop further down fans' feeds the longer your show goes on, set up an extra tweet to go out after a further 10 or 20 minutes to promote the live-stream. Pin this to the top of your Twitter feed.

Indeed, the longer the video, the more likely that most of the engagements will happen while it is still being broadcast. That's because longer videos require more investment to watch, and they're simply not as interesting or exciting once they're no longer live. In a 2016 interview with the *New York Times* conducted with Julian Assange, 50% of the total engagements of the 44-minute video came while it was live.[1]

Always encourage people to watch live, rather than on replay. Otherwise, over time, people will get into the habit of always watching the repeat, and your engagement level will drop.

Ask your viewers to promote you

Get your fans to do some of the heavy lifting! They're watching, so they like what they see, right? So ask them to share the show with their own fans. At the beginning, middle and end of your broadcast, remind them how they can do this:

- ▶ **On Facebook Live** – point out the 'share' button on the screen as they watch, that they can tap and tell their friends.

- ▶ **On Periscope** – draw their attention to the three dots at the bottom of the screen, which when tapped, brings up several options, including to share the link to the show.

- ▶ **On Twitter** – ask those people to re-tweet the tweet that brought them into the show in the first place.

And if you have a strategy that specific partners (other brands or individuals) will share your show as soon as you go live, then you are building in a bigger boost to your broadcast, to get an even larger audience.

Reciprocal viewing

When you start out, you may not have a following or indeed the 'influencer sta-tus' that other people have. The secret is: *other people's live-streams.* They've already accumulated an audience, so show up to those shows, contribute, be engaged and get known.

- ▶ Watch their broadcasts.

- ▶ Comment and comment on others' comments.

- ▶ Say hi to other people.

- ▶ Contact them afterwards to strengthen your relationship.

- ▶ Follow them on other platforms.

Engage with everyone you want in your sphere, and they will start to follow you, too. It's another way to get more viewers.

You can't expect people to follow you and watch your shows if you don't watch theirs:

▶ You get to see what they're doing, their ideas and their formats.

▶ It gives you an opportunity to be seen, as your name will pop up on the screen when you join, invite and comment.

▶ NOTE

1 Liam Corcoran, *How Much Engagement On Facebook Live Videos Happens While They're Live?*, www.newswhip.com/ September 7th, 2016

19

At the start
of the show

▶ **INTRODUCTION**

Some people mumble and stumble through the start of the show. Not only does this give a bad business image for their brand, but it will also dissuade early joiners (and replay viewers) from staying with them.

So here are the best-ever tips to help you thrive when you go live.

▶ **JUST BEFORE YOU GO LIVE**

Reboot your phone

Live-video takes a lot of processing power, and your stream will be smoother if your device can concentrate on doing just that: streaming. And that makes your connection the most important part of the whole production (after all, if you don't make it to air, there was no need to prepare).

We're all used to running several apps in the background of our phones even if they haven't been used in days. Before you start a show, do a bit of housekeeping: close these down and reboot the phone. It'll mean that the system will run more smoothly and you'll use less battery, too. And if the broadcast crashes, the phone will have less work to do to get you up-and-running again.

Run a speed test on your phone before you go live to see the strength of the connection. You need to aim for at least two megabits per second, although four or more is ideal. If you don't have that rate, move to a better signal area or a stronger, more resilient, less public Wi-Fi. You can get a speed test app from your app store.

Turn off any other phone you may have, desk or mobile, and remind any guests to do the same. That is unless you will use that second device as a prompt from your producer about what to do, or as a way of them sending you comments that have been received on the screen.

Basic checks

This is like checking the fuel and oil before a long journey:

▶ As well as checking the *signal* connection, also check *mic* connections by doing a 'private' stream first and looking back at it.

▶ Put a "do not disturb" note on the door.

▶ Mute your computer's pings.

▶ Consider putting up a 'crowd notice' to explain what's happening.

▶ Check behind you before you go live. Something untoward may be in the shot inadvertently.

Connect to Wi-Fi

Use a Wi-Fi network where possible. For one thing, the connection is likely to be stronger and your picture clearer.

After your phone has rebooted, turn off the capability of your phone to make and receive *phone calls*. Otherwise, if you get sent a notification, or someone calls you while you are streaming (or later while you are uploading to your camera roll/gallery or YouTube), you will be interrupted and may lose the whole show.

So, *turn calls off, but keep Wi-Fi on.* If you have to be on a phone connection, put your device on 'do not disturb'. Remember to reverse the process after the show *and after uploading,* to be able to receive and make calls again.

Save money while using live-streaming by finding free Wi-Fi spots near to where you regularly broadcast (e.g. local cafes, bars, and your journey to work). Then maybe suggest to the owner they advertise their free Wi-Fi, to encourage more live-streamers to eat there, stream from there and publicise their business!

Immediately before you start

First impressions matter!

▶ **Compose great eye-candy** – it could be your logo, or the best view, rather than just having the phone on your desk, or the pavement as you walk down the street. And if you use the same image every time, this could become part of your branding.

▶ **Have your camera at eye level** – so you are not talking down to your audience. *And so they're not looking up your nose!* It can look intimidating to your audience, and none of us looks very good from a low angle: we appear to have a wide face and two chins – not very flattering!

▶ **Make sure that you have the light facing you** – and not facing the camera. Your face needs to be lit from the front (whether it's by the sun or artificial light): if it's behind you and in the frame of the camera, you will have potential glare on the lens.

▶ **Correct the angle of the phone** – so, if you are wearing glasses, the glare from your phone is not reflected in them.

▶ **Tap and hold the screen** – to focus the camera.

Remember that people will be joining you throughout the time you are on air, so you have to keep them visually entertained all of the time, not just at the start.

Go early

You *may* want to start your show a minute or two before you have said you will. Why?

▶ To give you a moment to warm up rather than starting 'cold'.

▶ So you can set the scene.

You can always edit this off the start of the video when you later upload it to Facebook or YouTube as a new post.

FIGURE 19.1 Going live on Facebook Live

Source: Facebook

3,2,1... Live

When you start . . . start!

Not pause.

Once you press the broadcast button, you are potentially live to the world.

▶ Don't keep the people who join you on time waiting. (If you do this, you are essentially saying, "Thanks for showing up on time. We're now going to hang around for the late-comers.") Have respect for their time. It may be that you start saying what's coming up, welcoming and have to do so again, but *say something*!

▶ Consider starting with valuable content from the first few seconds to reward those who have turned up 'on time'. These are the people you should look after with a story or a bonus tip. (If you wait for more people to join before you get going, you will be rewarding 'bad behaviour'.)

▶ Replay viewers always see the show from the very, very start, and if there's a slow and lazy start, they may just turn off instead.

Give people time to get in before you start with the *main content* of the show (after all, people have to get the notification, leave what app they are already in and get a connection), but don't wait too long, or you'll annoy those who turned up at the start.

The First 111* Seconds

Not exactly 111 seconds. I chose that number because the digits look like three little periscopes! But the first, say, about 2 minutes, are really important.

You have to persuade the people who join you from the get-go, not to go. That's the people who are the eager ones who jump in as soon as they see your 'live now' notification and also those watching you on the replay. However or *whenever* people watch you, you have to persuade them to stay!

> *Statistically, by the time the clock on your video strikes 00:10, twenty percent of viewers will have already stopped watching the video and clicked away to some other website or moved on to some other video with cats playing the trumpet around a campfire.*
>
> Colin Hogan – DemoDuck.com[1]

▶ WHAT TO SAY AT THE START OF A SHOW

When you start your first few shows you may be a little nervous, and this will act as a checklist of what to do so you can concentrate on the unique and engaging body of your content.

Say 'hello'

Obvious perhaps, but make sure you say it anyway. The world turns on politeness after all. Or you may want to say 'welcome', but maybe *not* 'good morning'. Why?

- ▶ Because you're now global and people are in different time zones doing different things. They'll get that you are in Vancouver and they are in Prague, but it's best to keep things straightforward if you can.

- ▶ Because it will be a different time again when people watch the replay!

- ▶ And different again when someone watches the re-versioned video on YouTube in six months.

When you welcome people, use their names as people love to be personally acknowledged (it's what Greg Jarboe calls 'schmooze optimisation').[2] After all, this is live-streaming where you get to see who is watching you right now. On Periscope, broadcasters see a message on-screen when someone new to the app joins the audience. Be sure to give a warm welcome to those people specifically.

Counterintuitively you could at the very start of the live show say hello to the people *who aren't actually watching*! To explain: it will take a few seconds for the first *live* viewers to get the notification and join you. Before they do, greet those who will watch the show from the start, when it is posted as a replay: "Hi, thanks so much for watching the replay. I really appreciate your time and support. If you follow this account, you'll get a notification when we go live, and then you'll be able to interact during the show itself. Now I can see that some live viewers are joining us, so . . ."

You may also make an effort to include a mention to new viewers to make them feel special and included: "If this is your first time watching . . ." can preface a short sentence of welcome and explanation.

Tip: when you join someone else's broadcast as a viewer, say 'hello' in the text box the same way each time. This personal branding will help you stand out and get noticed by the host and other viewers.

Introduce yourself

This 'power statement' is your 'elevator pitch': 20 seconds or so saying who you are and what you do. Introducing yourself at the start and midway through each show helps establish your credibility, reinforces your brand image and is an opportunity to tell people who you are, your authority and your goal, and why they will want to stay watching the rest of the show.

Introduce the show

Like networked broadcasts, you may have a phrase that *succinctly sums up what your show is all about*, and becomes a slogan or catchphrase for your broadcasts:

- ▶ "Welcome to 'You and Yours', BBC Radio 4's daily consumer programme."

- ▶ "This is 'Saturday Night Takeaway': the only series on TV that says 'Don't just watch the ads – win them!'"

- ▶ "The promise I will make to you: you'll know more by one o'clock than you do now." (James O'Brien's 'Mystery Hour' on LBC Radio)

Or as we say:

> ▶ "Welcome to 'Live-Stream Insiders'. Live-streaming news from the last seven days, in the next 30 minutes."

Say what is in the show

Inspire and entice people to carry on watching as soon as possible. Remind them of the title ("Today we are going to share with you . . .") but without going into too much detail. You want to keep them hooked, but you also want to have forward momentum.

Say what's in it for them. In other words, *what they will get out of giving you their time and attention:*

> ▶ What they will know
>
> ▶ What they will experience
>
> ▶ What they will see
>
> ▶ How they will feel
>
> ▶ How they can save

So give them a take-away right away: say up-front what they will get from their investment of time.

Manage their time expectations

Viewers will start watching having no idea how much time (or data) they are committing to your show. So let them know. That could be in the title or in this introductory sequence at the start of the show. Try and make sure you stick to the duration you have promised or explain why it is longer or shorter. Don't mislead.

> *"Hello, I'm* [your name], *and I am* [your title], *and I help* [what you do]. *Over the next* [expected duration of the show], *I'm going to* [what you will show or where you will go] *so that you* [how they can use the content]."

Ask if anyone is new to the show

Again, this is another way to be friendly and to engage with your fans and encourages them to watch again. (Just mention a handful, and if you can, use their *actual* name rather than their handle as it's more personal.) They can let you know if they are new by making the comment 'new' (or any other word) on the screen. Then, when you have finished the show, go back and watch your own replay, grab their names, contact them on Twitter and thank them for watching. Yep, it's another way to build a stronger relationship.

If you spot someone start watching your show who you enjoy watching yourself, you may want to recommend to your other viewers that they follow this person. But explain *why* you recommend them. It's not really enough to say "they're awesome" without saying why, for example:

▶ "They do tours of the city, talking to great people, showing unusual sights and it's almost like being there."

▶ "They have great ideas and inspiring topics every week on saving time at work and home; the other day there were several tips I'm using already."

Ask where people are from

So you see that a viewer has joined, ask where they are watching. Again it's polite, but also you are encouraging people to start interacting, and in doing that you're building a relationship with them.

But try not to merely say "Oh, Belfast . . . hi, Canberra . . . hello, Hong Kong . . .". If you have something (positive) to say about the city or country that demonstrates your knowledge then do so, as another connection will be made. (You don't need to mention everyone, of course, just half a dozen, to give a flavour.)

> *If you are new to the show, send me the word 'new' and I'll say hi . . . and I also would love to know where you are today. Ah, Bonnie is in Scotland, great to have you with us Bonnie from the land of tartan and shortbread. Pierre is watching in Nice – I love the beach there, I was there a few years ago. Across Europe and Franz is with us from Berlin. Franz, I really must get to your city; it's on my wish-list for this year!*

Back-promote your previous show

Have some good content with which you can engage people from the start. It gets viewers chatting and gives time for new arrivals.

Why not use a moment or two while the audience is gathering to back-promote your previous show? Saying briefly what you talked about will reinforce your brand and help instil the 'fear of missing out' emotion (FOMO). In other words, viewers to your *current* show will realise what they missed and, if the content sounds valuable to them, they may go back and watch the replay and perhaps make more effort to catch your future broadcasts.

Say what is in the show

Yep, again!

> "Hello, thanks so much for taking the time to watch me today. During this show, I'll be helping you with . . ."

This is another form of words than you used previously, so as not to bore people, and because people are more likely to remember things if you repeat them.

It's great to say what you are going to do/show them/talk about, how their lives will be made better by investing their time with you or what problem of theirs you will solve.

Remind and explain

Remind viewers that they can comment on what you are saying at any time. You may at this point want to set any 'ground rules', perhaps that those who send inappropriate comments may get blocked.

Explain the icons and hearts and encourage viewers to tap on the screen if they like/ agree with what you are saying. *Reminding people that they can comment and send hearts encourages them to listen and engage more in your content: they feel obliged to do as you request.*

Suggest they could *subscribe* to your live-streams (on Facebook they tap the sub-scribe button, or they *follow you* on Twitter and Periscope) to get notified the next time you go live and invite their followers to come on over and watch as well.

Offer a roadmap

Explain how you will get to where you are going.

> *So today I'm going to show you some of the devastation caused by the fire at the historic Clandon Park mansion. We'll start with a look at the front of the house where the damage is the worst, before taking you to where the blaze broke out. Then we'll venture inside the shell of the building and talk to the person who's*

leading the team of surveyors and builders, and there'll be a chance for you to ask some questions. Finally, we'll go to the ornamental garden for a chat with the leader of the restoration team, and again we'll gladly try and answer as many questions that we can, and we'll also explain when you can come to the Park to see the work for yourself.

All that in, we reckon, 2 minutes. This should not be a 'welcoming people to your show' show!

Do a welcome, get their attention, and then get to the point.

▶ NOTES

1 Colin Hogan, *Grab Your Viewers' Attention in 10 Seconds*, http://demoduck.com/ September 28th, 2015
2 Greg Jarboe, *Schmoose Optimization: What It Is and Why It Expands Views, Engagements and Earnings on You Tube*, http://tubularinsights.com/ August 20th, 2016

20

During the show

▶ **INTRODUCTION**

It's easy to get caught up in the moment when you are presenting on a live-video. After all, there's a lot to think about:

- ▶ Being fluent
- ▶ Checking your notes
- ▶ Keeping on track
- ▶ Reading the comments
- ▶ Reacting to the comments
- ▶ Having an eye on the number of viewers
- ▶ Having an eye on the clock
- ▶ Maybe walking
- ▶ Possibly watching out for what you should *not* show
- ▶ And maybe doing an interview

There's no denying it: it's a non-multi-tasker's nightmare! In this chapter, we cover the considerations to have when you are in mid-flow. So here we go! And get ready to engage and inspire, explain and entertain.

▶ INVOLVE THE VIEWERS

If you don't interact, you are ignoring the 'live' and 'personal' aspects of streaming. That may reduce the benefit of someone watching (either watching live, or watching at all). It's a two-way street.

You may not be able to *hear* your audience, but you know they are there from the viewer-tally, the emojis or hearts, and the comments they make in the text box. So involve them! After all, one of the unique aspects of live-streaming is this live inter-activity that is achieved through the dialogue. So build ways for them to react and be part of an active audience and collaboratively contribute to the content using:

- ▶ Questions
- ▶ Calls to action
- ▶ Straw polls

Ask questions

Have the viewers confirm that they have a problem (one that you have already iden-tified), to *give you permission to help resolve it.* That way they will be more open to you helping them.

So ask a leading question:

- ▶ "Do you want me to explain the very best ways to make money with this new strategy?"
- ▶ "Who wants to see where the fire broke out?"
- ▶ "I was going to share the discount code now, is that okay?"

Viewers type 'yes' and that gives you 'permission' to continue with the content that you had already prepared, and they are more engaged because they have identified the 'problem' that they need to have solved.

And keep reminding yourself to ask questions and request feedback from the viewers to keep them engaged and involved throughout the show. For example:

- ▶ "Do you agree?"
- ▶ "Who here is going to do as I suggest/change their way of working/invest in/sign up for the discount?"
- ▶ "Should I move on now?"

Ask open-ended questions to get people to reply in a bit more detail:

▶ "Any questions, let me know what they are and how I can help."

▶ "How will you change what you are doing now?"

▶ "What should I cover in the next tutorial?"

Remember to leave a little longer for viewers to write their lengthier answers in the text-box.

And, of course, viewers don't have to reply in *text-form*. It may be more fun if you request they answer with an emoji, perhaps one with applause, a flame, a target, a money bag and so on.

▶ "Thumbs up if you think that's a good idea."

▶ "Drop me a smiley face if you understand what I've mentioned so far."

▶ "Put in the racing car if you want me to race to the top tip."

A few people will want to consume rather than participate, and that's fine. But give an opportunity for those who want to take part to do so: ask questions, invite people to respond, make it easy for them to comment about something you have said.

Don't forget about them. This is not a monologue!

And as well as asking questions, don't forget to answer them as well!

Acknowledge your audience

Acknowledge a few comments, say hi to a few viewers, and it will make the whole audience feel welcomed. If you spot a 'frequent viewer' join your show (someone who turns up and contributes on a regular basis), consider giving them a name-check. A personal acknowledgement and thanks will further build your relationship with them.

▶ MAKE THE SHOW STICKY

Remember that most people will watch with the sound down and for less than 30 seconds (probably considerably less). So make sure that what you show is visually captivating:

▶ Visual

▶ Colourful

▶ Interesting

▶ With movement

▶ Easily understood

And make sure that verbally you include as many of these as possible:

▶ Welcomes

▶ Acknowledgements

▶ Explanations

▶ Recaps and throw-aheads

▶ Reminders to share and how to do it

▶ Reminders to follow and how to do it

You need to improve your 'retention rate'. In other words, keep viewers watching for longer. Aim to retain!

Re-setting and re-introducing

There will be a continual 'churn' of viewers to the video, people coming and going at different times. So when new ones join, you have to explain who you are and what's going on. It's what the TV shows do brilliantly. Just before a commercial break, they tease ahead:

▶ "Still to come . . . will Michael complete the task on time? Jen spots something green and hairy in the bathtub . . . and discover how long it's been since Pablo walked more than five steps!"

And then after the break, they throw back:

▶ "Previously, we saw Kathryn lie to Pablo about her feelings towards him . . . Sarah failed spectacularly at the only task she's been given to do . . . and we discovered where it was that Mark's been hiding."

Use these techniques in your show when looking back and looking ahead. So you could structure that section like this:

▶ "If you've just joined us, hello and welcome. We're just going through how to winterize your car. Already I've shown how to save money when topping up your wiper fluid and the number-one thing not to do when clearing ice from your windscreen. Still to come . . . our 'no-pain snow-chain' lesson and 'staying alive if you skid when you drive'. But first . . ."

Keep an eye on the conversation and look for that new viewer to come in and ask who you are, what you're doing or where you are for opportunities to organically weave your message into the conversation.

Luke Watson[1]

But, and here's another trick, just before you do a 're-set', suggest to your viewers that they invite their friends to watch. That way, when they join, they'll arrive just as you are explaining what's going on.

Continual engagement

Grab your viewers' attention at the start of your stream, and keep grabbing them. That doesn't mean shouting or being outrageous, but giving them quality content. I've mentioned that phrase 'quality content' a few times. Obviously every show and subject are different, but what do I mean by it?

▶ New information

▶ Old information repackaged and explained in a new way

▶ Old information with a different or recent example

▶ Material someone can use immediately after watching

▶ Memorable stuff that sticks in their mind from the show ('take-aways')

▶ Content that keeps people watching for more of the same

Keep what you say simple, straightforward and to the point. Avoid jargon. Talk *with* the viewers and not *at* them.

Forward momentum

Remember the process of forward momentum: an eye on where you are going, and the occasional glance over your shoulder to remind your viewers where you have been.

Welcome late-comers, say who you are and what you are talking about, remind people what you've said so far and how to comment and 'heart', follow and share. At any stage in your show you have to:

▶ Be moving forward (to satisfy the *current* viewers)

▶ Have recently, briefly referred to what you have already said (to satisfy the *new* viewers)

▶ Be about to tease ahead to what's still to come (to keep *all* the viewers watching for longer)

THE A, B, C, D, E OF WHAT BEHAVIOURS DRIVE ENGAGEMENT

▶ **Amazement** – People are naturally curious, and live-streaming shows them new things.

▶ **Belonging** – Streams will usually only get a small number of live viewers because of their unpredictability and ephemerality. So when you watch, you feel part of a small, select group.

▶ **Control** – Naturally, humans like some control. The interaction in a live-stream satisfies this, as viewers may be able to affect the direction the content takes.

▶ **Desire for recognition** – The presenter can welcome viewers by name, and answer their questions and comments directly, thereby satisfying the desire in all of us to be recognised.

▶ **Exclusivity** – You have to watch live to be able to interact, and if the stream is to a closed group, viewers have the feeling of experiencing uniqueness.

▶ KEEPING GOING

Maintaining energy

Your energy will come from the passion you have for the topic. From that will come the comments and the emojis/hearts. From that engagement will come confidence and inspiration for future shows.

When we are nervous, our breathing cycle tends to be disrupted and becomes shallow and irregular. We breathe from high in our chest rather than deep in our diaphragm, and that means that we have less resonance, we can't say much before having to take another breath, and that causes our heartbeat to rise, our voice to sound thin and quavering, our presentation to become flat, wooden and uninspiring. You can see how one thing leads to another as being self-conscious about stress spirals out of control!

You need to relax so your energy is on slow-release. Like a valve, you will be able to increase or decrease it when it is needed. (If you are nervous, it'll either not be there at all or will come all at once like a fire-hydrant!)

This is an obvious way to relax: sit up straight (perhaps in a chair with a straight back), so your lungs aren't squashed, and so you can take a deep breath . . . and then go for it. Take a few deep ones: long breaths in through the nose, hold for five seconds and then s-l-o-w-l-y let it go, out through the mouth . . . and calm the whole thing down. (Here's another one: smile! It will relax your face and release endorphins, too.)

Maintaining focus

The focus will come from your preparation. Having some bullet points to hand will help you keep on track during your show. And so will a clock: it's easy to let the time slip away from you. We know that all too well. As TV and radio broadcasters, my colleagues and I often say to interview guests "You'll be on for about 5 minutes" and their reaction is one of horror! "How long? I can't possibly talk for all that time!" But they do, and what's more, they often say "Is that it? Was that 5 minutes? It went so fast!" Time can pass quickly when presenting, but often for a viewer, it's the other way around. Time d-r-a-g-s.

When you are broadcasting, have your notes and a clock. And when you start off as a newbie broadcaster, try not to cram too much content into each show. Better to do several short ones instead. Continually self-check that you are delivering what you set out to, in an orderly and timely manner. If it's a list, let the viewers know what's going on, what their journey is and how far down the road they are.

Whether you plan a show and stick to it, or viewers' comments lead you off course and you have to return to it, remember: people only have so much time and data allowance, so ensure you don't waffle.

Value your viewers' minutes and megs

On-location streams

One of the huge advantages of Facebook Live and Twitter Go Live/Periscope over the purely desktop-based video-streams is that you can take them (almost) anywhere and show people anything. Some of the best live-streamers have engaged and enthralled in equal measure by giving people a view of their workplace or their city. Here are a few tips to think about when 'on location' rather than at a desk.

Don't move the camera too much, but let objects appear naturally in the frame if you can. I don't mean 'don't walk around', but if you are on a barge up the canal, then let the view come to you, and if you are street-side during a parade, let the band march past you while you hold the camera steady. (Don't move the phone, as it's a better view to have the musicians walk towards you and see their faces and instruments, than away from you and only see their backs!)

The zoom is digital on the phone, which doesn't create a very good picture, so 'zoom with your feet'. In other words, walk towards something to make a close-up shot.

FIGURE 20.1 Consider having landscape orientation of your phone for shots which are obviously landscape-friendly! This sunset was streamed in portrait mode, and when the viewer turns the phone to landscape the image simply becomes smaller

Source: Periscope

If you lose the Wi-Fi or 3G/4G phone connection while you are on air, Facebook Live and Twitter Go Live/Periscope will both try to connect you. While this is happening:

▶ A message will appear on the screen.

▶ Don't give the phone too much work to do, so stop talking and moving the phone and just wait for a reconnection.

▶ The 'Go Live' button will be greyed out until a stronger connection can be established.

When you are back live, give a brief explanation "I'm sorry I lost the connection there for a moment" and continue.

If you never get back on live, don't worry: what you *did* broadcast will still have been saved to your profile (the show is captured remotely as part of the streaming process). If a half-recorded show isn't what you want to have posted, you can always delete it.

If losing the connection is a possibility, then consider writing in the text, or saying at the start of the show of your concerns.

But remember: if you have a poor and intermittent signal and your picture is fuzzy, pixelated or drops out too often, it may be all the reason viewers need to turn you off.

▶ QUALITY BEATS QUANTITY

Don't get hung up about having few people watching, for several reasons. One is, you don't actually want loads of people to watch your *early* shows as you are still on a learning curve! Also, later down the line, you'll build better engagement with people, the more specific your content is. *The quality of engagement beats quantity of people.*

You could do a general show about 'cars' and have a ton of viewers, but they may not stay around for long because they may consider your content unfocussed as the topic is too wide.

But do a show about *classic cars*, or *the latest models* or *racing cars* and you have started to narrow it down. You will get fewer viewers, but the ones you get will be much more interested and engaged in what you have to say and will likely stick around for longer. And that will increase your 'retention rate'.

Go deep, not wide, with your content. That way you will get a small, but more focused, more engaged audience that stays around for longer and comes back more often. And repeat viewers are really valuable as they are your biggest fans.

If you see that only *one* person is watching you live, don't give it up and give in. Present the show just as though 100 people were there. Give it your all:

▶ It's polite.

▶ To stop or do a half-hearted show will damage your reputation.

▶ Whoever is watching may love it and invite their followers to watch – they can't do that if you end early.

▶ There may be other people watching online whose attendance isn't noted in the tally number you see.

▶ People will also potentially still watch the show that you save and upload to Facebook Live, Periscope, YouTube, etc.

A single viewer

If you do decide to stop the stream, make a polite announcement (don't just throw in the towel!) before you stop. Take time out and restart with another title. This will mean you get another notification sent out, another chance to be redistributed and the new stream will go back at the top of your Facebook page, your Twitter feed and the 'live list' on Periscope, so you may catch new viewers.

▶ OTHER TECH TIPS

Swapping cameras

If you want to swap between cameras (the front-facing 'selfie' one that lets you see the comments and the back-facing one that shows what you can see ahead of you), tap the camera icon (Facebook) or double-tap the screen (Periscope). (Incidentally, the back-facing camera is usually the better of the two.)

You could have the phone screen towards you as you give a presentation, and then want to flip to the alternative camera to show something on your laptop, but still give your verbal explanation. But when you do this you will then be slightly 'off-mic', and the sound level will drop.

To get around this, use an external microphone so the sound picked up is always your voice (or whatever you point the mic at), wherever the camera is pointed.

A cheap and easy solution is to use the mic that's built into the headphones that come included with later devices. Plug them into the headphone socket to force the phone to always pick up sound from that mic.

Remember it takes a moment for a phone to switch between the two lenses and the two mics. So if you are using the built-in mics, pause talking for a second as you flip the view. Otherwise, people will miss what you have said.

Sketch

Both Facebook Live and Periscope have a feature that lets you draw on the screen. You can use this to highlight part of the scene to your viewers and work in a similar way: tap the pencil icon and pick a colour and then trace your finger on the screen. On Periscope, the doodle will disappear after a few seconds; on Facebook Live, tap the 'dustbin' icon to delete the sketch. There is no sketch feature in Twitter Go Live.

Screenshots

Unlike Snapchat where the screenshot is a big no-no, both of the main live-streaming apps encourage viewers to take screenshots of broadcasts. Indeed, on Periscope, when a viewer takes a screenshot a small camera icon appears so everyone knows.

How to take a screenshot varies by model, but it's usually by pressing the power button and home button at the same time. The picture will be saved to your camera roll. On Periscope you will then be given a prompt to tweet your screenshot (and a link to the live show) without leaving the broadcast you are watching. Encourage your viewers to take screenshots so there is more activity on the screen.

The value of vanity links

If you want to direct people to a website address, it can be a bit awkward for you to read and for them to remember and write down accurately. After all, they can't click on a link (unless you have a colleague putting it in the comments), so they need to be

FIGURE 20.2 The sketch facility in Facebook Live

Source: Facebook

able to remember it. That's especially the case if it's not the home page address, *but a page within it.*

But if you use a URL shortener (such as www.bit.ly), then you can easily personalise the long and cumbersome address to one which is more memorable and branded with your name. Use a shortener whose clicks you can track so that you can measure the effectiveness of your call to action and campaign.

No sound on your show?

If a viewer complains that they cannot hear, it may be that that person has the 'mute' switch still activated on their own device. Only worry if *several* people have the same problem. Then it's probably a bug in the system, so apologise, end the stream and restart.

 NOTE

1   *15 Best Practices for Facebook Live*, www.searchenginejournal.com/ May 12th, 2016

21

At the end of the show

▶ INTRODUCTION

As I mentioned previously:

- ▶ Don't just keep talking until you've got something to say.

- ▶ Before you start a show, know where you are going, so you know when you have arrived.

So, consider ending a show when:

- ▶ **You've said what you have promised to say** – 'loquaciousness' is a fantastic word to say, but not necessarily for the viewer to experience a demonstration of.

- ▶ **The numbers of live viewers starts to tail off** – but consider that more may be watching on the web.

- ▶ **The comments and questions start to tail off** – those watching on the web cannot necessarily contribute in this way, so you can only consider the app viewers. Maybe you have answered all their concerns and explained everything so well there is nothing more for them to ask.

Or, if you are not going to stop the show entirely after considering these points, then maybe change *content*.

▶ Q&AS

After you have delivered your main, prepared content, you may want to take some questions and open up the floor to comments, but the trick is not to get too distracted.

Of course, your live-stream won't be a hard sell for your product, service or experience, but here's a way you can promote what it is you do while answering a question: practice how you can pivot many questions back to your business, as you answer. So, even if you are doing a tour of a stately home:

Question: *How old is the oldest statue in the house?*

Answer: *Thanks for that. How interesting. It's probably one that we have from the Romans. We don't have time to show it just now, but next time you are here, pop by the Hadrian Room and be sure to check it out. Our opening times are right on our website.*

After a short while, tell viewers when you are about to take the last few questions, to signal to them that you will be ending the show in the next few minutes.

▶ AT THE END OF YOUR SHOW

At the end of the show, consider:

- ▶ **A summary of your main points** – Now would be a good time to ask viewers to share the show, just before you recap, as they know the value of what you have just said and will want to share that knowledge with their friends. (Remember, on Periscope, even if your followers' followers can't watch now, live, the replay of your show drops into their 'watch' timeline so they can see you later.)

- ▶ **Encourage late-comers to watch the replay from the start** – to get the full content.

- ▶ **A call to action**

  - ▷ Which could be as informal as "I hope you have now learnt how to make lemon drizzle cake, and you will be baking your own very soon", or something more formal: "and this is only available for this week, so get onto our website and order yours today!"

  - ▷ Or something more *specific*: "go to our website at xxxxxxx.com and download our free mortgage advice planner" and have a website landing page that you can point people to, or (in the days of double-screening) to drive people to a TV broadcast.

When you are broadcasting to an audience, you know that they are tuned in and highly receptive to messaging. But you need to hammer the right messages home if you hope to capitalise on this potential for driving leads.

Brian Honigman[1]

▶ A trail ahead to the content in the next show and say when it will be on, and a natural suggestion that people follow you to make watching that show easier.

Thank people for watching; they have, after all, given up their valuable time and have decided to spend it with you. Have an 'attitude of gratitude'. As we've said before:

Respect their minutes and respect their megs.

After all, if it wasn't for the live viewers, you might as well be doing the show for YouTube. (Some live-streamers have the occasional 'thank-you show': an episode with no other content apart from thanking their viewers for their recent support.)

Ask them to share the show. Why now, when it's all-but-finished? Because:

▶ They have seen the show to the end, so obviously they see it as worthwhile.

▶ Therefore, they are in a good position to recommend their friends to see it, too (rather more so than recommending the show at the start, before they have seen its content). People will rarely endorse to their friends what they haven't experienced themselves.

▶ The 'recommendation' will now appear in their friend's Periscope Watch list for the next 24 hours, and on their Facebook feed, so that they can view it at their convenience.

Get viewers to introduce themselves to others. Perhaps ask them to each send a message to the group saying their name, what they do and where they are ("Charlie, Cape Town, make windchimes from fishbones"). This all helps foster the image of you as a helpful person, bringing people together to network. Remember it's not all about you.

Why not repay their views of you, by watching them? A 'reciprocal watch' or tweet would really strengthen your relationship. Get to know your followers; build a relationship. (So-called 'follower trains', or 'follower orgies', are prompted by presenters who suggest that everyone watching should follow everyone else who's watching. This increases follower numbers for everyone, but doesn't necessarily increase viewers and certainly does nothing to increase the value of content.)

Remind them that if they are watching on replay, they can still:

▶ **On Facebook Live**: leave comments and emoticons

▶ **On Periscope**: 'heart' you

Remind people of who you are and what you do, how people can follow you or get in touch in 'real life'. This is another chance to build your relationship with them. You may not have seen, let alone responded to, every comment and question during the broadcast, so invite them to contact you in another way:

▶ **You can direct them to your website** – you can simply read out your website address or email, or you can have it printed out and show your viewers what it is and suggest they take a screenshot of it. Or have a colleague put it in the comments.

▶ **You can suggest they email you** – maybe as part of a VIP Club, or to get a free 'tip sheet' or sales code.

Then you can:

▶ Give them more help and advice.

▶ Answer more questions.

▶ Strengthen your relationship.

▶ Capture their email address for a newsletter or other marketing.

The power of live-streaming is in the community. Respect them, thank them, engage them, value their time.

Brian Fanzo

As part of my branding, I say the same thing at the end of each show. It started by accident, and now I am known for it:

"Thanks for the loan of your eyes and your ears. . .

And wherever you are on Planet Earth, have a great day!"

And having this means I don't have to think what to say at the very end of a show and let the show simply peter (!) out. Obviously, you won't want mine, but think up a phrase that's unique to you.

Having a surprise at the end of the show, or teasing during the show that there will be a 'reveal' or 'extra content' or a 'bonus tip' will increase the likelihood that people will watch to the end or tune in more regularly. "If you are watching right now, email or tweet me with the word 'klaxon', and I'll send you a special link." Doing this is like a 'secret handshake' and makes people feel special and part of an exclusive club.

Or finish on a cliff-hanger, an unresolved question, or the first part of a 'money off' catchphrase that will only be completed at the *start* of the next show . . . or in a 'private' stream that you present immediately afterwards.

▶ JUST BEFORE YOU END

Then, turn off the camera/stop the stream while people have this other image on their phone. That way their last memory of your show won't be you peering at the screen and jabbing at it with your finger trying to stop the broadcast!

Don't stop talking and then immediately stop the video. Instead, at the end of your final sentence leave a three-second pause before you close the video stream. That will give a buffer, so your final words are not cut off mid-stream. (On Facebook Live, wait for the 'ping' before you know for sure you are no longer live.)

To stop the streaming

On Facebook Live: tap 'Finish'

On Twitter Go Live/Periscope: swipe down and tap 'Stop Broadcasting'

THE DEBRIEF

How did the show go? Consider:

Content

▶ Did you follow through on what you set out to do?

▶ Were you side-tracked, and if so was this necessary or avoidable? Did it give you added content for another occasion?

Engagement

▶ Did you react to what viewers sent you on the screen?

▶ Did you react to people at the location?

▶ Was there as much use of the 'live' feature as possible?

Quality

▶ Did the technical requirements live up to expectation? The signal and camerawork?

▶ Did you show and go where you intended?

Value

▶ Did it inform people in a way they would have had difficulty sourcing otherwise?

▶ Was there knowledge, information and perspective?

▶ NOTE

1   Brian Honigman, *How to Be Compelling With Livestreaming*, www.brianhonigman.com/ October 7th, 2015

PART V

Post-show production

You have tapped 'Finish', but even though the show is over, the work isn't. Now comes the post-production. After all, it makes sense to get as much value as possible from the work you have put in. You need to analyse your viewing data and repurpose your content.

And that's what this final part of the book is about: helping you to evaluate and optimise your live-stream show.

22

Downloads and uploads

▶ **INTRODUCTION**

Of course, you can turn off your phone, turn off your mind and turn to other things. That's the simplest post-production. But it's probably best to finish the job you started. In this chapter, I'll tell you why you need to have a 'Post-Show Strategy' and how to run it.

There's quite a lot that you could do once your show is over, so let's start at the beginning of 'the end', if you see what I mean:

- ▶ 'Downloads' – to your phone and memory sticks.
- ▶ 'Uploads' – to the platform (usually Facebook Live, which has more options when you upload, than Periscope). Uploads to other sites (such as YouTube) are outlined in the next chapter.

▶ **DOWNLOADS**

As soon as you finish your broadcast, you will be given the option to download the video to your phone's camera roll. You will probably want to do this so you can 'do something else with it' later, in other words, so you can reversion it:

- ▶ Upload it to another site: your website or YouTube.
- ▶ Clip sections for tweets.

I'll show you more about those 'upload' options in a moment. First, let's take a look at saving shows locally on your device.

Saving the whole video to your phone will be a bit like a sci-fi story – it involves time and space:

▶ So, if you're trying to do one live-stream after another, you may need to dump the save so you can get on and do another show.

▶ Make sure that you have enough free space on your phone for the video to be saved.

How do you know if you have enough space? You can look in the 'settings' of your phone, which will tell you how many megs or gigs you have left, but that may not help you work out if that will be enough to save your video. There are plenty of apps that you can use that will tell you such detail; my favourite is the QuickSpace app on iOS.

If you don't have enough room on your phone to keep all of your videos, then consider uploading them straight from your phone to:

▶ A flash drive that you have with you (something like the SanDisk iXpand)

▶ A private YouTube account (so you have the videos, but no one else can view them unless you want them to)

FIGURE 22.1 In Facebook, tap on the download icon on the screen and choose to save and upload your live-stream

Source: Facebook

▶ A cloud service such as EverNote or DropBox, again which is accessed directly from your phone

In Periscope: you can configure your settings (in the People > Profile menu) to always save your Scopes to your phone. You can also choose to save your broadcast to your camera roll in high definition. You can find this option in the settings area of the app. This is the best quality but also the largest file.

If you decide *not* to save the Show, it's a bit awkward to get it back later (indeed, it's *impossible* to retrieve if you didn't upload *or* download). If it's on Facebook, you can:

▶ Open Facebook and find the video in your Photos.

▶ Click on the video to open it in Facebook.

▶ Click on the Options link under the video.

▶ Choose to download in SD or HD quality.

Or for Periscope, go to http://downloadperiscopevideos.com.

WHY YOU SHOULD ALWAYS SAVE YOUR SHOWS

Yes, even (or, especially) if you don't upload shows to the app's site, save your shows somewhere else, simply to protect yourself. Anyone could claim that your show included material that was:

▶ Illegal

▶ Against a copyright

▶ Defamatory

▶ Inflammatory.

▶ Or broke your terms of contract with your 9-to-5 employer

And even though it would be up to that other person to prove what they claim *was* on your show, how much easier if you could quickly and easily prove that it *wasn't*.

▶ UPLOADS

Once your live broadcast has ended, as well as having the opportunity to save the stream to your camera roll, you are also given the option to:

- ▶ Upload your processed live-stream to your Facebook or Periscope account, which will increase the chances for it to be seen, and more chances to market yourself and your product.

  - ▷ You can always upload it now but *delete it later* if you have second thoughts.

- ▶ *Not* to upload it, which you may choose if something went disastrously wrong in the show and you believe your brand may be damaged if people view it.

  - ▷ You can always choose *not to upload* it, but if you have saved the video to your camera roll to upload it later, it will then appear as a stand-alone video and not have the same appearance as the live-broadcast. And, of course, you can't upload videos to Periscope or ones over 140 seconds to Twitter.

On Facebook, before you can upload an HD version of your video, you will have to enable that feature in settings (more settings > video default quality > HD if available).

If you choose to save your live-video to your account, pin the post to the top of your feed so it is most visible for casual visitors to your page.

▶ EDITING FACEBOOK METADATA

(*A reminder that the layout may be different depending on which type of Facebook 'page' you are using and changes that may have occurred after the time of writing this book.*)

Once uploaded, you can make several changes or additions to the text and SEO content that will optimise it and help it get discovered.

This can only be done on the Facebook desktop site, not your mobile device.

From the desktop site, slick on the date stamp, and from the next screen you can add or change:

- ▶ The title and description. This is handy if you decide a different title, including key words, will be more alluring to potential viewers, or if the live-video ended up with slightly different content than you had anticipated when you originally wrote the text. Ensure the most important information is 'above the fold', that is, in the first few lines of the text box. Most people just glance at the text and won't click through to read more. Also put the 'call to action' here, such as a website link, and ask your viewers to share the show to their friends and fans.

▶ Who you were with, to help people find your video if they're searching for key words.

▶ Where and when the video was taken, including having it posted to your timeline at another time.

▶ Decide who sees the video.

▶ Change the settings regarding how the comments are displayed and add comments of your own (which are pinned to the point in the video that you made them).

Click on the 'options' button at the bottom of the page to:

▶ Share the video to another page or send it privately.

▶ Download the video in HD or SD.

▶ Get the link to the video (you can use this link to share this video with anyone, even if they don't have a Facebook account. Anyone with the link will be able to see it.)

▶ Delete the video.

▶ Edit the video (see the following section).

Editing your Facebook video

From the desktop site, slick on the date stamp > options > edit video, and from here you can make several additional changes to optimise your video.

You can enter up to ten tags (such as other people or businesses). These are not displayed, but they make your video more discoverable. You can also input the:

▶ Title

▶ Location

▶ Date

▶ Description of the video

And you are also able to select a category that represents your content (such as beauty, business, lifestyle, sport and several others); prevent embeds (when ticked, people cannot embed your video on third-party websites); and decide who can and cannot see the video.

Thumbnails

There is also the option to change the thumbnail, the small picture that illustrates your content and helps sell it. You will be given the choice of one of ten images to choose from so you avoid a still picture of you gurning to the camera, rather than the fantastic sunset you captured a moment later.

THUMBNAIL RULES OF THUMB

Little things mean a lot, and using this visual 'advert' that helps sell your video once it has been uploaded is another way to get views. It's the eye-catching 'book jacket' or the 'album cover' that will encourage people to click through to your content. You may have presented the greatest live show ever, but if you use a thumbnail that was chosen automatically by Facebook, then it may reduce the chance of your replay being watched. You are in a battle for eyeballs, and whatever you can do to help make your video stand out from the crowd is an opportunity you must take.

But you must know what frame from your video is the best to choose:

- ▶ One that's clear, bright and has good contrast, with a foreground that's distinct from the background. It has to jump off the screen at potential viewers.

- ▶ A close-up of a human face. We interact with other human beings, especially if the face is clear, you can see their eyes, and they are showing emotion.

- ▶ A scene that's visually interesting – a view, but not one of a brick wall.

- ▶ One that fits with your brand image.

- ▶ A frame that sums up the content of the show – maybe the product itself, not one that encourages click-bait (an unrelated but 'sexy' picture to encourage views).

Once the video has been uploaded, you can choose an alternative thumbnail from the video directly or create another one to upload.

▶ Take a 'composed' still image.

▶ Add contrast and other elements in Photoshop, or on an on-camera app.

▶ Add text (not too much as on a thumbnail it may be tricky to read).

▶ Add any branding such as a corporate colour to the frame, or a small logo.

Facebook Live subtitles

You can also embed subtitles onto your existing videos. Subtitling is important because so few people click through when a video is in their timeline to actually listen to the content. And if they can't hear what's happening, they won't get the full benefit. Indeed, if they don't click-to-hear then, unless the visuals are particularly captivating, the chances of them staying and watching the video on mute is pretty low.

The subtitling process takes more time, but:

▶ Makes your broadcast much more likely to be consumed either

▷ without clicking-to-hear

▷ with clicking-to-hear

▶ Makes it look more professional, especially if you upload it to your own website or YouTube, or the subtitles are a translation of the language being spoken.

▶ Makes it cut through the clutter of other video content in someone's feed.

There are two ways you can add captions: an easy way and a less-easy way! You can either automatically generate captions and edit them or you can upload a SubRip (.srt) file of your own transcription.

The easy way

Once your live broadcast has been uploaded:

▶ Click in your video library and open that video.

▶ Click on options (at the bottom of the video) and then 'edit'.

▶ Captions > Generate.

▶ Edit the captions on the right-hand side (these are tagged to the points the words are spoken in the video) and click 'Save to Video'.

The trickier way

Once your live broadcast has been uploaded:

▶ Click in your video library and open that video.

▶ Click on options (at the bottom of the video) and then 'edit'.

▶ Captions > Upload SRT file.

▶ Choose an. srt file from your computer (see following section).

▶ Select an optional Default Language. If you select a default language, captions will appear in this language when a viewer's preferred language isn't available.

▶ Finish adding details to your video and click Publish.

Creating an .srt file

SubRip or SRT files are created using a standard text editor like Notepad++ or TextEdit for Mac OS, and they can be a bit more time-consuming to produce than altering text that was automatically generated.

▶ Open the text editor such as Notepad++ or TextEdit for Mac OS.

▶ Play your video and prepare to transcribe what has been said.

▶ You need to divide each phrase into different numbered sections in the following format:

▷ Begin by typing "1" (without the quotes) and then press Enter to start a new line.

▷ The .srt format uses milliseconds to time when the text will appear, so divide each phrase like this:

```
1
00:00:11,000 --> 00:00:16,000
Humpty Dumpty sat on the wall,
```

▶ Press Enter, and then "2" (without the quotes) to get:

```
2
00:00:16,001 --> 00:00:20,001
Humpty Dumpty had a great fall,
```

▶ Press Enter, and then "3" (without the quotes) to get:

```
3
00:00:18,002 --> 00:00:22,002
All the king's horses and all the king's men,
```

▶ And so on until you have captioned the full video.

▶ Save the file in the (very specific). srt format: save > all files > [file name] ending in ".srt" (without the quotes) > save.

Ensure that the written words appear right as the spoken words are being said.

If there is no more commentary for a few seconds, don't let the text linger too long after the spoken word.

Limit the amount of text to one or two short lines each time.

People don't talk in sentences! Therefore, don't worry about breaking up long chunks of speech into phrases over a few screens, split with. . . . That way viewers won't be overwhelmed.

People who watch your Page's video with the sound turned off will automatically see captions. People who watch your video with the sound turned on will need to turn on captions to see them. The language people see captions in is determined by their preferred language.

23

Amplify your live-stream

▶ **INTRODUCTION**

When you repurpose your content to a new format, you can reach a new audience.

You've invested time and effort in getting this far, so this chapter is all about getting as much juice as possible from the fruits of your labour.

▶ **REPLAYS**

Watching a replay

When watching a replay of a Facebook Live, people can still send comments and emojis, which will be added to the video so others will see them subsequently. On Periscope they can tap the screen and send hearts but not comments.

On a **Facebook Live**, viewers can tap the timecode next to a comment and be taken directly to that point in the show. They will also be able to see a graph on the screen for when the most comments were made, and tap that to be taken to that point.

Periscope viewers can also scroll through a replay, forward and backward.

Why would they want to do this?

▶ To get past a lengthy introduction.

▶ To go back and hear a section again.

▶ Because they are busy.

▶ When you're watching a replay, you sometimes just want to fast-forward a segment and get to the part you're looking for.

▶ Or to the moment your friend told you about.

▶ Or you just want to seek through the whole thing quickly to get an idea of what happened.

Sharing a replay

Encourage your viewers to share your replays by mentioning how to do it in your video when you are live. This gives your show more traction and increases the potential number of viewers. Remember, you will have a unique URL for every single Facebook Live or Periscope you produce. Using it will save your followers from having to scroll through your entire newsfeed after being prompted with a vague "see the video on our Facebook page".

On Facebook: Click on the timestamp in your video post and copy the unique URL from the screen that opens up. You can then tweet this or put it in your email newsletter and so on. On mobile, tap the 'share' button and copy the link.

On Periscope:

▶ Start playing the show that you want to share.

▶ Tap the '. . .' and then 'share' and then either:

▷ **Share on Twitter**. This will automatically send a tweet from your account saying that you are watching this show and want to share it.

▷ **Copy to Clipboard** (the phone's memory). This makes it possible to post the link somewhere else. For example, if you wanted to email the link to someone so they could watch it on the laptop, then open a new email on your phone and simply 'paste' the link into the message.

▷ **Share on Facebook**

Boosting your replay

Scroll through the video to a great visual moment, perhaps where you pulled a strange face, showed a great view or the screen was filled with comments and emojis, and take a screenshot. Put that image (maybe with a text caption on top of it – I showed you how to do this earlier), together with an updated title and the link to the show, and re-tweet *that*. Schedule a few different versions of that tweet to go out over the next week.

On Twitter, you can also re-tweet the original tweet that was sent as soon as you originally went live on Twitter or Periscope. And you can take the text of that, and re-word it and send that out several times more with the link from Periscope.

On Facebook, you can also:

▶ Cross-post your video from one page to another.

▶ Pin that video to the top of your feed (as you can on Twitter).

▶ Boost its appearance in other people's timelines.

▶ Later you could take the address of that video and create another Facebook post to promote it, and include that link.

Also:

▶ Share the original 'live' link and add something along the lines of "Replay available until 5 pm Wednesday UK time" (a specific time is better than "for 24 hours" as you don't know when people will see the tweet). Make sure you say what time zone you are referencing.

▶ Or better still, add a sense of urgency and limited-availability: "Just 12 hours to watch . . .", "Link expires in three hours . . ." as you can create FOMO by deleting videos after a certain period.

▶ Then tweet links to all those other platforms where you have the repeat or repurposed videos of the original.

▶ Make sure all of these platforms give details of your show and how people can watch them *live*.

So where are those other platforms that you can post promotion of your video?

▶ As a screenshot and bit.ly link on Instagram (links aren't clickable on this platform, so you will need an easy-to-remember version)

▶ In your own blog post or as part of a comment in someone else's (then share that blog post back through the other platforms, for example as a tweet)

▶ As part of your email campaign to subscribers

A straightforward way of doing much of this is to use the Hootsuite app on your phone. So, as soon as you end your show, copy the link to it (as just explained), then open the Hootsuite app and add that link to a new tweet (with at least a title and a picture/screengrab). Then schedule that via the calendar option to be sent however often you like. Compile a 'Tweet Sheet' timetable of social media posts, together with links to content and dates and times to post.

All of this gives you more exposure and more chances to get follows, for only a couple of minutes' extra effort.

You can also schedule with other apps of course, including Twitter (desktop only). It's done via Twitter Ads:

Click on Twitter Ads > set your country and time zone.

And then put in your credit card details. Essentially, this is a bit of a hack. You won't be charged unless you actually set up adverts to run, but by giving your credit card details, you are getting access to the scheduling tool.

Timestamping

It may be quite a daunting prospect for some people to watch an entire show. After all, even though presenting a long broadcast will inevitably gather more viewers than a shorter one will, it's probably not a good experience for the viewer unless you are constantly engaging with them with fantastic ever-moving content and answering their questions.

So consider creating timestamps from the original broadcast to direct viewers to specific content. Timestamps:

▶ Are convenient for the viewer to use as they can jump to specific, relevant points in the show.

▶ Are reasonably quick and easy for you to produce.

▶ Reduce the requirement for your replay viewers to become 'scrubbers', fast-forwarding and rewinding through a show to find the content that they want.

You can produce a blog with the list of timestamps (essentially, a rundown of when you say what) of the entire show:

```
TIMESTAMPS
00:00 - Welcome
02:07 - How to implement a people-based marketing approach
12:41 - Generating Leads on Social Media
19:12 - Growing a digital marketing agency from China. . .
```

or you can write a series of tweets each linking to different, specific points in the broadcast:

How to implement a people-based marketing approach. www.facebook.com/ xxxxxxxxxx Timestamp: 02:07

Once in the broadcast, viewers can scroll through to that segment of the video and watch from that point.

Cross-posting videos on Facebook

Cross-posting video means that you can re-use the same production in other posts and pages, without having to share or upload it several times. It also means that viewer numbers will be consolidated from all the pages, to give one total on the *original* page. Doing this saves times and gives added exposure to your video.

To use this feature, go to the publishing tools for your page, and then enable specific pages to cross-post the video content. (Note: there are some exceptions about what can be cross-posted.)

▶ REPUBLISH, REPURPOSE AND RESURRECT

Don't run yourself ragged creating more and more content for all your social media platforms. Box clever and work out a work-flow to get what you have produced already into the eyes and ears of more people. You do this by republishing, repurposing and resurrecting content you've already created.

Republishing – simply putting exactly the same material on another platform, such as uploading a live-stream video to your YouTube channel with no alteration, to attract a different audience segment. You can do this immediately after your live-stream has finished.

Repurposing – taking previously produced content and editing it in some way before reposting. This may be:

- ▶ Another or a shorter version on the same platform (such as clips from a longer Facebook Live, posted on Facebook)

- ▶ The same content on *another* platform (the audio from a Periscope, as a podcast)

▶ A combination of the two (an edit from one platform, on another: for example, segments from a Facebook Live appearing as clips on Twitter)

Resurrecting – reviving content by linking to it, or reposting it with little or no alteration. This may well be something that you have previously repurposed. An example might be a tweet to the link of a video from a year ago, or reposting a previous live-stream. This may be done when the content becomes topical again, or simply as an automatically scheduled post of 'timeless' content. (Beware of resurrecting material which is out of date, and therefore which may harm your brand. Similarly, keep an eye on the news, so posts such as these don't clash with events. For example, you don't want to repost an interview with a guest who has since died; your title "how to avoid bombing in your next job interview" shouldn't go out on the day of an actual bomb attack.)

Why you should republish, repurpose and resurrect

▶ The hard work is already done. Make the most of it!

▶ You will increase your traction:

▷ You will inevitably reach more people than the original post did, as there's 'another chance to see'. Your followers may not have seen the original post as, because of algorithms, they simply weren't sent it.

▷ You may well reach a *different set* of people:

▶ On another platform – where the audience is different anyway.

▶ Because of how you rewrite the post – restructuring the title, using @names and #hashtags, will mean you are targeting different people to see the content.

▶ You are reinforcing your message and helping to brand your expertise.

▶ If you republish your live-stream to, say, YouTube, you will have a great source of evergreen content, which you can use to attract more fans and cross-promote back to.

▶ You'll build up an archive of shows which you can use to attract more fans. They can binge on the 'boxed set' of material, rather than wait for the next weekly instalment of the live show.

▶ Resurrecting previous content at an opportune moment shows you are in touch with what is happening in your niche. ("Congratulations to Joe Shmo who has today been appointed CEO of International Global Conglomerates Inc. Here's a clip from our interview with him when he joined the board a year ago.")

▶ Updating previous content, shows you are aware of developments and changes. ("The Fuzzballer XTC app has just had a makeover. Here's what's changed and our 'how-to guide' from when it was launched.")

Double, triple or quadruple your exposure all after just one live-stream. Here's how. . .

The ultimate RRR workflow

You may not want to follow all of these steps, but here is an extreme example of what you could do to revive your live and make it survive. Yes, it's additional work, but less than continually creating fresh content. (As many Android devices are different in their layouts, I have chosen to demonstrate this workflow using an iOS phone.) Doing this work on your mobile may eat into your cell-phone data plan, so use Wi-Fi to avoid the possibility of a hefty bill. (The iPhone app WifiMapper shows free Wi-Fi maps of 500 *million* hotspots: appsto.re/gb/9JUV3.i.)

Immediately after ending your live-stream, do the following:

Saving

Save the video to your phone

▶ You are prompted to do this whenever you end a Facebook Live or Periscope.

Upload it to your iCloud account

▶ Open iPhone > Settings > Network > Wi-Fi button.

▶ Move the slider from left to right to turn on.

▶ Settings > iCloud > Storage & Backup.

▶ Move the slider from left to right to turn Back Up to iCloud to on.

▶ Tap 'Back Up Now' to upload videos from your iPhone to your iCloud account.

Upload to Dropbox

First off, you need a Dropbox account. Be aware that iPhones save the videos in Quick-time Movie format (.mov), which may be tricky to use on other browsers, which usually prefer .m4v extensions. Also, you may want to rename the video file to something that is more personally memorable than the default title given to your video by the iPhone.

▶   Open Dropbox on your phone.

▶   Tap on the upper RHS > Upload > Select your video > Upload.

Save a Facebook Live video as an MP4

Go to the video on your Facebook page and download the video from it, so you can save it locally on your desktop and easily edit it.

▶   Play the video > right-click and copy the URL.

▶   Paste this URL into another tab > change the www. to an "m" (without the quotes).

▶   Play the video > right-click while it's playing.

▶   'Save video as' onto your computer.

▶ REPUBLISHING

Upload to YouTube

Share your video on this platform (on a 'private' account if necessary), so you have a backup copy. (Tip: don't post to YouTube too soon after your show has ended, because you want all your viewing stats combined in one place for maximum effect, not watered down across several different platforms.)

WHY IT'S GOOD TO USE YOUTUBE

Have the YouTube app on your phone, set up with your account, so then you can upload your video straight to it:

▶   What Facebook thinks is best for them may not be good for *you*, so drive your viewers where you want them to be and where you want them to experience your content, and make money for you and not for Facebook. On YouTube, if your content is popular you can make money from pre-roll ads.

▶   It's always a good idea not to house all your content in a single place (such as Facebook). You don't own it, or even pay rent on it, and even though it's unlikely to close down tomorrow, if it did you could lose all your work.

▶ It is difficult to point people to archived videos on Twitter Go Live/Periscope. Heck, it's even difficult to find your own material there! But it's much easier on a YouTube channel. (Possibly, set up a second YouTube account just for your live-stream shows.)

▶ YouTube is the second largest search engine after Google, so reposting your video here gives you more visibility.

▶ You will have all your videos in one easily searchable place, where potential customers or clients may find you.

▶ It's a 'digital CV' (or in broadcasters' lingo: 'a demo') of what you do, that you can show to a prospective sponsor.

▶ New fans who discover you some months later can see your material for the first time.

▶ You will have a back-catalogue of material that you can refer people to if the same topics or questions keep being asked.

▶ If you upload while 'in the field', you can free space on your phone ready for another live-stream.

Check that your phone settings do not have an 'auto-sleep' function 'on' (this is the function that will turn your phone off after a set time if you do not tap the screen). If your phone automatically turns off, it will disrupt the forthcoming upload. So, for iPhones: Settings > General > Autolock > Never (this is not available on every model, in which case keep touching your screen to keep the device awake as you complete the following procedure). Remember to reset the auto-lock time after the upload, otherwise your phone will never sleep!

▶ Go to your camera roll and select the video.

▶ Tap the Upload icon and then the YouTube logo.

▶ Complete the title and description, tags, category, quality and privacy sections.

▶ Tap 'publish'.

▶ From your desktop take the YouTube embed code for that video, and use it to show the video on your website.

Embed your Facebook Live video on your website

You can embed a Public post or video. When you embed a post that contains a video, the message that was posted with the video will be included. When you embed a video, only the video player will be included. To embed a video:

▶ Go to the video you want to embed.

▶ Click the down arrow in the top right of the post and select 'embed'.

▶ Copy and paste the code that appears and add it to your own website or web page.

If you embed a video and the audience of the video changes from Public, a message saying the embedded video is no longer available will appear on the website.

USING IFTTT

With 'If This Then That' (*https://ifttt.com/* a free web-based service), you can create a chain of simple conditions ('applets'), which are triggered based on changes to other web services. Here are just a few which have been created to automate various tasks to help you with live-streaming, such as republishing your content to other platforms. You will find others, or you can write your own:

▶ Post your Tweets to Facebook when you use a specific hashtag – Applet ID 112202p

▶ Autopost from Facebook Page to Twitter – Applet ID 263954p

▶ Promote Live Periscope on Facebook with branded image – Applet ID 300166p

▶ If I upload a #YouTube video, post about it to #Facebook – Applet ID 1836p

▶ If I'm going live on Periscope + my Twitter sees #Periscope, then post to FB page that I'm live – Applet ID 303609p

---

How to auto-share your stream to Google+, LinkedIn

If you want to maximise the reach and expose your live-stream to your social media audience, follow the tutorial here: *How to Automatically Share Periscope Video Across Social Media* https://blog.dlvrit.com

▶ REPURPOSING

Turn the audio of the video into a podcast

An assistant or colleague at a remote site can do this by downloading the video from the shared Dropbox account.

▶ Detach the audio from the video. If you've downloaded the video to your phone, run it through an app which separates the audio from the video (there are plenty available).

▶ Edit out the start and end, and any content that is 'video-specific', and edit in appropriate music (beware of copyright) and announcements at the start and end. You can do this on your phone using an audio editor such as Voddio (available on the Apple app store), or on your desktop with a free editor such as Audacity (www.audacityteam.org).

▶ Upload to your podcast platform, usually via a desktop. (Although Spreaker, www.spreaker.com, allows you to record, and then upload, a podcast directly from your mobile phone mic if you wish.)

Turn the audio insto text for a blog

Transcribe the audio and then turn the text into separate blog posts, each one linking back to the original video, or the podcast.

Take the text of your video:

▶ From your video captions or .srt file (described earlier)

▶ Or play the video through a voice-recognition programme (such as Dragon available in the Apple app store for your phone) to get the text

▶ Or play and transcribe the video by hand

Turn the text from the blog into Tweets

Identify quotes from the transcript to turn into scheduled tweets.

▶ Use one of the apps described previously (such as Canva or PicMonkey – both in the app store) to design quote-cards comprising a great original picture (or maybe an eye-grabbing screenshot from the original stream), with stylised text.

▶ Put a watermark or logo on your picture so it can be traced back to you if it is used by someone else.

▶ Compose a tweet with the graphic, together with a link back to the original video, or the podcast.

Segment the original video into soundbites

Create short sound-bites from the original live-stream to tempt people to watch the full version.

Still on your phone and using an app such as iMovie, edit out a short highlight clip each with a nugget of information (a top tip, a soundbite, a question/answer sequence, a blooper), and then:

▶ Share that on Twitter as an embedded video that auto-plays (on Twitter you are allowed up to 140 seconds of video),

▶ And/or put it on Instagram (which allows videos of up to a minute long),

▶ And/or another Facebook site,

▶ And/or as another Facebook post,

▶ And/or a blog post.

Include in these posts:

▶ A link to the original, longer content as a way to encourage people to watch the full show

▶ A link to details of your next scheduled broadcast to encourage people to watch live, and follow you to get the notifications

Create clips from the original video into a cut-down/highlights show

Do this easily by taking a series of soundbites (as described above), and sequencing them together with transitions.

Repurposing *other content* to create a live-stream

So far, I've looked at the most you can make from an existing live-stream, but you can also look at content-creation the other way around.

▶ If you are already producing a podcast, live-stream yourself recording it.

▶ Turn previous blog posts into notes for a live-stream.

We're also creating a show on Periscope as a forum to discuss what we covered in our last podcast. Our true podcast listeners will know to hop into the Scope and engage. It gives them a voice and reminds the community that we have a podcast. Those broadcasts extend the impact of our last podcast episode.

Mario Armstrong[1]

▶ RESURRECTING

With this technique, you manually or automatically redistribute previously repurposed content. The rotation of this will depend on your own business needs, but it makes sense to create a schedule so, for example:

▶ Valentine's day content from one year ("Why I #love #London. Live from one of the greatest views in Britain") goes on the same day the next year and so on.

▶ "The North by North West festival starts today. Here are some of my interviews with the best speakers at last year's event."

▶ "Devastating news that the Old Mill creative space was burned down last night. Here is my tour around it with the chief exec just three months ago."

▶ POST-PROMOTION

Now, you need to get in touch with as many viewers as you can. You have their contact details, and this information is gold-dust. Think what most companies would give to know the names and details of everyone who spent, say, 30 minutes engaging with their brand and so was interested in their messages service or product. Doing this may be tedious, but it's also worthwhile.

If you have used a unique hashtag in your title, search Twitter to see who has used it. They most likely re-tweeted your auto-tweet that was sent out when you went live on Periscope, or have mentioned a promotional tweet that you sent out before you went live on Facebook. Thank them either publicly or privately. Perhaps with a few of them, send a personal video message of thanks (that's easy to do, right in the 'compose tweet' screen, and think what it'll mean to one of your viewers to get that, moments after they've seen you live!).

On Facebook: put a "thanks for watching" comment under the feed, together with a way for people to contact you with further questions.

On Periscope: retweet the auto-tweet, with a quote from you to say "thanks for watching".

Now go to the feed of comments in the Facebook live-stream itself and reply, help and thank those who contributed to the broadcast. Yes, you can reply to comments after the broadcast, and yet how many broadcasters do? And that's why you should: you will stand out and become known for it. What about encouraging viewers to continue the conversation within the community? Incentivise them to contribute their own content on the theme: photos, opinions, links, and thank them when they do.

CAPTURE DATA

Re-watch the show and be your own critic:

- ▶ How did you do?
- ▶ Was the sound and light okay?
- ▶ What about your fluency and reacting to comments.

And while you watch:

- ▶ Note the comments and the names of the people who sent them.
- ▶ If you didn't answer them on air, now's your chance to re-engage with them and contact them on Twitter, thank them for watching, mention a sale code, invite them to a private stream, or offer to help further. Reply to relevant questions, and acknowledge other comments, posted on your Facebook Live.
- ▶ Or make a note of what they asked and do a follow-up show, repeating the questions and providing the solutions.
- ▶ Perhaps contact those whose questions you will answer and suggest they turn on for the next show.
- ▶ Start building a database of your Superfans – the people who always turn up and contribute.
- ▶ And create another of people who you may want to connect with for another part of your business (maybe a distributor or service provider).
- ▶ Consider a private stream for these Superfans to thank them for their support.

▶ NOTE

1 *This Entrepreneur Uses Periscope as a Growth Hack,* https://smallbiztrends.com/ August 30th, 2015

24

Measuring your metrics

▶ INTRODUCTION

Part of the professional marketer's job is to 'test and track':

- ▶ Know your goals:

    - ▷ What it is that you are trying to achieve

    - ▷ Why

    - ▷ Over what period

And, how you will *monitor and measure those goals* and evaluate success.

This data-mining will help you realise what is working, so you can improve your shows over time. Experiment with different content, formats, durations and so on and get to realise what works well and so, what you need to do more of to encourage more views, longer views, follows and shares.

Better content leads to greater interaction, which provides more accurate insight into your viewers.

> *Marketers need to set realistic goals, benchmark and work to grow, testing and learning along the way. Not every piece of content can and will be a winner, but that's part of the learning process.*

> Diana Gordony[1]

▶ QUALITY VERSUS QUANTITY

It is most likely that more people will consume your content once it's finished and has been uploaded than when it actually was live. It stands to reason because, if nothing else, they could only watch a show that was live for 30 minutes, within that 30 minutes, but the recording of it lives on eternally.

But remember, it's better to have 15 actively engaged followers, hanging on your every word, sharing your show, buying your product, than 1,000 passive viewers. And with smaller groups you can get to know individuals better and develop a stronger relationship.

The bad news

Go to your Facebook Analytics > Video Views and see how many people 'watched' the show. Now see the number of people who were so intrigued and engaged by the title or the images that they clicked through and watched with the sound on. And also take a look at the Average Watch Time: indicating the 'stickability' of your show.

You will probably notice a wide disparity. Just how many people loved what they saw so much they could be bothered to click though to hear a commentary? And how much of their time did they devote to it?

You may think this is a strange stat to draw your attention to in a book that espouses the benefits of live-streaming, but I want to be honest with you and also to remind you:

▶ It's not necessarily the quantity of people who watch, but the *quality*, those who *engaged* with you.

▶ You have this book, so you are already a step ahead of everybody else!

FIGURE 24.1 Thousands viewed this Periscope, but see how long on average they watched for. That doesn't suggest a very meaningful relationship was built by the broadcaster

Source: Periscope

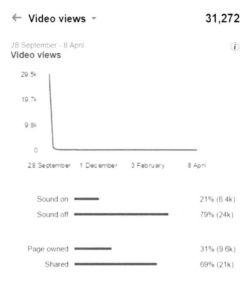

← Video views ▾   31,272

FIGURE 24.2 Viewing figures for a live-stream on Facebook Live

Source: Facebook

So, don't be misled by stats. When you get to the end of your show and you see your metrics and a high viewer-count, remember that a 'view' according to Facebook and Periscope is anything over three seconds, and most of them will be without sound. Yep: newsfeed views automatically play videos without sound, and if someone hovers over the feed for more than three seconds, bingo, it's registered as a 'view' (but obviously, not as a 'listen'). (Remember, if you stream through Twitter Go Live, you do not have access to any 'view stats'.)

WHAT IS A 'VIEWER'?

Live viewers – those who watch while the show is live.

Replay viewers – those who watch it after it has ended being live.

A 'view' –

▶   When, in auto-play, a Facebook Live, Twitter Go Live or Periscope live-stream plays for three seconds or more

▶   When a viewer taps the screen to be taken to the full-screen view with audio

WHAT IS 'INTERACTION'?

This is the term for all shares, comments and emojis/hearts and is a great (possibly the greatest) indicator of how well-appreciated your show. These stats show that a viewer was moved to 'do something'.

WHAT IS 'REACH'?

This is the number of people to whom the video *was sent*: it appeared in their timeline as something that may interest them. The show *may not have been seen* (if they didn't scroll down and didn't notice it was available) *or watched* for more than three seconds (thereby registering a view). It's only the 'most people available' to have seen it. Think of it like this: the number of the people who might drive past an advertising hoarding on a busy road and who have been *exposed* to it, but they may not have *seen* it, or if they did they may not have *read it, or remembered it, or acted on it.*

WHAT IS 'RETENTION'?

How long someone *stays watching* your video for; how long you can *retain* them.

▶ MEASURING IMPACT ON FACEBOOK LIVE

There's no way to see how long someone looked at your funny cat picture, or whether they actually read your oh-so-amusing status update. But you *can* get all sorts of information about how long they spent watching your *video*.

When a viewer comes to watch a 'once-live' video, they will see the 'engagement graph' superimposed at the bottom of the screen. This shows the peaks and troughs of engagement during the duration of the broadcast, and so they can skip to the 'best bit', the part which potentially had the biggest 'wow' response.

FIGURE 24.3 An engagement graph for a Facebook Live

Source: Facebook

As a broadcaster, you get to see several kinds of metrics in different places.

▶ As soon as you end your live-stream, you'll get a graph showing you how many watched and when the peak-viewing was.

▶ Go to your desktop > Facebook Page > Insights > Videos, and you'll see stats that compare your recent video with other ones that you have produced.

▶ Go to the desktop version of Facebook to see extra metrics via the Insights > Videos > and click through on that most recent video to see:

▷ Peak live viewers

▷ Minutes viewed

▷ Unique viewers

▷ Video views

▷ 10-second views

▷ Video average watch time

▷ Audience and engagement

Let's go through some of those in a bit more detail.

Peak live viewers

This shows the highest number of concurrent viewers who viewed your live broadcast for at least three seconds. The viewers during a live broadcast *curve* shows the number of concurrent viewers watching *different points of your live broadcast* for at least three seconds. In other words, which section of your video was the most watched.

FIGURE 24.4 Screenshot of additional metrics for a video on Facebook Live

Source: Facebook

Minutes viewed

The total number of minutes your video was watched by the total number of people, *including* replays and views *less* than three seconds.

Unique viewers

The number of different people who viewed your video at least once.

Video views

The number of times your video was watched for an aggregate of at least three seconds, or for nearly its total length, whichever happened first.

Ten-second views

The number of times your video was watched for at least ten seconds, or for nearly its total length, whichever occurs first. A low-completion rate of just 20 seconds or so is totally normal even on short videos.

Average video watch time

This is calculated as the total watch time of your video divided by the total number of video plays. This includes all replays. This metric doesn't count live-video sessions.

Audience and engagement

▷ People reached post engagement – the total number of reactions, comments and shares your video received on the original post and shared posts. This metric includes streaming reactions during and after the live broadcast.

▷ Video engagement – this curve shows the magnitude of reactions, comments and shares your video received on the original post and shared posts. This includes numbers received both during and after your broadcast.

▷ Top audience – this percentage shows the breakdown of total minutes viewed by age and gender for your video, compared to the audience that viewed videos on your Page over the last 30 days.

▷ Top location – this percentage shows the breakdown of total minutes viewed by region for your video, compared to the audience that viewed videos on your Page over the last 30 days.

On the Post tab, there are more metrics:

▶ People reached

▷ Video views

▶ Engagement:

▷ Reactions (what emoticons were sent)

▷ Comments.

▷ Shares

▶ Post Clicks

▷ Clicks to Play – the number of times your video started playing after a person clicked to play it

▷ Link Clicks

▷ Others – clicks not on the content of the post such as page title posts of clicks to see more

▷ Negative feedback

▷ Hide post

▷ Hide all posts

▷ Report as spam

▷ Unlike page

Remember that the more people watch your video, the more negative feedback you will get. Start to worry if it reaches more than 2–3% of your total reach.

Also on this page you can reply to any comments.

Boost your post

You can get your live-stream video to appear in more feeds, by paying. And if it's *sent* to more people, there's a greater chance it will be *seen* by more people. You can't boost the show to more pairs of eyes while you are live, but you can do so afterwards.

You will have to set up an account on the Facebook Ads Manager page first, and then select 'boost your posts', before choosing the kind of audience you want to be exposed to the broadcast (you can even target those people who only watched a few seconds, or a certain percentage, of your video), and then finally choosing the post you want to be given a boost.

Cheating

Facebook will boost any live-streaming video into others' feeds much more than it will any pre-recorded video that is uploaded, and even more than links to videos hosted on other sites, such as YouTube.

So some companies start a live-stream and then show pre-recorded, edited and produced content within that live-stream. That way they get the boost of live, but without the hassle of something potentially going wrong.

▶ MEASURING IMPACT ON PERISCOPE

The more information that you have about how your Scope has performed (i.e. who watched it, for how long, and so on) makes it easier to target those viewers or potential viewers. *(These stats are not available if you simply go live through the native Twitter app.)*

You can see which content works best, and what causes people to leave a show, or share a show, and then tweak your production to give people what they want more of and make it even more successful.

There are some basic analytics available when you end your broadcast. These Key Performance Indicators are:

- ▶ The number of live viewers you had
- ▶ The total duration
- ▶ The time they watched for:
  - ▷ The total time
  - ▷ The average time watched per viewer
  - ▷ The time watched per broadcast minute ("for every minute of this broadcast, viewers spent a combined total of XX watching it. This statistic normalises time watched across broadcasts of different durations.")
- ▶ The number of comments received
- ▶ How many times your video was replayed

Looking at other parts of Periscope, you will also be able to see:

- ▶ Your number of Followers

▶ The number of viewers of the replay

▶ The total number of hearts anyone has been given

▶ The number of re-tweets of your show's link that you had (track and trace these through Twitter's 'Advanced Search' feature – and of course only if you had the auto-tweet turned on in the Periscope app)

Your stats will pop up after every show, and you can also go back and review stats from all your previous shows, so you have them to compare with others over time.

▶ **Duration** – the basic duration of the show

And arguably the two most important:

▶ **Total Viewers** – this shows you the total number of people who joined you for at least part of your stream.

▶ **Time Watched** – this is usually a huge number of hours and minutes. How? Because it is the 'time spent watching the show' by each individual viewer, all added together.

Success for broadcasters means more time watched on their broadcasts. Success for the audience means more high-quality shows to watch and participate in.

Periscope stats online

As a broadcaster, you have access to an analytics dashboard for in-depth viewership and engagement data over time:

▶ Video duration

▶ Number of viewers

▶ Number of hearts received

▶ Time watched

▶ Time watched per viewer

Some of these stats are broken down into 'live' and 'replay', to give you better insight into how people are consuming your content.

See them at www.periscope.tv and tapping on your profile.

Other Periscope analytics tools

Other companies can provide data on your performance on Periscope shows. They aren't affiliated with the company and haven't hacked the app or use the API code, they just collate all sorts of information from your Scopes and put it all together in various graphs.

The different 'stats companies' will give you things like:

▶ Who watched

▶ For how long

▶ Who shared. . .

▶ and how. . .

▶ and with whom

▶ Who took screen shots

▶ How many hearts were given by each viewer and so on

Of course, the more Scopes you do, the more data the widgets will collect, to build a fuller, more-accurate analysis.

www.Delmondo.co

▶ *Measure an unlimited number of owned live-video channels simultaneously and watch your audience grow with real-time viewership and engagement graphs.*

▶ *Measure Average Minute Audience and Engagements per Minute for individual streams, or roll them up across series, channels and networks.*

▶ *See the data you're missing – track consumption for live and replay viewers.*

▶ *Optimise your streams with audience insights like age, gender, location and viewing habits like sound on vs. sound off and more.*

▶ *Build automated live-video reports based on keyword, hashtag, content tag and more – tracking cross-platform video views, reach and impressions, engagements, top performing streams and channels.*

▶ *Set custom campaign ROI metrics including CPV and CPM.*

▶ *Publishers can automatically break out branded content tagged streams into separate reports for advertisers.*

www.FullScope.tv

Fullscope.tv is a browser-based analytics and marketing software that provides you with the most detailed insights from your Periscope Broadcasts and Snapchat Stories. But also so much more:

- ▶ *View the results of your broadcast/Snapchat reach and influence.*

- ▶ *Compare your most recent Periscope broadcast to a previous one to determine what your audience likes and dislikes.*

- ▶ *Check out your most engaged viewers and tweet them back directly from the Fullscope Periscope interface.*

- ▶ *Run contests based on actions performed such as who sent the most hearts, screenshots, and shares.*

- ▶ *Add people to your email list.*

- ▶ *See how many hearts, screenshots, shares and engagement you had on your Periscope broadcast.*

▶ MONITORING YOUR METRICS

Having stats is no good if you don't use them. They should be a guide to what you are doing well and can do more of, and to help you develop your content over time to reach your desired goal. And, let's face it, so you can determine whether the time and effort are worth it or whether it's best to go with another marketing device.

So keep a record of each show on a spreadsheet:

- ▶ The date of the broadcast

- ▶ The page it was streamed via and published to

- ▶ A one-word content description

- ▶ The title of the show

- ▶ A direct link to the show

- ▶ Any production notes (audio problems, a clash with a major event elsewhere and so on)

Then the more specific drill-down data:

- ▶ The duration

- ▶ When the peak live viewing occurred

- ▶ The total of the peak

- ▶ The audience at the ten-minute mark (so you always have a standard comparison point)

- ▶ Total minutes viewed

- ▶ Unique viewers

- ▶ Views of the archived show (the 'post-live' video)

- ▶ The percentage of views with the sound on

- ▶ The average completion rate percentage

- ▶ The total number of people reached

- ▶ Reaction total

- ▶ Comments total

- ▶ Shares

- ▶ Clicks to play

- ▶ Link clicks

- ▶ The number of people who hid the post

- ▶ The number of people who hid all of your posts after this event

- ▶ And those who subsequently unliked your page

Each month you can create an overview report of these metrics (plus a total number of videos and total duration) to show your development over time.

When you have looked at and analysed your data, you can consider what you will do again and what you may change, such as:

- ▶ The time of the broadcast

- ▶ The content

- ▶ The duration

- ▶ The approach or production values and so on

All this will help you increase your audience in the demographic, geographical or lifestyle sphere that you are targeting. Remember, *sheer numbers* of viewers are not enough: if you are trying to call them to action, fewer people who *actually respond* is best.

Tweaks to your content and style may help in this regard, but it's a fine balance: what you do one day may not work another because of a thousand different reasons – some of them being outside influences (e.g. the weather, a TV event, another live-stream show by a competitor) that may affect the choices of your audience.

So be prepared to experiment.

One final thing to consider: Almost everyone will miss almost everything you live-stream. Until you make a mistake.

▶ NOTE

1 Quoted in *Best Practices for Facebook Live*, www.searchenginejournal.com May 12th, 2016

Thank You

Thanks so much for buying and reading this book.

I sincerely hope that you have found it an invaluable guide to (almost everything about) how to go live from your phone to the world.

The key is: have fun, experiment and overcome your fears.

You are at the forefront of an exciting new time in tech and communication. Never before have we each had a way to make our voices heard so far, so loud and so clearly.

And with the ideas and advice in this book, you will be leading the way.

I'd love to know how you get on. If you'd like to say "this book *is fantastic!*" and tell me about the brilliant and creative ways that you have been using these ground-breaking apps, do get in touch.

(And if you spot a mistake or think something could have been explained a little better, then it's the same contact details.)

Happy streaming!

Peter Stewart
@TweeterStewart
www.petestewart.co.uk

FIGURE 25.5 Screenshot of a live-stream ending

Index